THE
CATHOLIC
CHURCH
IN HISTORY

D0833468

THE
CATHOLIC
CHURCH
IN HISTORY

LEGEND AND REALITY

KEITH D. LEWIS

A Crossroad Book
The Crossroad Publishing Company
New York

The Crossroad Publishing Company
481 Eighth Avenue, New York, NY 10001

© 2006 Keith D. Lewis

This book is set in 11/13 Garamond Premier Pro.

Printed in the United States of America

Library of Congress Cataloging-in-Publication Data is available.

ISBN 0-8245-2389-X

1   2   3   4   5   6   7   8   9   10   10   09   08   07   06

To My Parents

Who Instilled in Me a Love of Learning

The first law of history is not to dare to utter falsehood; the second, not to fear to speak the truth; and moreover, no room must be left for suspicion of partiality or prejudice.

—Pope Leo XIII (1883)

To be a glorious Church, with neither spot nor wrinkle, is the ultimate end to which we are brought by the Passion of Christ. Hence, this will be the case only in the heavenly homeland, not here on the way of pilgrimage, where "if we say we have no sin, we deceive ourselves."

—St. Thomas Aquinas
(*Summa Theologica* III q. 8 art. 3 ad 2)

Contents

Introduction

It has often been said that church historians are troublemakers. They never forget, and they know where the bodies are buried, sometimes not just metaphorically. They do not hesitate to remind others that they are church historians and not theologians, yet, because of the nature of the discipline, they invariably poke their collective noses into theological matters. Sometimes, the work of church historians can be most unwelcome, such as the discovery of Lorenzo Valla (1406–1457) that the *Donation of Constantine* on which papal temporal claims to most of the Italian peninsula were based was in fact a medieval forgery.

Until the middle of the twentieth century, church history as a discipline was seen more as historical theology, in which the task of the church historian was simply to sift through the historical record to confirm the already-accepted doctrines of the church. The notion of historical objectivity gave way to an essentially apologetic approach, in which the Catholic Church as a theological concept became inseparable from the actions of its members. This type of church historiography gradually changed in the aftermath of groundbreaking historical works written by eminent Catholic historians such as Ludwig von Pastor (1899–1928), Josef Lortz (1877–1975), and Hubert Jedin (1900–1980), all of whom strove for critical objectivity in their efforts to present a comprehensive and clear portrait of various periods in the history of the church.

More recently, however, the task of the church historian has evolved to much more fundamental issues involving analysis and assessment of the unfolding and reception of abstract theologies *in the world*, where high ideals and love of God historically have often run headlong into the reality of original sin.

On the eve of the new millennium, in an action that was unprecedented in the 2,000 year history of the Catholic Church, Pope John Paul II called for institutional forgiveness: "The Church should become more fully conscious of the sinfulness of her children; recalling all those times in history when they departed from the spirit of Christ and his Gospel and . . . indulged in ways of thinking and acting which were truly forms of counter-witness and scandal"

(*Tertio Millennio Adveniente,* 33). The comments of the pope were of profound importance, in that they called the Catholic Church to come to terms with points in its history that have been less than edifying in a way that is honest, objective, and conciliatory. Elsewhere, John Paul II speaks of these darker points in the history of the church as "the mystery of iniquity, at work in the human heart" (2 Thessalonians 2:7).

This was no passing thought on the part of the pope. During the liturgy of the "Day of Pardon" on March 12, 2000, in an act of honesty and in a spirit of reconciliation that has received far too little attention, John Paul II sought public forgiveness for the historical role the church played in

> sins of intolerance and violence against dissidents, wars of religion, and acts of violence and oppression during the Crusades, methods of coercion employed in the Inquisition, excommunications, sins regarding relations with the people of the first Covenant, Israel: contempt, hostility, failure to speak out, sins against . . . the rights of peoples and respect for cultures and other religions which took place during the work of evangelization. . . .

The pope called the church to no less than a *purification of memory and commitment to the path of true conversion.* What precisely is meant by this? This was perhaps best articulated in 1999 by a report of the International Theological Commission entitled *Memory and Reconciliation: The Church and the Faults of the Past.* Study of the topic was suggested to the theological commission by its president, Cardinal Joseph Ratzinger. The study defines purification as aimed at "liberating personal and communal conscience from all forms of resentment and violence that are the legacy of past faults, through a renewed historical and theological evaluation of such events. This should lead—if done correctly—to a corresponding recognition of guilt and contribute to the path of reconciliation. Such a process can have a significant effect on the present, precisely because the consequences of past faults still make themselves felt and can persist as tensions in the present." It is an act of *courage and humility,* which recognizes that though we are not today personally responsible for the faults of the past committed by the church, we nevertheless bear the burdens of those wrongs in the tensions of today and have an obligation to come to terms with them.

The task of the church historian is an essential part of this task of coming to terms with past faults of the church, in terms of presenting a clear, objective reconstruction of the historical event. Though there is a complex interplay between theology and church history, it is not the task of the historian to pass ethical judgment on past actions, just as most secular historians strive to present historical reconstructions that are interpretive rather than judgmental. It must be further borne in mind that ethics and theological interpretation are conditioned by historical context, and what might seem outrageously unethical to us today was not necessarily seen as such at the time. Thus for example, a crusading knight in the Holy Land would in good conscience and with full church support see his activities in the Holy Land as a pious pilgrimage that had the potential to bring him closer to salvation. This is by no means to suggest, however, that everything is relative to its historical context and thus there is no need for remorse or forgiveness.

The work of the church historian in this regard must above all else be bound by a solemn commitment to "patient, honest, scholarly reconstruction, free from confessional or ideological prejudices, regarding both the accusations brought against her and the wrongs she has suffered." And it is a task from which the church historian must never be put off. As Cardinal John Henry Newman (1801–1890) stated in 1872, "There is an endemic perennial fidget which possesses us about giving scandal; facts are omitted in great histories, or glosses are put upon memorable acts, because they are thought not edifying, whereas of all scandals, such omissions, such glosses, are the greatest."

The present work is not intended as a rigorous or comprehensive historical analysis of each topic. Rather, emphasis has been placed on some key fundamental points about each topic, intended to suggest a different way of looking at the subject, which it is hoped will lead the reader to a clearer understanding of how objectively to place the topic within the larger context of Roman Catholicism. The purpose of this book is not one of apologetics, in which the reader is provided with the "right answers" to refute any objection that one might raise about historical events and how they reflect negatively on the Catholic Church. This is particularly true with regard to the last chapter on Pope Pius XII and the Holocaust.

Chapter 1 examines the rise of Islam, some of its basic tenets, and its common roots with Judaism and Christianity. The seventh-century classification of Islam as a Christian heresy and the impact this had on subsequent perceptions of Islam will serve (somewhat paradoxically) as the basis for the contention that it is only with acceptance of a notion of a "Judaeo-Christian-Muslim" tradition that true mutual tolerance will occur.

Chapter 2 surveys the crusades between 1095 and 1291. Rather than the simplistic notion of the crusaders as pure bloodthirsty mercenaries—the term "crusade/crusader" is not used until the fifteenth century—the crusades are addressed in their religious context, albeit different from modern notions of religiosity. Consideration is given to the notion of "just war" in the context of the crusades, as well as the impact of the crusades on Muslim-Christian and Orthodox-Catholic relations in the present.

Chapter 3 addresses reality and legend concerning the Spanish Inquisition and challenges the popular notion of an omnipresent and invidious institution that executed hapless individuals by the hundreds of thousands, as is often portrayed in modern media. Yet, though now many scholars refer to the Spanish Inquisition as the "Black Legend," there is still the reality that an inquisition did operate in Spain and that approximately 5,000 people lost their lives in the four centuries of its existence. How did it operate and who were the targets of this institution? How did the "Black Legend" come into being?

Chapter 4 discusses how the scrupulous and exemplary Augustinian friar Martin Luther emerged in sixteenth-century Germany as the leader of a movement that would dramatically reshape the ecclesiastical map of Europe. The only Protestant reformer ever excommunicated, Luther in many ways was swept up in the ecclesiastical and political circumstances of his time. What is the place of Luther with regard to the Catholic Church today?

Chapter 5 looks at key personalities and methodologies in the spread of Catholicism to the Americas, Africa, and Asia in the sixteenth century in the aftermath of Pope Alexander VI's division of the world between the Portuguese and the Spanish. A comparison and contrast will be made between those regions where indigenous culture was largely disregarded and those regions where there were efforts at inculturation, which though as a word was anachronistic to the sixteenth century, nevertheless was a concept that came to be applied successfully in some areas.

Chapter 6 recounts Galileo's scientific contributions and the key issues surrounding his stormy relationship with the church. Although never excommunicated, Galileo's impasse with ecclesial authorities has taken on an almost mythical quality and has come to be synonymous with the notion of incompatibility of science and faith. What were the origins of his dispute with the church, and how did his personality figure into the unfolding of events?

Chapter 7 explores the relationship between the Catholic Church and Nazi Germany from the beginnings of the National Socialist Workers Party in 1929 to the end of the Second World War. The Vatican policy of impartiality during World War II is portrayed as a continuum of papal policy since World War I and is sometimes misunderstood as silence, or even as tacit acceptance by Pius XII for the racial policies of the Nazi regime. What in fact did Pius XII do on behalf of the Jews of Europe, and how have perceptions of his actions evolved radically since the end of World War II?

Although the chapters are in chronological order and share common themes, each may be read as an independent essay. For the convenience of the reader, dates for an individual are given parenthetically when their name is first mentioned. In the case of popes, monarchs, and bishops, the dates given are for the term of their rule or administration rather than birth and death.

It is hoped that the Catholic reader will learn that it is only on the basis of historical accuracy rather than uninformed defensiveness that one can speak with credibility, integrity, and faithfulness concerning the historical record of the church, and ultimately draw closer to the "fuller consciousness" and "purification of memory" of which John Paul II speaks. Concomitantly, it is hoped that the non-Catholic reader will be less eager to adopt sometimes-facile assessments of the historical record of the Catholic Church, often based more on a "canon of perceptions" than on fact.

1

People of the Book

Islam and Division among the Children of Abraham

The mutual suspicion and frequent animosity that has predominated in relations between Muslims and the Western world for centuries is for the most part based on negative perceptions of Islam formed shortly after its foundation. Yet a religion that seems so "other" to the average Westerner in fact has roots in the Judaeo-Christian tradition. An understanding and acceptance of this fact is an essential part of any real dialogue between the three great monotheistic religions of the world.

◄○►

Over the centuries many quarrels and dissensions have arisen between Christians and Muslims. The sacred Council now pleads with all to forget the past, and urges that a sincere effort be made to achieve mutual understanding; for the benefit of all men, let them together preserve and promote peace, social justice and moral values.
—*Nostra Aetate 3*, Second Vatican Council, October 28, 1965

On May 14, 1999, at the conclusion of an audience for representatives of the Shiite and Sunni branches of Islam, Pope John Paul II was presented with a copy of the Qur'an, the holy book of Muslims. Then, in a move that shocked many at both ends of the ideological spectrum, the pontiff spontaneously bowed and kissed the cover of the leather-bound volume. Five months later in London, a noisy group of protesters gathered outside Pleasance Theatre in London, where Terrence McNally's controversial play *Corpus Christi* had just opened. Angry

7

over the portrayal of a homosexual Jesus, the largest and most vocal contingent in the group was in fact Muslim, incensed at what they termed a "grave insult to a messenger of God." Two years later, on September 11, terrorists claiming to represent Islam crashed their hijacked jets into their chosen targets in the United States, and for the first time in several centuries, the West was again collectively fearful about a "Muslim threat" to the mostly Christian West.

How are we to understand Islam, particularly from a Christian perspective, in the midst of the conflicting images mentioned above? The purpose of this essay is not to provide a detailed and comprehensive look at Islam, nor is it designed to settle or even gloss over fundamental theological differences between Islam, Judaism, and Christianity. Rather, its primary purpose is to place Muhammad and the rise of Islam within the Jewish, Christian, and polytheistic context of the Arabian peninsula in the sixth century, in an effort to create a more objective vantage point from which the reader can view Islam, and ultimately come to a deeper and more tolerant understanding of a religion which is not as "other" as one might think.

Coming Down from the Mountain

In A.D. 610, in the hills of Mt. Hira on the western side of the Arabian peninsula, a forty-year-old Arab nomad and caravan trader from Mecca emerged from the solitude of a cave, where he had withdrawn for a month of prayer and meditation. Such seclusion was a common practice among the holy men of late antiquity, but what the merchant Muhammad ibn Abdallah (A.D. 570-632) proclaimed after he emerged from the cave was anything but commonplace. The archangel Gabriel—the same archangel Gabriel who had announced to Mary the role she was to play in the salvation of humanity—had visited him during his seclusion and revealed to him that he too was a prophet, a messenger of the one (and only) God.

Who was this seemingly self-proclaimed messenger of God? There are few concrete and reliable sources regarding the details of the early life of Muhammad. What we do know is that he was born in 570 in Mecca, into a modest family of the Hashim clan, which was part of the larger Quraysh tribe. Tribal affiliation and loyalty was for Muhammad, as it was for all Arabs, of paramount importance, since it was the predominant social structure. Largely isolated and inaccessible to outsiders, Arabia was never directly dominated by a foreign power, and there was very little in the way of foreign alliances. Nor was there any sense of government, law in the politico-juridical sense, or nationhood.

Thus it was tribal code and conduct that provided the norms for the smooth functioning of society.[1]

The Quraysh tribe to which Muhammad belonged was the most powerful in the Arabian peninsula. As traders, they controlled the important city of Mecca, which was at the crossroads of the Yemen–Syria and Yemen–Iraq trade routes. Also under the control of the Quraysh was the ancient shrine of the Ka'ba, or "cube," founded on the site of a sacred spring. In the center of Mecca, the large black stone cube structure was surrounded by 360 idols, and was the shrine to *al-Llah*, the supreme god of the various deities of the Arabs. All of Mecca within a twenty-mile radius of the Ka'ba was considered a sanctuary and was a major cultic center, attracting pilgrims from all over Arabia, and especially from the Hijaz, the west-central region of Arabia, which would be the main territory for Muhammad's religious activities.

Muhammad's father died before his birth, and his mother died when he was only six, so he was raised by his grandmother. Without attempting to delve into the relatively new realm of psychohistory, it is commonplace in such circumstances for an individual to experience feelings of abandonment, and long for what modern psychology would term object constancy.

As a young caravan trader, Muhammad traveled the deserts, leading caravans from Arabia to Syria and Iraq.[2] When Muhammad was twenty-five, he married a widow named Khadija, a distant cousin. The first of an estimated dozen wives during his lifetime, Khadija was supposedly fifteen years older than Muhammad, which is somewhat questionable since she would eventually bear six of Muhammad's children—two sons who would die in infancy, and four daughters, including Fatimah, who would be instrumental in the spread of Islam after the death of Muhammad.

Little else reliable is known about the early life of Muhammad, until 610, when we find him on Mt. Hira announcing his prophetic visions. As his message continued to unfold, Muhammad would highlight his place as a champion of monotheism and the final prophet in the Judaeo-Christian tradition. His very first revelations were written down in summary form by his followers and circulated among them, thus forming the beginnings of the Qur'an, to which we will return shortly. No belief system arises in a cultural and religious vacuum, and it is thus to the religious atmosphere in the Arabian peninsula at the time of Muhammad that we now turn.

The Arabian period prior to Muhammad is referred to by Muslims as the *jahiliyah*, a kind of "Dark Ages," from which Muhammad rescues his people. Fetishism, animism, and polytheism were widespread, and religious leadership was usually to be found in the ubiquitous Arabian shamans known as *jinn* (genies). Underpinning all this was a kind of "tribal humanism," which provided a basic system of ethics for nomadic society and would later be foundational for the strong ethical dimension in Islam. Yet the ignorance and superstition of the *jahiliyah* have often been overstated, and in fact the difference between pre- and post-Islamic Arabia may not have been as radical as sometimes argued.[3]

In addition to the presence of polytheism, there was also a Jewish and Christian presence, as well as approximately a half-dozen known Arab monotheists prior to Muhammad, who ascribed neither to Judaism nor to Christianity. Further enriching this religious tapestry in Arabia is the fact that Jews, Christians, and polytheists were culturally and ethnically Arabs, and often lived in mixed settlements, which on occasion led to cross-fertilization of ideas. Ultimately, it is not so much a question of whether, but rather to what degree and how early these communities influenced Islam.[4]

Many Jews in Arabia had fled Roman persecution, while others had fled Persia and its Zoroastrian state religion. Judaism was especially strong in the southern Arabian kingdom of Yemen, where one of its kings had adopted Judaism as his official religion, but it had also found a firm place in the Hijaz region in which Muhammad grew up. Particularly important to our story were the Jewish tribes in Medina, where Muhammad would spend ten years in exile. Often, these weaker Jewish clans in Medina would attach themselves to larger, more powerful non-Jewish tribes for protection, which as we will see, eventually proves disastrous for them.[5]

If we bear in mind that culturally and geographically the Arabian peninsula did not stop at the borders of the present-day Saudi kingdom but extended northward as far as Iraq (Mesopotamia) and Palestine, then we see that the Christian presence in Arabia was more at the periphery than Judaism. An important point to remember is that northern Arabia was a large part of the frontline in ongoing warfare between the Byzantine Empire, which was the surviving eastern half of the Roman Empire, which had fallen in A.D. 476, and the Persian Empire in the east. In addition, northern Arabia had often been a place of refuge in the early church for those individuals whose Christian beliefs were not in line with the orthodox position.[6]

In the northeast, in Iraq, although largely Persian territory, the Nestorian Christian Church flourished, especially in the Christian city of Edessa. Declared heretical in A.D. 431 because of its belief that Jesus was two separate and distinct persons, Nestorian Christianity was nevertheless for the average individual indistinguishable from orthodox Christianity, and eventually spread its influence southward along the Arabian shore of the Red Sea. The Arab Lakhmid Dynasty seated in the city of Hira in northeastern Arabia adopted Nestorian Christianity and, under Persian protection, served as a buffer state against the

Roman Empire. Some neighboring tribes are also known to have adopted Christianity, but more important in terms of our topic, the court at Hira attracted visiting poets from all over Arabia, whose poetry now carried at least superficial references to Christianity to the interior of the Arabian peninsula.[7]

Syria in the northwest, always predominantly Arab in character, was a regular destination for caravans from Mecca. They adhered to Monophysite Christianity, declared heretical in A.D. 451 because of its belief that Jesus had only one divine nature rather than a human *and* a divine nature. The Ghassanid Dynasty in northwestern Arabia adopted Monophysite Christianity and, subsidized by the Byzantine Empire, provided a counterbalance to the above-mentioned Lakhmid Dynasty. The influence of the Ghassanids may have extended even as far south as Medina.

It would be almost inconceivable that at least rudimentary knowledge of Christianity would not have flowed southward into the desert of the nomads. As a caravan trader, Muhammad himself made at least two trips to Damascus, and his visit of A.D. 595 is of particular interest to us. While in the Syrian city of Basra, Muhammad mentions contact with a Christian monk he calls Bahira, although this was likely a confusion of the Syriac word *bhira* ("reverend"), and would thus have been the monk's title.[8] Although Muslim tradition holds that the monk immediately recognized the holiness of Muhammad, later Christian critics would regard Bahira as an apostate Christian who used Muhammad to attempt to denigrate Christianity. In any event, the encounter does establish that Muhammad did have contact with Christians.

In the west, Ethiopia (Abyssinia) was also Monophysite Christian. Also a client-state of the Byzantine Empire, Ethiopia had regular trade relations with Mecca, and some of Muhammad's followers would in fact later find refuge there during a period of persecution. Monophysite Christianity was also well established in South Arabia, which was under the control of Ethiopia. A persecution of Christians in A.D. 525 in the city of Najran is even mentioned in the Qur'an [Sura 85], and in 560, the governor of South Arabia built a large Christian church in the city of Sana'a. But there was also fear in Mecca of the power of South Arabia, after this same governor tried to attack Mecca and destroy the Ka'ba, in an effort to divert trade to south Arabia.[9]

The point is not to diminish the religious insights of Muhammad, or rather to suggest that he is simply another religious renegade in the Arabia that the church had called "a breeding ground of heresies." Rather, it is simply to demonstrate that he was born into a highly diverse, syncretic, and loosely structured religious atmosphere which facilitated his ability to develop and proclaim a message that in other parts of the Mediterranean world would have been immediately brought to heel.

A Prophet in His Own Land

Muhammad traveled to Mecca around A.D. 612 and began a frustrating struggle to convert the people of Mecca to monotheism. He did not at first know what to call God, since the Arabic of the polytheistic culture from which he came did not seem to have an appropriate term. At first, he used the term *rabb* ("Lord"), then *Allah*, but soon found that many associated it with pagan subdeities, especially the *banat al-Lah*. Muhammad switched to *ar-Rahman*, but finally went back to the name *Allah*, perhaps recognizing that with proper explanation in a monotheistic context, the more recognizable term would more readily attract converts from paganism.[10]

At first, Muhammad called his religion *tazaqqa,* that is, the virtues of compassion and generosity, which the individual was exhorted to cultivate. This was coupled with a strong apocalyptic bent borrowed from the Judaeo-Christian tradition, in which Muhammad emphasized that it was the actions of the individual and the life he lived which would determine his fate at the end times: "Those who have believed, the Jews, the Nasara [Nazarenes] and the Sabi'in, whoever believes in God, and the Last Day, and acts uprightly, have their reward with their Lord. There is no fear upon them, neither do they grieve" (Sura 2:59). Soon however, Muhammad adopts the term *Islam,* from the Arabic *'aslama* ("surrender"); the idea was that one surrenders or submits to God. Related to the same root word, a *Muslim* was simply one who had surrendered or submitted.[11]

It is interesting to note that Muhammad initially seems to have envisioned his prophetic role as one specifically intended *for his community* at Mecca rather than a new worldwide religion, and there is no evidence to suggest that his campaigns toward the end of his life were designed to export Islam. The injustice of social abuses was something that inspired Muhammad in his prophetic mission and may reflect at least the Judaeo-Christian atmosphere regarding such issues, although there is no evidence of direct borrowing.[12]

Muhammad struggled to make converts but alienated many in Mecca in 616 when he announced that his converts could no longer worship Arabian deities, especially the *banat al-Lah*. This antagonized his own Quraysh tribe in particular, which, as has been pointed out, was responsible for the Ka'ba in Mecca, and thus had a vested interest in preserving pagan worship. It may also have been the occasion for what are commonly referred to as the "Satanic verses." According to tradition, at one point, in an effort to patch things up with the Quraysh, Muhammad conceded that there were three pagan deities (*Al-Lat, Al-'Uzza,* and *al-Manat*), to whom one could look for intercession with

Allah. Later realizing that it was in fact Satan who had led him to these thoughts, Muhammad then insisted that the supporting verses in the developing Qur'an be withdrawn.[13]

While in Mecca in A.D. 620, Muhammad revealed to his followers an event that is usually referred to as the "night journey." While asleep one evening, Muhammad explained that he was awaken by the archangel Gabriel. Then, a horse from heaven named *Buruq* transported Muhammad to Jerusalem, where he and Gabriel set down on the Temple Mount and were met by Abraham, Moses, and Jesus, as well as some other prophets. After praying together, Muhammad says that he was offered three goblets, each respectively containing water, milk, and wine. He chose the milk, he explained, to demonstrate that Islam would pursue a path of moderation between extreme asceticism and hedonism. Then, a ladder suddenly appeared, and Muhammad and Gabriel climbed through seven successive levels of heaven until they reached the throne of God. What happens when Muhammad is before God is not explained, but the Dome of the Rock in Jerusalem is sacred to Muslims today because of their belief that this was where Muhammad last touched the earth before he was taken up into heaven.

A Prophet in Exile

By A.D. 622, after ten years in Mecca, Muhammad had made only a handful of converts, and continued hostility from the Quraysh tribe eventually forced Muhammad and his followers into exile in the nearby city of Medina. Known as the *hijra,* this period of exile marks the beginning of the Muslim calendar and would prove to be a profoundly formative period for Islam both socially and theologically.[14]

In Medina, Muhammad was immediately faced with a very important practical matter of how to provide for himself and his followers; so he began to send out raiding parties against caravans from Mecca. Although unacceptable to our modern mindset, one must not be too quick to judge Muhammad or Islam on the basis of this. Raiding parties and the resultant redistribution of resources was in fact an accepted tool of survival in the harsh desert nomadic culture in which Muhammad lived, and it must be remembered that in Medina, he was cut off from the resources of his tribe. Nomadic code called for bloodshed to be avoided, and to conduct raids only against outsiders or those from other clans.[15]

In Medina, Muhammad claimed further revelations from God, as he would for the rest of his life, and each of these revelations was added to the growing Qur'an. Text and meaning of the Qur'an, however, would tend to be fluid throughout Muhammad's lifetime, until the first complete Qur'an was compiled two years after his death.[16]

Divided into 114 chapters, or *suras*, the Qur'an was regarded as God's word, and had to be read in Arabic. Numerous Jewish and Christian stories in the Qur'an are reminiscent of the biblical text. In particular, Muhammad had an interest in the prophetic stories, such as those of Moses, Noah, Abraham, and Lot. At first glance, one might assume that Muhammad had simply lifted passages and had given them a Muslim spin to suit his own ends. However, there were no translations of the Bible into Arabic at the time, and even if there had been, it would have made no difference, for like the majority of people living in the strongly nomadic and oral culture of Arabia, Muhammad was illiterate. Muhammad's knowledge of the Bible and biblical references in the Qur'an were in fact based on Arab oral traditions, which had taken many biblical stories and retold them in a more Arab context. By the time Muhammad heard them, he had no reason to doubt their validity or accuracy, and he utilized them, as well as some secular stories from oral tradition, with full sincerity and integrity. This oral tradition would in fact become an important wellspring for the development of the Qur'an, especially with regard to knowledge of Judaism and Christianity.[17]

Muhammad initially reached out to the well-established Jewish community in Medina in an effort to convert them, and in the process, incorporated many of their practices into Islam. The Feast of Atonement became the Fast of the Ashura, and Muhammad tells his followers to pray in the direction of Jerusalem. Dietary prohibitions in Judaism regarding shellfish, predatory birds, pork, blood, animals that have died of natural causes, or any meat which has not been slaughtered and prepared according to religious ritual, are mirrored in the Muslim *hallal*. The Torah forbade coming before the tabernacle after having consumed alcohol (Lev. 10:9), and similarly, the Qur'an admonishes believers not to come to prayers after drinking until one's mind is clear (Sura 4:43). Initially, although Muhammad was generally negative toward wine, he only forbade imported wine (*khamr*) but not *nabidh*, the local date wine. Eventually however, alcohol would be forbidden altogether (Sura 2:219).[18]

But perhaps most important, in Medina Muhammad discovered Ishmael. In the Old Testament (Gen. 16), when Abraham is unable to have a son by his wife Sarah, she gives to him her Egyptian concubine Hagar, who eventually gives birth to Abraham's son Ishmael, who initially enjoys great favor: "As for Ishmael, I am heeding you: I hereby bless him. I will make him fertile and will multiply him exceedingly. He shall become the father of twelve chieftains, and I will make of him a great nation" (Gen. 17:20). But when Sarah eventually gives birth to Isaac, she becomes jealous and demands that Abraham send Hagar and Ishmael into exile. What we are told in Genesis 25:18, is that the twelve tribes who descended from Ishmael "settled in the area from Havilah to Shur, near the border of Egypt." Long before Muhammad, the story of Ishmael had found its way into the oral traditions of the Arabs. Ishmael was believed to be the ancestor of the Arabs, and in fact, the ancient Israelites were quite conscious of their common cultural and linguistic roots with the Arab people. But at the same time, there was also a very clear sense of maintaining separation, no doubt in large part because of the rabbinic tradition that associated Ishmael with enemies of the Jews.[19]

When Muhammad became aware that Ishmael was the son of Abraham, it provided him with an essential basis for establishing the kinship of the Arabs to the people of the covenant. Whereas in Mecca, Muhammad had emphasized the importance of Moses, Abraham now became paramount. He and Ishmael were the first Muslims, and in post-Islamic traditions, Abraham was regarded as the progenitor of the northern Arabs from whom the Quraysh tribe to which Muhammad belonged claimed descent. Other pre-Islamic oral traditions also held that Hagar and Ishmael eventually settled in Mecca, and that Abraham came to visit them and established the first monotheism there. While on a visit, Abraham then built the Ka'ba, in some versions of the story by himself, and in others with the help of Ishmael.[20]

But it was all too much for the Jews of Medina. Although Muhammad had made a large number of converts outside of his clan, he had failed to win over the Jews, and they now began to accuse him of distorting scripture. Muhammad responded with the same accusation, as his growing knowledge of the Jewish scriptures conflicted more and more with what he regarded as the authentic Arab oral versions. In particular, as Muhammad began to understand the differences between Jews and Christians, especially the former's rejection of Jesus, he saw a fatal flaw in Judaism. He had presented himself as the prophetic heir to Jesus, so a denial of Jesus was a denial of Muhammad.[21]

Raids against caravans from Mecca continued, but in A.D. 624, an event took place that heightened the tension between Mecca and Medina. Muhammad's followers conducted a raid on Nakhla, which took place during one of the four sacred months. According to nomadic custom, fighting was strictly forbidden during these months, so that pilgrimage could safely be made to sacred sites. To make matters worse, a camel-driver from Mecca was killed during the raid, also violating nomadic code. This marks the first instance in which the followers of Muhammad engaged in violence. Muhammad agreed that it was in fact wrong to violate the sacred month but that it was an even more serious matter to oppose the truth of Islam, which further infuriated the Quraysh in Mecca.[22]

Those who had made the *hijra* to Medina were now regarded in Mecca as traitors who had broken the sacred bonds of kinship, and a large army of nine hundred Meccans soon showed up at the gates of Medina. To everyone's surprise, they were repelled by Muhammad and his army of only three hundred men at the so-named Battle of Badr. Just as the Roman emperor Constantine at the Battle of the Milvian Bridge in A.D. 312 had attributed his victory to God's intervention, so too did Muhammad regard his victory at Badr as a sign that he was truly a prophet, not just to the Jews of Mecca but to the world. In commemoration of the victory, Muhammad instituted the Fast of Ramadan.[23]

Emboldened by the victory, Muhammad felt that he no longer needed the support of the Jewish tribes. He dropped the Fast of Ashura and told his followers to pray toward Mecca instead of Jerusalem. More ominously, he began to expel Jewish tribes from Medina, in part because he was suspicious that they were allying themselves with the Quraysh in Mecca. After an unsuccessful siege of Medina in 627 by the Quraysh, Muhammad became convinced that the attackers had been supported by the Jewish tribe of Qurayzah. In a decision that would have major ramifications down to the present, he ordered the seven-hundred men of the Jewish tribe to be executed.[24] On the one hand, it is important to understand that according to the norms of the time, the tribe represented an imminent military threat to Muhammad's hold on Medina. On the other hand, one cannot help but wonder how much of an impact the deteriorating relationship between Muhammad and the Jews of Medina might have had on his decision.

An important social development in Medina was Muhammad's establishment of the Medina Agreement, which was a sort of constitution by which his followers would live. Collectively, his followers in Medina who lived according to the agreement were referred to as the *umma,* from an Arabic word meaning "people." It was not uncommon in nomadic culture for a holy man (*mansab*) to create a sacred enclave over which he would exercise authority, but what is significant about the *umma* is that it contained converts from outside Muhammad's clan. In addition, Jews and pagans had responsibilities as well as benefits within the *umma* as long as none of them sought alliances with Mecca. Very rapidly, the *umma* became a kind of super-tribe, based not on pre-Islamic kinship ties but rather religious principles. This was a profound social change for Arabia.

A natural result of the fall from favor of the Jews was that Muhammad now became more favorable toward Christianity: "Thou wilt find that the most hostile of men towards those who have believed are the Jews, and the Polytheists, and the most favorable towards those who have believed are those who say "We are Nasara" [Nazarenes]. That is because there are among them priests and monks, and because they are not proud" (Sura 5:85). After all, the Christians had been able to recognize and accept the prophet Jesus.[25]

Although it is true that most of Muhammad's direct formal contact with Christianity would come much later, he did find it advantageous while in Medina to enter into negotiations with Christian chiefs and tribes beyond the Hijaz in an effort to make them part of the *umma*. When a Christian delegation from the town of Anuran in southern Arabia came to him with their refusal to join, Muhammad agreed that in return for protection, they could pay annual tribute instead, thus establishing an important precedent for non-Muslims in other regions.[26]

In addition, there is very clear evidence of influence from a Christian ethos on Islam during this formative period in Medina, particularly in terminology. Muhammad emphasized the importance of *rugz*, which was from a Christian Aramaic word meaning "fleeing from the wrath to come." The very name "Qur'an" was from the Christian Syriac *qeryana*, which meant the "ritual reading" or "scripture lesson." And *salat,* one of the five pillars of Islam and which called for prayer five times a day, was not only a word of Christian origins but also seems conceptually to have come from the prayer practices in Christian monasticism. Even the frequent prostrations during Muslim prayer mimic the numerous prostrations during the recitation of the Psalms which characterized Christian monasticism at the time. Throughout his life, in fact, Muhammad seems to have had a particular affinity for Christian monasticism, which he called *rahbaniyya,* and which was also often respectfully mentioned in pre-Islamic poetry.[27] Furthermore, the rich Muslim mystical and ascetical tradition that would later develop into Sufism, a name derived from the *suf,* or coarse woolen garment worn by its adherents, sought to mirror Christian monasticism and asceticism.

Muhammad was aware of the Christian Gospel (*injil*) but did not seem to have had a detailed knowledge of it. Nevertheless, Jesus is in fact mentioned twenty-eight times in the Qur'an, and Mary, who holds a place of high honor in Islam, is mentioned thirty-one times, more so than in the New Testament. The Qur'an repeats an apocryphal account of the birth of Jesus that seems to have come from the Protevangelium of James, which like so many Jewish biblical stories had found its way into Arab oral lore. Muhammad also suggests that Jesus had not actually died on the cross but rather it simply *appeared* as such, again reflecting an understanding of the crucifixion called *docetism*, which had been rejected by the early church but which also had likely found its way into Arab oral tradition.[28]

One of the most interesting facets of Christian influence on Muhammad is his contact with individual Christians. Muhammad seems to have maintained a high degree of respect for the *hanifs,* who were the half-dozen or so people associated with him who chose not to adopt Islam. Several of them were Christians

and may have been related to Muhammad. Even more significantly, Muhammad eventually took as a concubine an Egyptian Coptic Christian slave girl
named Maryam, by whom he would have a son. It is hard to imagine that
Muhammad was not conscious of the parallels with the Egyptian concubine
Hagar, mother of Ishmael, particularly given the fact that Muhammad chose to
name his son Ibrahim.[29]

The Return of the Prophet

Finally, after eight years in exile, Muhammad triumphantly returned to Mecca
and established Islam as the sole religion. He is said to have ridden his camel
seven times around the Ka'ba, forbidden any further pagan religious practices,
and ordered the sanctuary cleansed of idolatry. According to one tradition,
there were frescoes of Jesus and Mary on the walls of the Ka'ba, along with
images of pagan deities, and Muhammad allowed the former to remain.
Muhammad had readily accepted the belief that Abraham had built the Ka'ba,
and now insisted that it was in fact God who had commanded Abraham to
institute the pilgrimage to the holy sanctuary (Sura 22:27). Pre-Islamic pilgrimage to the Ka'ba and votive offerings were simply regarded as a temporary
aberration and deviation from its original monotheistic purpose.[30]

Yet just as he had had a falling out with the Jews of Medina, so too did
Muhammad now find fault with the Christians of Northern Arabia. They too,
he now learned, regarded Ishmael as having been rejected from the covenant
with God. Furthermore, they had corrupted the scriptures with their doctrine
of the Trinity and their insistence that Jesus was the Son of God, which in
Muhammad's mind was incompatible with monotheism. That Muhammad
would seize on this last point is not surprising, given the fact that Trinitarian
disputes within the Christian church were widespread throughout the Mediterranean world. Jews and Christians together were now regarded by Muslims as
having distorted the bible in order to bury the revelation about Muhammad.
Thus, we find: "O you who have believed, do not take the Jews and Christians
as friends; they are friends of each other; and those of you who take them as
friends belong to them; God does not guide the people who do wrong" (Sura
5:56). Yet in spite of this, Muhammad still found it expedient to enter into
direct negotiations with some of the Christian communities on the borders of
Arabia.[31]

In very short order after Muhammad's return to Mecca, Islam had taken on
its most definitive shape. Monotheistic to the core, the overall framework of
Islam was now found in the *shahada,* that is, the formula "there is no God but

God, and Muhammad is his prophet." The law of Islam, called *shari'a*, spelled out the five essential ritual obligations for Muslims that are regarded as the "five pillars of Islam." First, recitation of the *shahada* before two witnesses, which was the Muslim equivalent of baptism. Second, *salat*, or ritual prayer, repeated five times a day in the direction of Mecca. Third, *zakat*, or alms, which were owed to the state but were to be used for assistance to the poor. Fourth, *Ramadan*, the annual thirty-day fast during which one was not allowed food or drink from sunrise to sunset. Fifth, the *hajj*, or pilgrimage, to Mecca, which all adult Muslims were expected to make at least once, if they were financially able.

After Muhammad's return to Mecca, Islam spread rapidly throughout Arabia, largely because the *umma* that Muhammad had established in Medina and which now controlled Mecca was regarded as a kind of megatribe for which the other smaller nomadic tribes were no match. Conformity with Islam, albeit in some cases only outwardly so, became the order of the day. Muhammad's influence was now felt over all Arabia, and he began to flirt with the idea of expansion to foreign lands, but did not make it a reality. Then, in A.D. 632, Muhammad died in Mecca, and Islam exploded across the borders of Arabia.

Muslim horsemen from the now-large *umma* quickly conquered the waning Ghassanid and Lakhmid dynasties in northern Arabia, which opened the gateway respectively to the Byzantine and Persian empires, where local Christian populations would in fact often look on the Muslims as liberators from Byzantine and Persian oppression. By the middle of the seventh century, the Muslims had conquered Persia and Iraq and had also taken Syria and part of Armenia. In the west, Egypt quickly fell, and in Alexandria, the Muslim horsemen from the desert discovered the advantages of ships. A Muslim fleet soon swept across the rest of North Africa, and by the early eighth century, most of Spain from Gibraltar to the Pyrenees had passed into Muslim control. Sicily was invaded in 832 and would be ruled by the Muslims until it was retaken by the Normans in 1060. And much to the consternation of the papacy, Muslim invaders even established themselves on the Italian mainland at Bari and Taranto, less than two hundred miles from Rome itself.

How did this conquest occur so rapidly? The casual observer would be tempted to say it was because of religious fervor. Yet there is nothing explicit in Islam that stressed proselytization, and even in areas conquered by the Muslims, it was never the policy to offer the vanquished a choice between Islam or the sword. Rather, in keeping with the practice instituted by Muhammad in Medina, non-Muslims were allowed to continue in their faith under the status of *dhimmi* and pay an additional annual tax which was probably not much different in amount than that which was paid to the Byzantine or Persian authorities. The observation has been made by one historian that subjugation more than conversion was the goal of those carrying Islam beyond Arabia, and that the Arab conquest was more a business proposition than a religious crusade. Although a bit overstated, the fact remains that there were few cases of forced conversion, and relations between Christians, Jews, and their Muslim overlords seem on the whole to have been amiable. Furthermore, if the Islamic Empire outside of Arabia appeared more political than religious, it was understandable since that is what Muhammad and his followers had observed around them in the close church–state model of the Byzantine Empire. But the "how and why" of the rapid growth of Islam was secondary to an inescapable fact. The Mediterranean had rapidly become a Muslim lake, and the obscure caravan trader on Mt. Hira was now seen as the nemesis of western Europe, whose religious beliefs seemed to threaten the very fabric of Christendom.[32]

Muhammad in History

Islam and Muhammad have traditionally been portrayed in extremes. On the one hand, there has been a tendency, mostly by Muslim writers, to attribute to Muhammad as factual even the most fantastic of legends. His critics, on the other hand, portray him as a cunning political creature, insatiable in his appetites (mostly because of his numerous wives), and intent on destroying Judaism and Christianity. Much of the negative portrayal of Islam in Christian circles began less than a hundred years after Muhammad's death, with the Christian writer John of Damascus (675–749). Fluent in Arabic and well versed in the Qur'an, this son of a court official of the Muslim Umayyad caliphate in Damascus penned his *Defense of the Orthodox Faith*, in which he classified Islam as a Christian heresy. His *Dialogue with a Saracen*, in which an imaginary Muslim and Christian debate each other, focused on freedom of the will and the divinity of Christ as the two principal points of departure between Islam and Christianity.

Thereafter, Muhammad was seen by most other Christian writers as an apostate from Christianity rather than a founder of a new religion, just as Jews would think of Christians as Jewish heretics. Throughout the Middle Ages, Islam continued to be regarded as a Christian heresy and Muhammad an apostate. In particular, medieval writers ascribed a major role in the religious formation of Muhammad to the above-mentioned Bahira, who was declared to be an embittered apostate Christian monk, intent on using Muhammad as his instrument in the destruction of the church. Such views seemed to be confirmed by the seemingly unstoppable spread of Islam into Christian territory, and Muslims became the arch-enemy of the West—the scourge against which medieval crusaders were willing to fight and die in battle. Muhammad and Muslims became fixed in Western literature as the antithesis of all that was good and heroic: "Like well-loved characters of fiction, they were expected to display certain characteristics, and authors faithfully reproduced them for hundreds of years."[33]

The first Latin translation of the Qur'an was produced in the thirteenth century, which gave educated people a first-hand acquaintance with the "great heresy from the East." The poet Dante (1225–1321), because of his belief that Muhammad had authored a great heresy, placed him in one of the innermost circles of hell in the 28th canto of his *Inferno.* Even today, editions of the *Inferno* sold in Muslim countries routinely omit the 28th canto, and recently, Italian authorities claimed to have thwarted a plan by an Al-Qaida cell to blow up the Basilica of St. Petronius in Bologna, which contained a 1415 fresco by Giovanni da Modena portraying Dante's fate for Muhammad.

The rapid advance of the Muslim Ottoman Turkish Empire toward western Europe in the fifteenth and sixteenth centuries renewed fears of an imminent threat from the followers of Muhammad. There were impassioned but unsuccessful calls from the papacy for a new crusade, and the Protestant reformer Martin Luther deemed the growing threat of the Muslim Turks a "scourge sent by God" to punish Christendom for its sins. But the looming invasion of the West by the Turks came to a halt outside the gates of Vienna, and the Spanish monarchs Ferdinand and Isabella banished all Muslims from Spain. Gradually in the West, fear of Islam subsided.

During the eighteenth century, Islam and Muhammad began to find favor with Enlightenment thinkers because of perceptions that it was a religion that conformed more to rationality and natural law, and seemed to be relatively free of what many regarded as abstract dogmatism in Christianity. Even Voltaire's play *Muhammad,* at first glance an attack against Islam, is in fact more of an attack against Christian extremism than anything else.

By the nineteenth century, serious efforts were made by Western scholars to *understand* the religious mind of Muhammad and the essence of Islam. British explorers and scholars became fascinated with Islam and oriental studies, particularly after Sir Richard Burton, who had taken the trouble to learn Arabic and live incognito among Muslims, fired the imagination with books about his exploits. But more ominously for the fate of Muslims, the nineteenth century also saw industrialization and superior weaponry in the West, which rendered the idea of a Muslim threat unthinkable. From there, it was a small step to retaking Muslim lands in North Africa and the Middle East, especially by Britain and France, and it surprised no one, when in 1917 as he entered Jerusalem, British General Edmund Allenby (1861–1936) announced that "the crusades had been completed."

In the twentieth century, less hostile perceptions of Islam began to emerge. Lutheran bishop and Islamic scholar Tor Andrae (1885–1947), in his 1932 biography of Muhammad, insisted that the founder of Islam had to be portrayed as a true religious leader: "Like any movement in the realm of ideas, a religious faith has the same right to be judged according to its real and veritable intentions and not according to the way in which human weakness and meanness may have falsified and maimed its ideals."[34]

Relating to Islam Today

Particularly in the wake of September 11, there is renewed fear of Islam by many in the West. Yet it would be wrong today to judge Islam on the basis of its small, fundamentalist sects, just as one cannot judge all of Christianity according to the actions of some of its more extreme branches. Furthermore, secular Middle Eastern rulers who loosely cloak themselves in a mantle of Islam for the purposes of retaining power cannot be considered representative of the faith of Muhammad.

Islam has unfortunately in the minds of many become synonymous with *jihad,* or holy war, which it must be pointed out, is *not* one of the five pillars of Islam. Nevertheless, it has led to stereotype, pointed out by Jewish historian of Islam Reuven Firestone: "Among our most secure images are those of the Arabs: dark warriors grasping scimitars in one hand and Qur'ans in the other, a close-up of a swarthy giant, robed and bearded, brandishing a curved blade while breaking into a cunning grin—or a guerrilla aiming his Kalachnikov at innocent bystanders, a lone figure wired with explosives boarding an airplane or a city bus." Semantically, the word *jihad* has nothing intrinsic to do with war, but rather refers to a great striving or exertion of oneself. Distinction has often been made between a greater and lesser *jihad*, the former being an internal struggle and the latter warfare on behalf of God.[35]

To be sure, a Muslim doctrine of holy war did develop, but its exact origins are difficult to discern. The Qur'anic verses on warfare are numerous. Some place many restrictions on fighting, while others condone fighting when one has been wronged, even if the aggrieved party is Jewish or Christian. But often, Qur'anic passages on warfare directly contradict each other.[36] Thus, in Sura 29:46, we read "Only argue nicely with the People of the Book, except with the oppressors among them. Say: We believe in what has been revealed to us and revealed to you. Our God and your God is one, and it is Him to whom we surrender." It seems to be the essence of toleration, until we read in Sura 9:5, which is one of two so-called sword verses in the Qur'an: "When the sacred months are past, kill the idolaters wherever you find them, and seize them, besiege them, and lie in wait for them in every place of ambush; but if they repent, pray regularly, and give the alms tax, then let them go their way, for God is forgiving, merciful."

Traditional Muslim explanation for the inconsistencies is that Muhammad responded to each specific situation at the time each was written, and shows an evolution of a doctrine of religiously sanctioned warfare which reflects the growing strength of Islam from a weak minority in exile to the dominant religion in Arabia. Thus, a contradictory passage determined to have been written later in Muhammad's life would be regarded as an "abrogating verse," and would be the final say on the matter. Some, however, have suggested that since the Suras in the Qur'an are not arranged in chronological order of composition, but rather according to length, it is difficult to ascertain what verses should be taken as definitive. This has led to a suggestion that regarding warfare, there were in fact diverse opinions in the young Muslim community during Muhammad's lifetime, and that in fact it is possible that one can speak of "many Islams" during this formative stage.[37]

As stated at the outset of this essay, John Paul II's decision to kiss the Qur'an surprised many. Yet it should not have. In a 1985 address to young Muslims in Morocco, John Paul II reached out to them in unequivocal language. He spoke of his respect for the rich spiritual traditions in Islam and the shared religious values, such as prayer, fasting, repentance, and almsgiving. He also affirmed their common belief in the same just and merciful God, and concluded, "that after the resurrection He will be satisfied with us and we know that we will be satisfied with him." The words of John Paul II were also fully consistent with the position taken by the Second Vatican Council in 1965 in its decree *Nostra Aetate,* which had praised Muslims for their submission to God, their commitment to the "faith of Abraham," their veneration of Jesus as prophet, their honoring of Mary, and their belief in a day of judgment and reward of God for the upright.[38]

Yet implicit in such thinking lay a challenge. If there is to be meaningful dialogue and peaceful coexistence between Christians, Jews, and Muslims, we must be prepared to speak not just of a Judaeo-Christian tradition, but also a *Judaeo-Christian-Muslim tradition.* Such statements would in bygone centuries have been referred to as "offensive to pious ears." However, Christians must bear in mind the presumptions they make when they capriciously speak to Jews of "our common Judaeo-Christian tradition." From the perspective of most Jews, Christians abandoned the Jewish tradition two thousand years ago, yet most Jews are expected to, and in fact do tolerate the phrase for the sake of harmonious relations. It would seem, then, that a Muslim would have every right to speak to a Christian or a Jew of "our common Judaeo-Christian-Muslim tradition," and indeed, that Christians as well as Jews who are serious about improved relations among the three monotheistic religions of the world should welcome it. There are twenty million Jews worldwide, compared with one billion Muslims, and by the year 2050, Muslims will outnumber Jews a hundred to one. Furthermore, there are projections that by the year 2025, Islam will have 5 percent more adherents than will Christianity. It is difficult to disagree with the conclusion of Philip Jenkins in his recent book *The Next Christendom,* wherein he suggests that we exclude Muslims from the Judaeo-Christian equation at our own peril.[39] In Genesis 25:9, we are told that after Abraham died, Ishmael and Isaac came together to bury their father. It would be hard to find a more fitting paradigm for future peaceful coexistence between the descendants of Isaac and the descendants of Ishmael.

Questions for Reflection and Discussion

1. What has been your basic perception of Islam, particularly with regard to how it relates to Judaism and Christianity?

2. Can you accept and value the concept of a "Judaeo-Christian-Muslim" tradition without feeling as if you are compromising what you might believe individually?

3. Does knowledge of the Jewish and Christian roots of Islam help you see it less as an "alien" religion? (If you are a Muslim) Can you appreciate the Jewish and Christian roots of Islam without feeling as if you are "taking something away" from the Prophet Muhammad?

2

Neither for Money Nor Honor

The Crusader Response to Islam

The very word *crusade* conjures up images of bloodthirsty mercenaries from Europe slaughtering innocent Muslims in the Holy Land. Although atrocities were indeed committed by both Western crusaders and their Muslim counterparts, an essentially religious motivation was behind at least the initial phase of the century-long period that has come to be called the crusades. It was in the complex military and political scenario that resulted that religion gradually took second place to pragmatism—and often avarice—as crusader leaders often allied themselves with Muslims against other crusaders in an effort to maintain a hold on the territory that had been gained during the First Crusade.

To make war in the service of God is imposed on some as a penance, as is evident from those who are enjoined to fight in aid of the Holy Land
—Thomas Aquinas, *Summa Theologiae*

Iraq is the lever which will set in motion the whole Arab east; it is the point of division and center of resistance, and once it is set in its place in the chain of alliances, the whole armed might of Islam will be coordinated to engage the forces of unbelief
—Saladin, A.D. 1182

Quietly and without fanfare in 1945, the diocese of Pueblo, Colorado, became the last Roman Catholic diocese worldwide officially to end the *cruzado,* or crusading tax, which for centuries had been the principal opportunity for the faithful to demonstrate tangible support for the campaign against

25

the "infidel." This was, in a sense, the "official" end to a long and problematic chapter in the history of the church. Perceptions nevertheless persist in the Muslim world that the West is still engaged in a crusade against Islam. One need only recall the furor that erupted in the Muslim world, when a week after the attack against the World Trade Center, President Bush unwittingly pledged a "crusade against evil-doers."

Pilgrimage, holy war, a general passage, an expedition of the cross, the business of Jesus Christ—all were euphemisms for what we will call the "crusades" in this essay, even though the term was not used until fifteenth-century Spain. The First Crusade, in many ways the paradigm for all later crusades, has been correctly described as a "violent and brutal episode during which the crusaders cut a swathe of suffering through Europe and western Asia."[1] Yet, in the context of the eleventh century, the crusades were also profoundly religious. The penitential element of the crusades and the desire of the crusader for salvation were its defining features, and once an individual had made the commitment to go east, it became a religious obligation. How did this strange combination of religion and irreligion begin?

A Call to War in the Service of God

On November 27, 1095, the assembled crowd was silent outside the cathedral in Clermont, France, as Pope Urban II (1088–1099) sat on his papal throne and addressed them. Born Odo de Lagery, into a French knightly family from the province of Champagne, Urban II had fought hard to establish his legitimacy as pope and to bolster the authority of the papacy. Just ten years earlier, the great reforming pope Gregory VII (1073–1085) had died in exile after the German emperor Henry IV (1056–1105), insisting that his temporal authority was superior to the pope's spiritual authority, occupied Rome and created the antipope Clement III (1084–1100). Urban himself, although elected in 1088, had not been able to occupy St. Peter's Basilica until 1093, when Clement III finally relinquished possession of it.[2]

Although the exact content of Urban's speech is not certain, we know that he called upon the nobility of Western Europe to go as armed pilgrims to the East, assist their Christian brothers against the attacks of the Muslim Turks, and liberate the holy city of Jerusalem. Those who acted not for honor or money but rather out of a desire for salvation and to liberate the church of God in Jerusalem were to be "relieved of all penance imposed for their sins, of which they have made a genuine and full confession." If one died in battle or even on the way to battle against the "pagans," one would still gain immediate remission of sins. A church council in the cathedral had already passed two canons in support of Urban's plan, proclaiming the Truce of God between those at odds with one another in western Europe and supporting the plenary indulgences just announced by the pope.[3]

The call for help against the Turks had not been Urban's idea but that of the Byzantine emperor Alexius I Comnenus (1081–1118) in Constantinople. The Byzantine Empire, which was the Eastern Greek-speaking half of the Roman Empire that remained after the Western empire collapsed with the fall of Rome in A.D. 476, was in trouble. After Muslims in the sixth century took over Persia, the longstanding nemesis of the Romans, the Byzantines had quickly lost territory. By A.D. 638, Palestine, Syria, and Jerusalem had fallen, and soon, all of formerly Byzantine coastal North Africa was in Muslim hands. By 711, Muslim invaders had established themselves in Spain and by the ninth century occupied Sicily and parts of southern Italy. In A.D. 846, Muslims even sacked Rome itself. Yet there was no large-scale movement of Arabs or Arab culture into these conquered areas other than the introduction of the Arabic language, and because Islam officially condemned forced conversions, Christians generally lived quite well under Muslim rule. Furthermore, the Byzantines showed an interest in the culture and court of the Muslim caliphs in Baghdad, who were regarded as monarchs equal to the Byzantine emperor, and even allowed Muslim worship in Constantinople itself. [4]

The problem, as Alexius saw it, was not the Arabs but rather the Turks. Turkestan had been ruled by the Persians in the tenth century and had been converted to Islam, but now the converts became the invaders of Byzantine as well as Muslim Fāṭimid territory. The Byzantine emperor Romanus IV (1067–1071) in 1068 had attempted to repel the Turkish invaders at the Battle of Manzikert, but the imperial army was soundly defeated and Romanus taken prisoner. It was a humiliating wake-up call, and by 1081, when Alexius came to power, almost all of Asia Minor was in Turkish hands. Alexius knew he had to respond, but the Byzantine army was depleted. Why not, he thought to himself, look to the West?[5]

Alexius had made similar requests in the past, and before his death, Gregory VII himself had hoped to lead 50,000 men in battle against the Turks and liberate the Holy Sepulcher, although his main agenda had been the reunion under papal authority of the Eastern and Western churches, in schism from each other since 1054. Urban had no intention of emulating Gregory and going himself, but promoting an expedition to the East under papal sponsorship would almost certainly boost the damaged prestige and authority of the papacy. He had already tested the waters in 1089, when he announced that anyone in Spain who would participate in rebuilding the frontier outpost at Tarragona would receive the same spiritual benefits as pilgrims to Jerusalem. France now seemed the ideal recruiting ground for a much bigger venture, since the French had already proven themselves able defenders of Christendom when they had helped reconquer northern Spain from the Moors.[6] But although popes had on occasion exhorted the faithful to the defense of Christendom, it had always been the task of monarchs to summon forces for the actual purpose of warfare. How had Urban justified his groundbreaking speech?

Initially, Christianity had an ambivalent attitude toward warfare, but after the Roman government became officially Christian in the fourth century, guidelines were established for the use of violence. Relying largely on St. Augustine, it was determined that although violence was evil, *always* to remain passive when faced with violence might in fact be an even greater evil. Therefore, a Christian could legitimately engage in warfare if the war had a just cause, if it were waged under due authority, and if the Christian combatant had the right intentions. More recently, it had been determined that the pope himself could legally summon men to arms in defense of the church and that death in such a battle was equivalent to martyrdom. The first application of this principle was two decades earlier when Pope Alexander II (1061–1073) created the "faithful of St. Peter"—knights pledged to protect the pope. Now, Urban applied the concept broadly and formally. The war against the Turks was in his mind just, since it involved the reclaiming of Christian territory and the recovery of the patrimony of Christ.[7] And as for being waged under legitimate authority, the German emperor Henry IV would normally have made the summon to arms, but he had been excommunicated, so it seemed logical that Urban himself should act.

At the conclusion of Urban's speech in what was likely prearranged, the bishop of Le Puy, Adhémar of Monteil (d. 1098), stepped forward and dramatically proclaimed his willingness to take the cross. Described as "a fighting prelate and good horseman who knew how to wear the armor of a knight," the bishop was quickly designated by Urban II to be his papal legate on the armed pilgrimage to the East. Everyone was to obey his commands as if it were the pope himself speaking.[8] The council at Clermont had already fixed the departure date as August 15, 1096, the Feast of the Assumption. In the meantime, Urban urged bishops to promote the campaign in their dioceses and set out himself to preach the armed pilgrimage all over southern France. As he traveled and word spread, many nobles as well as commoners enthusiastically came forward to take the pledge.

It was not a hard sell. The theology of indulgences held that although one could be given a penance for one's sins, an additional work of merit might be necessary to receive God's grace and release from temporal punishment and possible purgatory. The plenary indulgence offered to those who took up the cross effectively wiped away the need for any such works. Reasonable certainty of salvation was intensely important in the Middle Ages, and members of the knightly class in particular often had consciences weighed down by participation in warfare and bloodshed against fellow Christians. In a revolutionary blend of theology and pragmatism, Urban had woven together pilgrimage, penance, and pious violence, into "penitential war," which offered the knight or foot soldier the opportunity to make his peace with God through a profound act of self-sanctification, normally only accomplished by renouncing the world and entering monastic life. Now the knight could use those same skills which jeopardized his salvation to *improve* his chance of salvation and then return to his family and landholdings. It is in fact primarily in this context that one can regard the crusader as taking the cross for personal gain, in that service to God and church were usually secondary to his desire for personal spiritual benefits.[9]

Urban absolved the crusaders of the traditional canonical penalties for carrying weapons to the Holy Land (the Muslim prohibition notwithstanding), since these "Jerusalemites" were to be fighting pilgrims who would make the way to Jerusalem safe from the Turkish threat. Ironically, pilgrimage had actually been rare in Christian antiquity, and sometimes even frowned upon, such as by St. Augustine and St. Gregory of Nyssa. Nevertheless, there was a growing belief that the spot where a martyrdom occurred had a kind of remissory power, and by the eighth century, the king of the Franks, Charlemagne (771–814), was on good enough terms with the Baghdad caliph to have a hostel set up in Jerusalem for pilgrims. In the mid-ninth century the first pilgrimage to Jerusalem as a penance is recorded, and as Italian maritime powers began to enter into business arrangements with Muslim ports, it became even easier for pilgrims to make the journey. The approach of the year A.D. 1000 saw even heavier pilgrim traffic, fueled by millennial beliefs in the imminent return of Jesus to Jerusalem, as well as by the warm reception Muslims gave pilgrims because of the foreign capital they brought to Jerusalem.[10]

The only significant interruption in pilgrim traffic prior to the Turks occurred under the Shiite caliph Hakim the Mad, Fāṭimid ruler of Egypt and Palestine. Hakim, whose mother was Christian, began to persecute Christians and vandalize churches, including the Church of the Holy Sepulcher in 1009. Completely contrary to Muslim tradition, he forced Christian conversions to Islam and outraged his fellow Muslims even further when he declared himself to be God incarnate. Not surprisingly, Hakim soon disappeared, rumored to have been killed by his own sister, and his chief supporter fled to Lebanon where he founded the Druze Islamic sect, still active to this day. Stories of Hakim's harsh rule may have been mistaken in the West for a fundamental policy shift, but the reality was that after the Hakim debacle, a treaty was entered into with the Shiite Fāṭimid caliph in Egypt, who restored the rights of Christians and provided for the rebuilding of churches: "In the 1040s, Jerusalem was so full of Byzantine officials that the emperor seemed to have taken over the whole city . . . the lot of the Christians in Palestine had seldom been so pleasant . . . never before had Jerusalem enjoyed so plentifully the wealth and sympathy brought to it by pilgrims from the west."[11] Pilgrimages to Jerusalem continued on a massive scale, one group alone in A.D. 1065 numbering around seven thousand individuals.

Preaching of a crusade was supposed to be undertaken only by clergy, and the vow to go on armed pilgrimage was sworn in the presence of a priest, bishop, or higher cleric, after the crusader's wife had given permission, since his long absence would deprive her of what were delicately called "marital rights." Immediately after the vow was taken, a red cloth cross was sewn onto his clothing to identify him as one of the *cruce signati*, "signed with the cross." It was serious business. He was now a temporary ecclesiastic and faced excommunication and outlaw status if he removed his cross before he had fulfilled his vow by praying at the Holy Sepulcher and then returning home, or at least dying in the process. If one died before setting out to complete his vow, his son inherited the vow. Some who took the cross and had second thoughts paid someone to go in their place or paid a large amount of money to support a crusade, a process known as *substitution* or *redemption*.[12]

The journey was a daunting two thousand miles, which under ideal conditions, could be made in as little as five months. Before departing, a crusader thus had myriad legal, financial, and spiritual matters to attend to, especially since there was a great chance that he would not return. First and foremost, he had to ensure that he could afford the cost of raising and provisioning an army, which required on average four times his annual income. Many incurred heavy debt, and reluctantly mortgaged or sold land, which usually only the religious communities could afford to buy. Godfrey of Bouillon (1060–1100), however, raised money by more nefarious means, extorting money from local Jews. A perennial stereotype portrays the crusades as a calculated colonial venture for material gain, but although wealth and status would eventually preoccupy some crusaders, there is no clear evidence to support the notion that it was a significant factor in the planning or execution of the First Crusade, and few of the returning crusaders in 1099 would have anything material to show for their travails.

A crusader also had to make sure that his will was in order and settle any legal claims that one might have against him or his property. These "renunciations of claims" usually involved cash settlements, which was yet another expense that had to be covered, although on occasion crusaders' claims against others would also be settled. All that having been done, the crusader received the "Privileges of the Cross," which meant that his property and family were henceforth protected by the church and that no legal action could be taken against him in his absence.[13]

Hopeful for a safe return, the crusader also sought ways to insure prayers during his absence. Often, he made a large cash bequest to a religious community, or in the case of wealthier knights, completely endowed a brand new religious house or church. For the First Crusade alone, there is a record of eighty such endowed churches. Sometimes, a crusader might waive any debt claims he might have against religious communities in return for perpetual prayer on his behalf, or he might convince a younger family member to enter a religious community, which would guarantee the prayers of that community during his absence.[14]

The plenary indulgence announced by Urban was aimed ideally only at fighting men or those who could otherwise contribute to a military effort. Urban did not want any elderly or infirm, women without husbands, clergy without permission from their superiors, monks, or laymen who had not received a clerical blessing. However, because it was technically a pilgrimage, none could be refused, and as word of this new path toward salvation spread, Urban got exactly what he did not want. Many older men *wanted* to die in Jerusalem and wives often accompanied husbands. Monks went, in spite of the prohibition, and even the occasional criminal, whose sentence would be commuted for taking part. [15]

Especially problematic was the self-styled itinerant French preacher Peter the Hermit (1050–1115), so-named only because of his hermit's cloak. Described by contemporaries as "short, barefoot, and filthy," he claimed to have a letter "fallen from heaven" that prophesied that Christians would drive the "infidels" from the Holy Land. Peter insisted that during an earlier pilgrimage to Jerusalem, the Greek patriarch had appealed to him to persuade Urban II to preach the crusade. A congenital embellisher, Peter nevertheless had an uncanny ability to win people over. In his preaching, he tapped into the strong apocalyptic millennial reservoir of the eleventh century, particularly prophecies that confused the New Jerusalem with the Jerusalem of Palestine, and thus insisted the latter would *have* to be recovered before Jesus could return. Peter's followers numbered 20,000 in April of 1096, when the ragtag army set out four months ahead of the August commencement date set by the Council of Clermont. But the so-named People's Crusade of mostly poor French and Germans, along with a handful of lesser knights, was long on religious enthusiasm and short on military prowess, and it was only a matter of time before serious problems arose.[16]

Preaching about the crusades had emphasized the liberation of Jerusalem, the scene of the suffering and death of Jesus, and soon a violent wave of anti-Semitism began to follow the route of the People's Crusade toward Constantinople as some became convinced that the battle against Christ's enemies ought to begin at home. Peter does not seem to have been directly responsible, but rather others who set out in the wake of his preaching. Emich of Leisingen, a petty and disreputable count from the Rhineland, ordered the massacre of hundreds of Jews as he and his army journeyed through the Rhine and Moselle valleys. An obscure follower of Peter named Volkmar instigated pogroms in Prague, while a German priest named Gottschalk inspired his followers to massacre the Jews of Regensburg in southern Germany. These unprovoked attacks were in no way sanctioned by the church, which in fact went to great effort, albeit largely unsuccessful, to suppress the anti-Semitism.[17]

Meanwhile, more prudent and professional preparations for the "official" crusade were underway. Approximately seven thousand nobles and knights took part, and when support personnel were added, the army numbered approximately 24,500 men, the various "camp followers" of elderly men and female pilgrims notwithstanding. No kings participated in the First Crusade; the leadership was made up of several high nobles and the above-mentioned papal legate Adhémar, bishop of Le Puy, whose two brothers also joined the pilgrimage. The next most senior churchman after Adhémar was William, the bishop of Orange. Raymond of Toulouse (1052–1105), age fifty-five, headed the largest military contingent. The first layman of stature to join the crusades, he was the only notable with whom Urban II had discussed his plans for the crusade, and Raymond would work closely with Adhémar. Other of the better-known participants included Hugh of Vermandois (1053–1101), Godfrey of Bouillon, Baldwin of Boulogne (1058–1118), and Robert of Flanders (1065–1111).[18]

Bohemond of Taranto (1058–1111) and Robert of Normandy (1054–1134) each headed Norman contingents. Descendants of Vikings who had plundered and then colonized the northwestern coast of France, the Normans (Northmen) were known for battle prowess. Just thirty years earlier in 1066, Robert's father, William the Conqueror (1028–1087), marching under a papal banner of St. Peter, had defeated Anglo-Saxon England. Normans had also ousted Muslims from Sicily, set up their own kingdom, and protected Pope Gregory VII in southern Italy during his exile from Rome. In a dramatic gesture,

Bohemond announced his intention to take the cross by doffing his scarlet cloak and tearing it into crosses for those who would join him.[19]

Constantinople

The Byzantines had planned to control the heavy flow of crusaders through Byzantine territory by opening or shutting local markets, but it was based on the August 15 departure date announced by the Council of Clermont. Alexius was thus surprised when in mid-summer, he learned that a large crusading army had already entered Byzantine territory and had begun to forage and pillage. Sixty had been killed in retaliation. Alexius was even more surprised as the army of Peter the Hermit made its way into Constantinople in July of 1096. It was no fighting force, but rather a ragtag group of overzealous pilgrims.[20] Nevertheless, Alexius was cordial to them, fed them, and invited Peter to the palace. Within days however, reports of petty theft committed by Peter's followers caused Alexius to move the entire group across the Bosphorus, the narrow waterway that separated European Constantinople from Asia Minor, with the exception of Peter, who remained at the palace.

In Asia Minor, they began to pillage indiscriminately, and in October of 1096, a large group of French members of the army confiscated herd animals and slaughtered the Christian Greek population of the Christian villages on the outskirts of Nicaea, the capital of the Seljuk sultan. Ironically, retribution came from the Turks, and it was swift and powerful. Almost the entire army of the People's Crusade was wiped out; only a handful of survivors made their way back to Constantinople. The People's Crusade had collapsed, and a few days later, the first of the formal crusaders arrived in Constantinople,[21] after embarking from Adriatic ports, signaling the beginning of a lucrative business for the Italian maritime powers of Genoa, Pisa, and Venice.[22]

Alexius knew that as the main bulwark of Christendom the crusaders could either be a tremendous help or a tremendous threat. In the best scenario, they would fight as mercenaries, recapture Turkish-held lands, return them to Byzantine control, and then go home. However, Alexius was not naive. The Greek Church had been in schism from the Latin Church since A.D. 1054, and the *Dictatus Papae* of Pope Gregory VII in 1075 had declared the right of the pope to depose emperors, proclaim uncatholic those who were not at peace with the Roman Church, and absolve subjects from their fealty to "wicked men." Alexius was vulnerable. In addition, Alexius had been playing the Turkish princes off against one another and did not want them to unite prematurely against the crusaders until he was ready to make his move. Alexius needed some control over the crusaders, so he required that the leader of each army swear allegiance to him and pledge to return to Byzantine control any territory retaken from the Turks. The only leader who did not take the oath was Raymond of Toulouse, with whom Alexius had reached a private understanding.

Alexius also feared that the crusaders might pose a threat to Constantinople itself and was particularly concerned about the Normans; Bohemond and his Normans had already destroyed a town on the way to Constantinople simply because it was inhabited by Paulicians, a dissident sect of Christianity. Accordingly, as he had done with the People's Crusade, he quickly moved them across the Bosphorus, and must have breathed a sigh of relief in May of 1097, when the last of the crusader armies arrived in Asia Minor. Remarkably, in less than a year, between 60,000 and 100,000 Westerners had passed through Constantinople, and Alexius seems to have provided for all of them. It seemed at the time a small price to pay to have the Turks driven out of Asia Minor.[23]

The First Crusade (1096–1099)

Accompanied by a contingent of Greek troops, the crusaders set out for Nicaea, the site of the very first ecumenical council. Now the Seljuk capital, the city was the gateway to Asia Minor; it had four miles of walls and 240 towers, and it was inhabited mostly by Christians, except for the large Turkish garrison. Nicaea fell fairly quickly in the siege of June 1097, but not before the crusaders had catapulted the heads of some of the slain Turks into the city to demoralize the defenders. Many crusaders were unhappy when the sultan's family along with their possessions were taken to Constantinople, where they eventually ransomed themselves for their freedom, but the enterprise was still under Byzantine control.[24] After Nicaea, towns conquered along the way were at first handed back to Byzantine control, as had been promised, but there was growing tension and mistrust between Latin and Greek troops. Even more ominous, there was growing factionalism among the crusader princes.

Four months later in October, the crusaders laid siege to Antioch. Its importance was more symbolic than strategic; the name "Christian" had first been used there, and the city had been established as a bishopric by St. Peter. It had already been recovered once from Muslim control by the Byzantines in the tenth century and had subsequently become a thriving crossroads of Byzantine and Muslim trade, until it fell to the Turks. The Greek, Syrian, and Armenian Christians initially had been left alone by the Turks, but as a crusader attack became more imminent, the Greeks and Armenians were sent out of the city so they could not form a disloyal fifth column. The Syrians were allowed to stay, since the Turks perceived them to hate the Armenians and Greeks. The patriarch of Antioch was then imprisoned and periodically suspended over the walls of the city in a cage, as a warning to any would-be attackers that the cost would be great.[25]

The siege dragged on for months. In the meantime, two hundred miles away in northern Mesopotamia, Baldwin of Boulogne assumed the reigns of government in Edessa after he had wrested the city from Turkish control. By all rights, he should have given Edessa back to Alexius, but Baldwin defiantly proclaimed himself "Count of Edessa" and thereby established the first crusader state in the region. But Baldwin's army was small, so he pragmatically entered into treaties and alliances with both his Christian and Muslim neighbors, and invited them to take part in his administration. Much to the shock of other crusaders, Baldwin even allowed Muslim worship to continue in areas he conquered, perhaps in imitation of Islamic toleration of religious pluralism.[26]

As the siege of Antioch continued, an embassy from the Egyptian Fāṭimid caliphate arrived and tried to make a deal. They would let the Franks have Syria if they could have Palestine. The innovative notion that religious considerations could be treated as secondary to political considerations did not go unnoticed by the crusaders, but unlike Baldwin in Edessa, they balked at the idea. In June of 1098, they brought the siege of Antioch to a successful end, after bribing one of the Turkish defenders to let them into the city in the dead of night. In the fighting that ensued, the entire Turkish population, men, women, and children, were all massacred, as well as some Christians. The streets were strewn with corpses, and the houses of the inhabitants, both Muslim and Christian, were pillaged by the crusaders.[27]

Baldwin had set a precedent in Edessa, and as the crusaders now argued over whether to return the city to Byzantine control, the Provençal servant Peter Bartholomew (not to be confused with Peter the Hermit), approached papal legate Adhémar and Raymond of Toulouse. He claimed that visions of St. Andrew had told him that the lance that pierced the side of Christ was to be found in the cathedral of St. Peter in Antioch and that the city should remain in Latin hands. Adhémar, who was the great peacemaker among the sometimes-factious crusaders and universally liked (except by Peter Bartholomew), was determined to pursue rapprochement with the Greek Church and insisted that Antioch be given back to the Byzantines. Then, Peter suddenly produced a piece of iron, after a group of crusaders had already dug unsuccessfully in the cathedral, and it was quickly accepted by most as the true lance that pierced Christ.

Subsequent "revelations" from St. Andrew gained Peter an even wider following. A skeptical Adhémar continued plans to give Antioch back to Byzantine control, but he died of typhoid. Peter wasted no time and proclaimed yet another vision, not just of St. Andrew but also of a now-contrite Adhémar. Not surprisingly, both insisted that a Latin patriarch should be appointed for Antioch and that the crusaders should then march immediately to victory in Jerusalem. Peter's revelations carried the day, and Bohemond, arguably the most bellicose among the crusaders, proclaimed himself prince of Antioch. There would be no more help from the emperor Alexius. The army, however, quickly tired of Peter's revelations, and an outraged Peter requested an ordeal of fire to prove his legitimacy. Apparently, he sincerely believed in himself, because he subsequently died of his burns.[28]

As the crusaders approached Jerusalem in June of 1099, there was an eclipse of the moon, which they took to prefigure a victory over the crescent of Islam. The Fāṭimid caliphate in Egypt had recruited Arab and Nubian troops to help defend the city, and the governor had expelled all the Christians from Jerusalem—about half the population. The Jews had been allowed to remain. Approximately 1,400 knights and 12,000 infantrymen prepared to lay siege to the city. They first fasted, as they did before all major engagements. Some excitedly took the time to go to the Jordan River for rebaptism.[29] In a liturgical procession before the city walls, bishops, priests, and crusaders prayed that Jesus would intercede to deliver the city and the Holy Sepulcher.

When six weeks passed and the prayers still had not worked, the crusaders constructed two large siege engines, and on July 15, 1099, wheeled them before the city walls. The defenders rained down stones and Greek fire, the napalm-like substance which had for centuries been such a formidable weapon in the East, but Jerusalem was overrun. The crusader Raymond d'Aguiliers proudly described what followed:

> Our men had captured the walls and towers of the city and wonderful sights could be seen. Some of the merciful crusaders cut off the heads of their enemies; others shot them with arrows so that they fell from the towers of the city; other crusaders tortured the Moslems longer by throwing them into fires. Piles of heads, hands, and feet were littering the streets of the city. We had to step over bodies of men and horses in the streets. These were small matters compared to what happened in the Temple of Solomon, a place where religious services were normally held. . . . Here men rode in blood up to their knees and bridle reins. It was a just and splendid judgment of God that this place should be filled with the blood of unbelievers. . . . This day will be famous in all

future ages . . . it marks the justification of all Christianity and the humiliation of paganism.

The Dome of the Rock was pillaged, and those who had taken shelter inside were killed. Men, women, and children were slain throughout the city, and Muslims who had taken refuge in the Al-Aqsa mosque were slaughtered. Most of the Jews of Jerusalem took refuge in the chief synagogue, where they were burned alive by the crusaders. In a horrific display of pseudopiety, the crusaders had exacted revenge against not just "those who had stolen the Holy Land" but also against "those who had killed Christ himself." This thinking would be echoed in the 1099 crusading epic *La Chanson d'Antioche*, in which Christ on the cross assures others that he will be avenged by the crusaders. [30]

After the capture of Jerusalem, most of the crusaders set out for home. The eager anticipation of battle during their journey to the Holy Land was replaced by the weary realities of deprivation, disease, and battle fatigue. When finally reaching home, they placed Jerusalem palm fronds on the altar of their parish church as evidence they had fulfilled their vow. As stated above, there is scant evidence of crusaders returning home wealthy, with the exception of the Montlhéry family, but many crusaders made additional donations to churches and even foundations in gratitude for a safe return. Some, perhaps disillusioned with secular life, even became priests or monks.[31]

Those who did not come home built up the society known as *Outremer*— Old French for "across the sea." They set up a Latin patriarchate in Jerusalem, and only Latin religious services were now allowed in the Church of the Holy Sepulcher. When the Kingdom of Jerusalem was proclaimed, Godfrey of Bouillon took the secular title "Protector of the Holy Sepulcher," since the consensus was that only Jesus could be the "King of Jerusalem." When Godfrey died a year later however, he was replaced by Baldwin, who, less concerned about religious sensitivity, became "King Baldwin of Jerusalem."

The crusaders could now look with considerable satisfaction on a string of city-based Frankish states—the County of Edessa in the northeast, the Principality of Antioch in Syria, the County of Tripoli (present-day Lebanon), and the Kingdom of Jerusalem, which extended south all the way to Gaza. Their continued existence, however, was precarious. With the exception of Edessa, all were along the coast, were isolated from one another, and could do little to support one another in the event of attack. Political pragmatism finally became unavoidable, and crusader–Muslim alliances soon protected the crusaders not just from other Muslims but also from other crusaders who might covet their fiefs and territories. It was not, however, without cost, as the Latins quickly became just another player in the game of shifting alliances, counter alliances, and temporary treaties which characterized the Middle East.[32]

Pope Urban II died in Rome two weeks after the fall of Jerusalem, before word of the conquest could reach him. He had exercised unprecedented papal power in launching the First Crusade, but it quickly became a juggernaut that he could not control, especially given the ability of a few powerful crusading families to manipulate the flow of events. However noble and religious the motives had been for those first crusaders to Jerusalem, the subsequent decision not to hand territory back to the Byzantines changed the crusading dynamic and replaced knightly honor and commitment with pragmatism and avarice. All of the subsequent crusades would be aimed at preserving the crusader states, and the religious dimension of these armed pilgrimages would fade even further. And when the emperor Alexius died in 1118, he would have little to show for all the "help" from the West. He had regained part of Anatolia, but no other region in which the crusaders had fought was now under his control, and he now had what seemed to be permanent Frankish states in his own backyard.[33]

The Second Crusade (1147–1149)

The success of the First Crusade had been due in large part to Byzantine help and Muslim disunity, but almost fifty years later, circumstances were very different. In the aftermath of the siege of Jerusalem, the Iraqi poet Abu l-Musaffar al Abiwardi had penned an impassioned call for Muslim resistance: "This is war, and the infidel's sword is naked in his hand. . . . For fear of death the Moslems are evading the fire of battle, refusing to believe that death will surely strike them. Must the Arab champions then suffer with resignation, while the gallant Persians shut their eyes to their dishonor?" The poet's exhortation was not ignored, as new Muslim leaders tried to reunite the Islamic world in the aftermath of Turkish and crusader invasions. An Islamic "counter-crusade" *jihad* began, especially fierce in tone because of the memory of the massacre during the siege of Jerusalem, which "was the bloodthirsty proof of Christian fanaticism that recreated the fanaticism of Islam."[34] The first major blow was struck by the Muslim general Imad ad-Din Zengi (1087–1146) and his troops, who captured far-off Edessa on Christmas Eve, 1144, and killed all the Franks. Pilgrims returning from Jerusalem to Europe in 1145 reported the unbelievable news of the destruction of the oldest of the crusader states, and before the year was out, former Cistercian abbot Pope Eugene III (1145–1153) called for another armed pilgrimage in his papal bull *Quantum praedecessores* of December 1, 1145.

The Second Crusade lacked the novelty and enthusiasm of the First Crusade, and the pope's call was more of a "charter" than the dramatic appeal of his predecessor, Urban. Pope Eugene, however, had learned from the mistakes of the First Crusade and spelled out the status and privileges of crusaders with much greater precision. They were exempted from legal action and interest payments on all debts until their return and were permitted to mortgage their properties in order to fund their expenses. Only authorized preachers were to promote the crusade, in an obvious effort to avoid another Peter the Hermit. More experienced military leaders and logistical planning was needed, and leaders through whose territories the pilgrims would travel now had to give permission. This was not just a diplomatic courtesy but would also prepare local markets for the influx, thus avoiding the foraging and looting of the First Crusade. Pope Eugene was supported by the ecumenical First Lateran Council, convened in 1123 by French Pope Calixtus II (1119–1124), whose three brothers had been crusaders. The council had decreed that those who set out for Jerusalem in defense of Christians were to be granted remission of their sins and that "all their houses and families and all their goods be placed under the protection of blessed Peter and the Roman Church." Any who violated this protection would be excommunicated. The council further warned that any who took the cross and did not complete their obligations would be forbidden entry into church, and no sacraments, except baptism and confessions for the dying, would be allowed to be celebrated in their lands.[35]

In *Quantum praedecessores,* Pope Eugene invited all the faithful to take part, but aimed his remarks especially at King Louis VII of France (1137–1180). Louis was in fact a little too eager. He tried to make the crusade his own and enlisted the help of popular St. Bernard of Clairvaux, who, in impassioned language, preached the crusade in a series of public homilies throughout France: "What are you brave men doing? What are you servants of the cross doing? Will you thus give a holy place to dogs and pearls to swine?" Eugene saw the Second Crusade slipping from his authority and became even more concerned when King Conrad III of Germany (1138–1152) also took the cross, since a crusade united under *two* sovereigns could only further weaken papal control. Eugene hurriedly reissued *Quantum praedecessores* to reassert papal authority over the enterprise and designated not one but two cardinal papal legates for the Second Crusade—one for the French and one for the Germans.[36]

To underscore further papal authority, Eugene expanded the scope of the Second Crusade. He granted the request of the king of Castile to extend crusader privileges to those willing to fight in the Iberian peninsula against Spanish Muslims and, similarly, extended crusader privileges to a contingent of Germans who decided that instead of fighting in the Holy Land, they would do battle with the neighboring Slavs east of the Elbe River. Eugene even designated a papal legate to accompany the Germans and, contrary to church tradition, seems to have allowed for forced conversion of the Slavs. In the end, however, the so-named Wendish Crusade would accomplish little, either in terms of territorial acquisition or conversions.[37]

The armies of Conrad and King Louis, accompanied by Louis's wife, Eleanor of Aquitaine (1122–1204), finally set out for the East in the summer of 1147. Once more, there were sporadic uprisings against the Jews along the way, mostly attributed to a monk named Radulf. When they arrived in Constantinople in the fall, the emperor Manuel I Comnenus (1143–1180) was nervous. Although he already had an informal alliance with Germany, the sight of a large combined German and French army raised the specter of a united Europe against the Byzantine Empire. As his grandfather Alexius had done during the First Crusade, Manuel insisted on an oath of fealty and hinted at the reunion of the two churches, but only if King Louis pledged to return to Byzantine control any city recaptured in Anatolia. In return, Manuel was willing to concede the rest of Palestine and Syria to Latin control. Negotiations unraveled quickly though, when the crusaders learned that, in true Byzantine fashion, Manuel had for good measure also concluded a treaty with the Seljuk sultan of Iconium, whose burgeoning army threatened the Byzantines. The Byzantine–crusader alliance had collapsed, and the subsequent lack of Byzantine assistance complicated the already-daunting plan to retake Anatolia from the Turks.[38]

The crusaders wasted no time in crossing over to Asia Minor. Because of their superior tactical skills, the Knights Templar and the Hospitallers of St. John were given a leadership role. A fusion of monasticism and knighthood, these military orders had originated in Jerusalem after the First Crusade. Pledged to protect pilgrims traveling to and from the Holy Land, they took vows of poverty, chastity, and obedience, just as religious did.[39] But in spite of the additional support, the Germans and the French suffered defeats in separate battles in Asia Minor. By the time they reached Antioch, half of the French army had disappeared, and those that remained were quarreling with the Germans. Even worse for King Louis, he discovered that his wife, Eleanor, had become "involved" with Prince Raymond of Antioch (1136–1149). Louis decided that Edessa was not worth saving, so in July 1148, they laid siege to Damascus but suffered a humiliating defeat, mostly due to a recurrence of infighting among the Latin leaders. The emperor Manuel no longer had to fear a German–French alliance.

The degree of commitment and resolve of the First Crusade was absent, and many crusaders now simply completed their pilgrimage to the Church of the Holy Sepulcher and went home, defeated and humiliated. King Louis felt betrayed by the lack of Byzantine support and began to speak of revenge, while the opportunistic Conrad of Germany entered into a more formal alliance with the Byzantines, which earned him the scorn of the French.[40] It would turn out that the conquest of Lisbon was in fact the high point of the Second Crusade, and was one of the few real territorial acquisitions. Even worse, the crusader states were now in an even more perilous state, as the failure of the Second Crusade emboldened and unified the Muslim world even further.

The Third Crusade (1189–1192)

Forty years after the debacle of the Second Crusade, armed pilgrimage had long lost its luster. Then, in 1187, shocking news reached the West, and it had to do with Kurdish general Salāḥ-ad-Dīn Yūsuf ibn-Aiyūb, or "Righteousness of the Faith, Joseph son of Job," better known in the West as Saladin (1138–1193).

Arguably the greatest of Muslim generals, Saladin possessed a charisma recognized even by his enemies. He had held some minor administrative posts in Syria, had an interest in religious studies, and was a skilled polo player,[41] but prominence came when he assisted the Fāṭimid caliph in Egypt in putting down an internal revolt by one of the viziers who had conspired with the Franks. Saladin soon found himself as the new vizier and shortly thereafter sultan. Saladin restored an alliance between the Abbāsid caliphate in Baghdad and the Shiite Fāṭimids in Egypt, and when he was invested with the governments of the newly unified Egypt and Syria, the poetic diploma recited clearly foreshadowed his role against the crusaders: "As for the jihād, thou art the nursling of its milk and the child of its bosom." Damascus could no longer be courted by the crusaders as a friend in order to counterbalance the threats from Egypt and northern Syria. Saladin systematically negotiated peace with every potential adversary of the Franks and simply conquered those Muslim states and leaders who refused, reducing the ability of the crusaders to play them off against one another or to enter into an alliance with them. Saladin also concluded trade treaties with Pisa, Genoa, and Venice and successfully sought improved relations with Constantinople, evidenced by the restoration of Muslim worship in Constantinople.[42]

The crusaders had already met Saladin in earlier battles, and there was a certain measure of respect for him. William of Tyre (1128–1186), who had been born in Jerusalem, remarked that Saladin "was a man wise in counsel, valiant in war, and generous beyond measure." But aware that Saladin was a force to be reckoned with, they also tried to use him to their advantage. In 1183, Raymond of Jerusalem allied with Saladin to put down a rival crusader's attempts to take control of the city, and Saladin negotiated a truce with Bohemond of Antioch, which allowed Saladin to retaliate against the Franks in Jerusalem for their forays into his territory. Saladin also negotiated a four-year truce with Raymond of Tripoli (1142–1187), which allowed Saladin to move against the eastern Seljuk princes, but in the end also strengthened his position against the crusaders.[43]

Finally, in July 1187, Saladin made his move when he surprised and annihilated the entire army of the Kingdom of Jerusalem at the mountain pass known as the Horns of Hattin, near the Sea of Galilee. Victory was made even easier because of a series of strategic blunders by the crusaders and infighting among the principal Franks. Two months later in October, Saladin and his troops recaptured Jerusalem, and again, crusader infighting simplified the task. The native Christian population was allowed to remain, but some Christian churches were pillaged. The Byzantine emperor Isaac II Angelus (1185–1195), great-grandson of Alexius, sent his congratulations to Saladin, suggested a renewed alliance against the Latins, and asked that Greek places of worship be restored.[44] Saladin now controlled the entire Muslim world from Egypt to Iraq, with the exception of Tyre, Tripoli, and Antioch.

In the West, the faithful were urgently exhorted to take up arms. Henry II of England (1154–1189), Philip II Augustus of France (1180–1223), the Count of Flanders, and Holy Roman Emperor Frederick Barbarossa (1155–1190) agreed, and when King Henry II levied the "Saladin tithe" to raise funds, there was no doubt as to the enemy. Henry II, however, married to the same Eleanor of Aquitaine who had gone on the Second Crusade with her then-husband King Louis, died before he could embark, so the crown and responsibility for the crusade passed to his son, Richard the Lionhearted (1189–1199), who was hesitant because of potential political instability in his absence. Nevertheless, Richard set out from Dartmouth with an English contingent of approximately one hundred ships in the fall of 1189. As a sort of training exercise, the advance squadron of the English fleet reached Lisbon in September 1189 and vanquished the Muslims in the nearby town of Silves, which was then handed over to Portuguese control. A number of English sailors also engaged in rape and plunder.[45]

The German emperor Frederick and his eager troops had set out early and were the first to arrive in Asia Minor. They took the town of Iconium from the Turks in May 1190, but just weeks later, disaster struck when Frederick drowned in a river crossing near Antioch. German participation in the crusade was over, and the dispirited troops returned home. Ten months later in April 1191, French king Philip Augustus and his fleet arrived at Acre, and shortly thereafter, King Richard and the English fleet arrived, after stopping in Cyprus to seize the island from the Byzantines. The combined French and English forces laid siege to the city of Acre, which quickly fell. Richard and Philip divided the city between them, but King Philip abruptly sailed for home, which raised Richard's concerns that Philip would try to assert rights to the English throne. Richard set his sights on Jerusalem, but although "reckless and fool-hardy as a soldier," he was also "intelligent, cautious, and calculating as a com-mander," and quickly realized that the costs of retaking the city would be too high. Instead, he negotiated a treaty with Saladin. Jerusalem would stay in Mus-lim hands; the crusaders would retain a narrow strip of land on the coast; Chris-tians and Muslims would have free passage throughout Palestine; and, best of all for Richard, no French were to be allowed access to Jerusalem. The treaty now agreed to, Richard set sail in October 1192 but was delayed two years after being shipwrecked and then rescued by the Venetians, who turned him over to the duke of Austria, who imprisoned him for ransom.[46]

At best, what can be said about the accomplishments of the Third Crusade, besides the recapture of Acre, was that through the treaty, the remnants of the Kingdom of Jerusalem were protected from further conquest at a time when in hindsight, it would have been easy for Saladin to do this. Yet minimal territory was secured, and the city of Jerusalem itself remained in Muslim hands. Largely through his singleness of outlook, his ability to lead and unify, and his sense of moral outrage and determination to take a stand against the crusaders, Saladin had reestablished Muslim hegemony in the Middle East.[47]

The Fourth Crusade (1202–1204)

In 1198, just eight years after the fiasco of the Third Crusade, the great medieval pope Innocent III (1198–1216) was elected. Intensely interested in crusading, he hoped for the reunion of the two churches and the preservation of the holy shrines and disintegrating Latin states of the East, but was also determined to reestablish papal control of the crusades, particularly since Holy Roman Emperor Henry VI of Germany (1191–1197) had just failed in his own efforts to launch a crusade. Innocent repeated now-standard language about the suffer-ings of Jerusalem and the Christians in the East, the laxity of Western princes, and the need for peace among them so they could turn their attentions to the real enemy. Innocent sent two cardinals out to enlist support, one in France and the other in Venice. To help keep the crusade under papal control, Innocent appealed not to monarchs or higher nobility, but rather to cities, counts, and barons. Innocent admonished King Richard of England and King Philip Augustus of France, at war with each other since the end of the Third Crusade, to make a five-year peace, not so they themselves could participate in the crusade but rather to make it easier to recruit troops.[48] The pope also chastised in a letter the new Byzantine emperor, Alexius III Angelus (1195–1203), for ignoring the Muslim threat and exhorted him to recognize papal primacy.

Innocent engaged in an unprecedented level of aggressive fundraising, informing bishops that they were either to raise an army or provide a monetary equivalent. The cardinals of Rome were ordered to give a tenth of their income, while the clergy throughout the church were to remit one fortieth of their annual revenues. A chest was placed in each parish, and the faithful were to receive an indulgence commensurate with the amount of their contribution. King Philip of France and King John of England (1199–1216), who had succeeded his recently deceased brother, Richard the Lionhearted, were also expected to contribute. But in spite of, or perhaps because of, Innocent's intense efforts, there was resistance on all levels, and the entire financial effort largely failed.[49] Nevertheless, some did heed the call for yet another crusade.

The core of the crusading army came from the highest levels of the French nobility, and approximately 10,000 men were recruited in France within a year. Only Venice had a fleet large enough to carry such a large army, which the optimistic French had told the Venetians would number about 35,000. The huge colonial, maritime, and commercial power already had a reputation for being more interested in profit than religion, evidenced by their lucrative trade relationship with Muslim Egypt, which various popes had tried unsuccessfully to curtail. Their iron-fisted ruler, the ancient and blind doge Enrico Dandolo (1107–1205), agreed to transport 33,500 men and their gear, along with 4,500 horses, for a fixed price, and to supply and personally accompany fifty additional, fully manned Venetian war galleys in return for acceptance of Venice as an equal partner. The ostensible Venetian and crusader plan was to pretend to be heading to Jerusalem, but then divert to Egypt and strike a blow at the Turkish leadership there. Innocent III reluctantly approved the plan, fearing that not to do so would cost him further control of the expedition.[50]

But there was apparently another secret plan afoot. Envoys of a young claimant to the Byzantine throne named Alexius showed up in Venice and presented a plan whereby Alexius and the crusaders would divert instead to Constantinople and restore Alexius and his father as legitimate emperors in return for an alliance with the West. The plan appealed to the French and to the German king Philip of Swabia (1198–1208), who was the brother-in-law of the young Alexius.[51] Venice readily approved, since they felt their trading privileges, in place since the First Crusade, were being jeopardized by the current emperor, Alexius III. But this time Innocent III refused and wrote to Alexius III that he would not permit the attack, although Innocent pointedly remarked that many had urged him to allow it because of the disobedience of the Greek Church.

When the day of departure came, only about a third of the expected 33,500 men actually showed up in Venice. A few had reneged on their crusading pledge, but the bulk of the discrepancy was due to misguided French optimism. The Venetians demanded the full negotiated transport price, so the French leaders tried to make up the difference from their own funds but were still short, so the doge proposed postponement of the remaining debt until there was booty from the crusade to pay it back. In return, while en route to Constantinople, the French crusaders were to aid the Venetians in the reconquest of the Christian Dalmatian city of Zara, a former Venetian vassal city now under the protection of the king of Hungary. Pope Innocent forbade the attack, but the crusaders ignored him.[52]

As they approached Zara, the papal legate and some of the French nobility also protested, but the city was attacked and plundered, and the crusaders incurred automatic excommunication. While the crusaders wintered in Zara, Philip of Swabia pushed the plan to attack Constantinople and reestablish his brother-in-law Alexius, enticing the crusaders with 200,000 silver marks and the promise to provision the crusade for an entire year. The majority of the crusaders agreed and sought papal absolution from their excommunication, insisting they had attacked Zara unwillingly. Innocent, again fearing a loss of control, responded with a mild reprimand and rescinded the excommunications.[53] Nevertheless, he then excommunicated the Venetians and reiterated his prohibition of the plan, but the document unfortunately did not reach Zara until after the crusaders had already set out.

In July 1203, the crusaders broke through the defenses of Constantinople and crowned the young Alexius co-emperor with his father, Isaac. Then, in what had now become a standard desperation tactic of Byzantine emperors, Alexius wrote Pope Innocent and promised reunion, but it was too late. Detested by the Byzantines because of his Latin sympathies and unable to pay the crusaders the 200,000 silver marks that his brother-in-law Philip had promised, Alexius rightly began to fear for his life. In February 1204, he and his father were murdered, and a new anti-Latin Byzantine emperor assumed the throne as Alexius V (1204).

The crusaders acted quickly. On April 13, 1204, they took Constantinople by force and sacked it for three days. Eyewitness and Byzantine historian Nicetas Choniates (1155–1217) recounted that in the churches icons were stepped on and relics strewn about; reliquaries were stolen for their jewels and used as drinking cups. The cathedral of Hagia Sophia was plundered, and the spectacular altar, comprised of precious metals, was broken into bits and distributed among the soldiers. Throughout the city, there could be heard weeping, cries of grief, groaning from wounds, and the shrieks of women as they were raped. Another Byzantine eyewitness commented that even the Muslims would have been more merciful. But the crusader and participant Robert de Clari had a different point of view about the attack: "the bishops and the clergy in the army debated and decided that the war was a righteous one, and they certainly ought to attack the Greeks. For formerly the inhabitants of the city had been obedient to the law of Rome and now they were disobedient.... And the bishop said that for this reason one ought certainly to attack them, and that it was not a sin, but an act of great charity."[54]

Alexius V was put to death, the Latin Empire of Constantinople was created, and when the new Latin emperor donned the sacred purple boots and jeweled eagles, which were reserved exclusively for the Byzantine emperor, the emperorship of the East passed to Westerners for the first time ever, where it would remain for the next fifty-seven years. But the Venetians were the big winners. They insisted on three-fourths of the booty, a controlling role in the selection of each emperor and veto-power over his decisions, possession of Crete, and the rights to control the division of Byzantine territory. The property to be left to the Greek Church was only enough for the clergy to subsist.

Innocent III vigorously condemned what the crusaders had done: "How can the church of the Greeks be expected to return to devotion to the apostolic see, when it has seen the Latins setting an example of evil, and doing the devil's work, so that already, and with good reason, the Greeks hate them worse than dogs?"[55] But as on previous occasions, the Latins gave no heed to the papal admonition and continued in their occupation of the Byzantine Empire. Over the decades, Latin greed and mistreatment of the Greek peasantry led to widespread resentment, and conditions became wretched as the Latin Empire steadily weakened. Cash-strapped Franks began to mortgage relics, such as the purported crown of thorns, to the Venetians, while one Latin ruler even mortgaged his only son. A thousand Franks even sold their military services to the Turks.[56]

When Constantinople was finally recaptured in 1261 and a Greek emperor installed, the empire was only a pale shadow of its former self. The century-long cat-and-mouse game between Latins and Greeks, in which each party had sought to advance its own interests under the guise of cooperating with the other, had come to an unfortunate conclusion. It would be an easy victory in

1453 when Constantinople fell to the Ottoman Turks and nearly two thousand years of Roman imperial rule in the East ended, though not before the Byzantine emperor, for one last time, appealed to the West for help and offered reunion between the two churches. What Alexius I had feared during the First Crusade had finally come to pass, but with consequences far worse than he likely ever imagined. On the balance sheet, however, it was no victory for the crusaders, for their half-century occupation of Constantinople was a financial disaster and had transformed the long-standing enmity between the Greeks and Latins into outright hatred.

By 1291, less than two centuries after the First Crusade, there were no more crusader outposts on the Asian mainland, and the Holy Land was once again completely in Muslim hands. Nevertheless, a crusading mindset had taken hold in the West and evolved and adapted to changing circumstances and needs. In the so-named Children's Crusade of 1212, thousands of unarmed French and German children set out against their parents' wishes to rescue the Holy Land, only to be sent back home when they reached ports of embarkation.[57] The Albigensian Crusade in southern France against religious dissidents, the Spanish reconquest of the Iberian peninsula from the Moors in the fifteenth century, the Spanish Armada sent against Protestant England in 1588—all exhibited technical characteristics of a crusade. Various other minor crusades vainly attempted to recapture Jerusalem, protect remaining Latin settlements outside the Holy Land, and curb the growing problem of Turkish piracy.[58] When Urban II gave his speech in Clermont in 1095, he most certainly could not have foreseen the unparalleled chain of events his speech would unleash, the enduring mark it would leave on the Western imagination, and the centuries of animosity it would create between the Christian and Islamic worlds. And in the end, one can neither dismiss these "armed pilgrimages" as pure secular ventures nor praise them as wholly religious. Similarly, it would be simplistic to condemn crusaders categorically because of the excesses and materialism of some of the more powerful and influential among them, for as T. S. Eliot writes of them, there "were a few good men, many who were evil, and most who were neither, like all men in all places."[59]

Questions for Reflection and Discussion

1. Can you understand the fundamentally religious motivation of the first crusaders, at least within the medieval context of what it meant to be pious and religious?

2 .Do the largely negative attitudes and perceptions formed during the Crusades still continue to dominate relations between Muslims and Christians today?

3 .Are there differences between the Catholic concept of a "just war" and the Muslim concept of "jihad"?

3

The Spanish Inquisition

Legend and Reality

The Spanish Inquisition has become synonymous with a belief in a repressive Catholic Church. Fueled in no small part by literature and film, the pope is seen as having had at his disposal a ubiquitous institution of terror to torture, and often execute, any who dared to demonstrate spiritual innovation. Though the Spanish Inquisition did, in fact, mete out justice that by modern standards would be considered cruel, the institution was largely created by the Spanish monarchy. A number of popes even tried unsuccessfully to curtail the excesses of the Spanish Inquisition, only to be defied by the Spanish monarchs.

————◄o►————

Even if my own father were a heretic, I would gather the wood to burn him at the stake.

—Pope Paul IV, 1558

Perhaps no other event in the history of the Catholic Church has become as synonymous with religious repression and violence as the Spanish Inquisition. Even in many Catholic minds, mere mention of the word "inquisition" invariably conjures up images of dark-hooded persecutors torturing and executing hapless victims by the hundreds of thousands, not just throughout Spain, but in most of Catholic Europe. Yet the notion of *The Inquisition* as an all-powerful, omnipresent institution with which the Catholic Church crushed all attempts at spiritual and intellectual innovation is a myth. On the basis of a collection of second- and third-hand accounts of various local inquisitions, the Golden Age of Spain in the fifteenth and sixteenth centuries became irrevocably identified with torture, oppression, religious persecution, and the absence of any political liberty. In what one scholar has called "one of the most enduring public relations victories ever accomplished," this long anti-Spanish literary and artistic polemic created what is now called *La Leyenda Negra*—the Black Legend.

Legends notwithstanding, there is still the reality that the Spanish Inquisition *did* exist and *did* prosecute allegations of heterodoxy, sometimes employing methods which by any modern standard would be described as brutal. It is our threefold purpose to demonstrate how the inquisition in Spain came into being in the first place, describe the reality of its day-to-day operations, and, finally, to explain how a collection of local ecclesiastical tribunals in Spain metamorphosed into such a powerful myth that the very word "inquisition" in the English language no longer has any benign definition. In exploring these questions, I have adopted the terminology of inquisition scholar Edward Peters. Thus, the term "inquisition" designates the technical term for any kind of inquest; "Inquisition" refers to an ecclesiastical tribunal specific to a certain region, such as the Spanish or Venetian Inquisition; and *The Inquisition* refers to the myth.[1]

Convivencia—Peaceful Coexistence

The richly woven religious tapestry of Spain throughout most of the Middle Ages is best understood in the term *convivencia,* or "living together." Six million Christians, 500,000 Muslims, and 100,000 Jews had co-existed fairly peaceably for centuries, with a high degree of cross-fertilization of religious, intellectual, and artistic traditions.

Spanish Christians were descendants of the barbarian Visigoths who had converted to Christianity in antiquity, while Islam had been a strong presence in Spain since the eighth century when Muslim invaders from North Africa crossed the Straits of Gibraltar and displaced the Visigothic king of Toledo. Jews had been in Spain, which they called *Sefarad,* since the third century—the largest single Jewish population in the world.

Until the mid-fifteenth century, Spain was not a nation but rather a patchwork of smaller, regional kingdoms. Christian kings ruled some regions, and their Muslim subjects were called *Mudéjares.* Muslim caliphs ruled other regions, and their Christian subjects were *Mozárabes.* No region was under Jewish control. As was the case between crusaders and Muslim rulers in the Middle East, military alliances in Spain often took place between Muslim and Christian rulers, and King Alfonso X El Sabio (1252–1284) of Castile pragmatically called himself the "king of the three religions."[2] Though limited efforts to reconquer Muslim Spain had begun in 1118, by the end of the thirteenth century, the southern Spanish Kingdom of Granada in Andalusia was still a thriving Muslim stronghold. Furthermore, mutual toleration among Jews, Christians, and Muslims continued to be the rule rather than the exception.

Jews in medieval Europe had become an institutionalized minority, for which the church was at least partially responsible. The Fourth Lateran Council had decreed in 1215 that Jews in all Christian provinces must distinguish themselves from Christians by the character of their dress, and that from Good Friday through Easter Sunday, they were not to go out in public at all.[3] England expelled its entire Jewish community in 1290 and France did the same in 1306. Yet in Spain, the Jewish community fared significantly better. Many exiled Jews from England and France had joined the well-established Sephardic community, and Spanish Jews worked as royal physicians, civil officials, and even married into some of the leading aristocratic families in Spain.

Yet change was in the air. In the fourteenth century, an increasingly militant Christian nobility, which billed itself as the rightful heirs of the Christian Visigoths of antiquity, began to believe that Spain properly belonged to them. Judaism and Islam were increasingly depicted as inferior, even harmful. The Black Death of 1348–49 was blamed on the Jews, and increased royal taxes also led to greater resentment toward Jews, who often worked as tax collectors because Christians were forbidden to enter this profession.

Anti-Jewish uprisings began, the flames of which were fanned by popular preachers. In 1391, archdeacon and vicar-general of the archdiocese of Seville, Ferrant Martínez, began to preach against the Jews of the city. Large-scale pogroms resulted, and over the next several months spread throughout Spain, leading to the murders of over a thousand Jews. Dominican Vincent Ferrer (1350–1419), later canonized by the Spanish pope Callistus III (1455–1458), capitalized on the situation and preached about the errors of the Jews and the need for baptism. In the midst of such rising anti-Semitic fury on a popular level, many Jews faced a choice between baptism and persecution or even death.[4]

Those Jews who accepted baptism, forced or otherwise, from that point on created a new class in society known as *conversos*, or "converts." They began to intermarry with "Old Christians," and, with each succeeding generation, seemed to become more integrated with Spanish society. Yet, theirs was in reality a tenuous place in Spanish society. The Jews regarded them as false Jews who had betrayed the faith of Abraham. Many Old Christians and lesser members of the aristocracy, on the other hand, believed that *conversos* were insincere Christians, whose baptism was insufficient to remove their "Jewishness."[5] *Limpieza de sangre*, or "purity of blood," became the watchword for many in the aristocracy, and although blood purity was never part of Spanish law, eventually a "green book" would be drawn up to trace the pure lineage of the nobility. Some cities attempted anti-*conversos* legislation, such as the town council of Toledo in 1449, which barred *conversos* from holding any civil jobs. Pope Nicholas V (1447–1455) denounced the decision in Toledo, insisting that *all* Catholics constituted a single body, but in an action that would foreshadow a long and difficult relationship between Spain and the papacy, the pontiff was simply ignored.

Ferdinand and Isabella

The marriage of Ferdinand of Aragón (1452–1516) and Isabella of Castile (1451–1504) in 1469 united the kingdoms of Castile and Aragón, the latter of which included Valencia, Catalonia, the Basque region, Navarre, Sardinia, and Sicily. Almost all of Spain was under one crown for the first time. The two large pieces of this geographic puzzle that were still missing were Portugal to the west and the Muslim kingdom of Andalusia to the south.

Measured against the norms of the fifteenth century, Ferdinand and Isabella are said by scholars not to have been personally anti-Semitic, and do not seem to have been preoccupied with establishing religious uniformity in Spain.[6] The position of Jews did not get progressively worse in the fifteenth century, and in fact they had remained an important part of Spanish society under Ferdinand and Isabella, who relied on Jewish doctors as their personal physicians. Furthermore, the monarchs initially seemed little concerned about the sincerity of the *conversos*, evidenced by the fact that large numbers of *conversos* continued to serve in an official capacity. What Ferdinand and Isabella *were* concerned about was the growing friction between Jews, *conversos*, and Old Christians, prompted by growing accusations in anti-*converso* literature that many *conversos* in Castile were Christian in name only and were in fact secretly observing Jewish practices—so-called judaizing. A Dominican in Seville convinced Isabella that the *conversos* were secretly practicing and spreading Jewish rites *throughout* Spain and that only an inquisition could deal with this problem. Ferdinand and Isabella, fearful that such discord would blur the lines of division and cause severe social instability, received permission from Pope Sixtus IV (1471–1484) on November 1, 1478, to appoint three priests to investigate the alleged judaizing in Castile.

It is important to note that the establishment of the inquisition in Castile was intended to be a low-key, localized attempt to put an end to growing religious and civil unrest, rather than a foundation stone of a grand edifice of religious uniformity. There had had been a remarkable absence of any kind of formal heresy in Spain on the eve of establishment of the inquisition, which may in part have been due to the fact that in the atmosphere of religious pluralism, there was a concerted popular effort to remain conscious of what differentiated each faith from the other.[7] Although an earlier inquisition had been authorized in Aragón by Urban IV (1261–1264), this was mostly because of its proximity to Languedoc, where French inquisitors were quite active in the pursuit of religious dissidents.

How had Christendom dealt previously with dissident religious beliefs? In the early church, heresy more often than not resulted in the formation of separate Christian communities, where dissidents were left to develop in their own direction. It was only with the adoption of Christianity as the official religion of the Roman Empire by the emperor Constantine in the fourth century that heresy now became a civil crime against the empire and ecclesiastical community. Though possessing almost no theological acumen himself, Constantine repeatedly used the force of the state against heresy, especially with his sponsorship of the Council of Nicaea.[8] In an ecclesial context, St. Augustine himself would later suggest that disciplining of heretics by civil authorities was acceptable in order to avoid "polluting the entire community."

Since the sixth century, Roman civil law had had a broad range of sanctions against heretics, but by the eleventh and twelfth centuries, when bishops rather than the state were responsible for enforcing orthodoxy, these disparate punishments were not as easily applicable. Religion and society were considered inseparable, and preserving orthodoxy was thus considered essential, since dissent seemed to invite God's disfavor on *all* of society rather than just the individual. Bishops, however, were not always clear on how to proceed. Traditional criminal procedure in medieval Europe was based on the concept of *accusation*, in which it was fairly easy to level charges against an individual. However, the burden of proof was upon the accuser, and an individual who failed to prove the veracity of the accusation was made to suffer the same punishment that the accused would have experienced, if he or she had been found guilty. Furthermore, excommunication seems to have been the most severe punishment for heterodoxy, and "heretics" lived openly, which indicates that there was little fear of punishment.[9]

In the twelfth century, however, as practitioners of the new discipline of Canon Law began to sift through Roman civil law, concrete procedures for dealing with heterodoxy began to be spelled out. Similarly, councils and popes began to promote a more aggressive stance toward heresy. The Third Lateran Council, in 1179, decreed excommunication and denial of Christian burial for heretics, and, as has been seen in the previous chapter, extended crusader-like privileges to those who fought heresy. Pope Lucius III (1181–1185) issued *Ad Abolendam* in 1184, which has been called the "founding charter of the inquisition" and was the most comprehensive statement to date by the Western church concerning heresy. Innocent III, in 1199, relying on ancient Roman law, equated heresy with treason, and declared that the goods of heretics could be confiscated and that their children suffer "perpetual deprivation."[10]

Theory found application in 1208, when Innocent III approved the Albigensian Crusade in the southern French region of Languedoc. Innocent was interested in reform, not persecution, but many who were declared heretics as well as lay leaders who seemed indifferent to heresy were killed, often without due process. As was the case in other crusades during Innocent III's pontificate, the pope had difficulty controlling what he had unleashed.

As the Languedoc Inquisition tried to finish off the Cathars and the Waldensians, religious dissidents began to secret themselves, and authorities thus found it necessary to "inquire" after them. There had been precedent for this in Roman law, in which an *inquisitio* was made in a potential criminal case, much like a grand jury inquest today determines whether allegations of criminal wrongdoing are sufficient for a formal accusation. As the accusatorial procedure declined, the inquisitorial procedure became the standard form of criminal prosecution in Europe, especially because its proactive nature meshed with the centralizing tendencies of local governments.[11]

Previously designed for the settlement of disputes, courts now became the forum for the enforcement of conformity to abstract notions of justice and belief, as defined by secular ruling powers. These judicial systems rapidly became a major tool for the extension of political power in late medieval Europe, including the belief of the monarch that he alone was responsible for preserving religious orthodoxy in his kingdom. In 1229, Louis IX of France (1226–1270) committed royal officials to the seeking out and punishment of heretics, and in Germany, Holy Roman emperor Frederick II (1215–1250) decreed in imperial law that unrepentant heretics were to be burned at the stake—an innovation that unfortunately quickly became the norm throughout most of Europe, with the exception of Spain, where the practice was unknown until the fifteenth century.[12]

But as secular rulers attempted to tighten their jurisdiction over heretics, the papacy further delineated its own juridical authority. Pope Innocent IV (1243–1254) created a formal office of "inquisitor of heretical depravity" and appointed members of mendicant orders as local ecclesiastical judges, usually Franciscans and Dominicans, since unlike secular clergy, mendicants would not be accountable to the local bishop or monarch but to the pope. Medieval inquisitorial tribunals were little different from other canonical or civil proceedings, other than the secrecy of witnesses, a restricted defense counsel, and the penitential rather than punitive context of the proceedings. It must be stressed that there was *no single inquisition in Europe*, but rather tribunals scattered all over, which had no central organization, formal office, or leader. They were exempt from episcopal control and did not need to wait for an accusation to be made before proceeding against someone. In the secret proceedings, virtually anyone could make accusations, and the accused usually was not told who they were. Furthermore, the accused swore a solemn oath to testify against himself. The ultimate objective of the inquisitor was not conviction but rather to save the soul of the accused and thus preserve the unity and well-being of the church.[13]

The inquisition in Castile came into definitive existence on September 27, 1480. Other than the fact that the accused was placed under the authority of the inquisitors rather than the local bishop, the inquisition was operationally almost identical to the earlier inquisitions in Languedoc and Aragón, due in large part to the use of the procedural manual of famed Dominican inquisitor Bernard Gui (d. 1331). Each tribunal had two inquisitors, who could be either laymen or priests, a *calificador* (assessor), whose job it was to determine whether a case for heresy existed before an arrest could be made, an *alguacil* (constable), and a *fiscal* (prosecutor). Lay servants of the inquisition were called *familiars*, and functioned like bailiffs.[14]

In terms of how it operated, the primary objective of the inquisition when it arrived in a new town and set up near a target community of "judaizers" was to instill fear of denunciation by one's neighbor. Following almost to the letter the practice of the Languedoc Inquisition, the local clergy would preach against heresy and teach how to identify it. Then, the inquisitors would arrive, and, at High Mass, would announce the Edict of Grace. This thirty day period allowed one to confess one's heresy and, after a cash payment to the inquisition, not be subject to any further accusations of heresy. Clergy and people were then called upon to denounce known heretics, and if an unfortunate individual, guilty or not, had not availed himself of the Edict of Grace and was now accused of heresy, things would go far worse for him.[15]

Unlike our modern concept of law, an inquisition tribunal presumed guilt, and it was up to the accused to prove otherwise. Though clearly undesirable procedurally, one could at least take small comfort in the fact that the *calificadores* were expected to look thoroughly into the veracity of allegations before an arrest could be made in the first place. Charges were not revealed for days, sometimes even months. Conviction required the testimony of seven witnesses, whose names were *never* revealed, though one could draw up a list of enemies, whose testimony would then be disallowed. The accused also had the right to call witnesses on his behalf and, if he somehow learned the identity of a witness against him, had the option of attempting to prove that that witness had a personal vendetta against him. The accused could also object to the choice of judges, although not always successfully. Specific evidence that had prompted accusations was often not presented but only the conclusions that might be drawn from that evidence. Thus, the most frequent recourse for defense was simply to present counter-witnesses, although under some circumstances, drunkenness or insanity might be accepted as a defense.[16]

As was the case in Roman law, it was the practice of the inquisition in Spain to order the sequestration of the goods of the accused. This meant that for the duration of that individual's trial, his property could gradually be sold to pay for the costs of his imprisonment as well as the expenses of his trial. If the individual were exonerated, he was simply given what remained of his possessions. Contrary to the popular image, however, tribunals did not grow particularly wealthy as a result, and in fact the various inquisitions throughout Spain for most of their existence would struggle to find adequate financing for their operations.[17]

Again derived from Roman law, virtually all ecclesiastical and secular courts, with the exception of England in the thirteenth century, had torture as an option. There were, however, strict guidelines, and it was actually used only infrequently, mostly in cases where there was a preponderance of partial proofs, but no conclusive proof. Contrary to the popular image of a variety of elaborate instruments designed to mutilate and kill, the strict rules for ecclesiastical tribunals was that torture was never to be used as a punishment; the person tortured should not be permanently injured or killed, and no blood was to be shed.

The three main forms of torture that were used were overall less severe than those used in secular courts, although this in no way suggests that *any* form of torture was appropriate. The *garrucha* involved being hung by the wrists, heavy weights attached to the feet, and hoisted by pulley off the ground, then dropped with a jerk. The *toca* involved being tied down and a cloth stuffed in the mouth, which gradually conducted water into the throat and simulated drowning. The *potro* involved being bound with cords, which were then gradually tightened. Confessions made under torture were invalid and would have to be "verified" the next day. One could be tortured only once, so multiple sessions were "suspended" rather than ended.[18]

There was a number of possible outcomes for one who found himself before the inquisition. Ideally, a person would be successful in proving his or her innocence. Otherwise, sentence was pronounced in public at an auto-da-fé, or "act of faith." The purpose of this was to demonstrate the faith of the heretic for all to see. It was about reconciliation, albeit in a way foreign to our mindset. As for punishment, a guilty person who admitted transgressions might be given penance and absolved. The penance might involve a reprimand, flogging, a period of imprisonment, further confiscation of goods, or rowing in galleys. Seemingly innocuous, one of the most dreaded punishments was the wearing of the *sanbenito,* a special garment that readily identified one as a penitent. In some cases, an individual would be forced to wear it for the rest of his or her life, thus destroying any vestige of honor for the individual, and even for his or her entire town. But the shame did not end with death. The family of the individual would then be forced to hang the *sanbenito* on the interior wall of the local parish church with the family name under it for all to see and would be required to maintain the condition of the *sanbenito* for succeeding generations.[19]

In extreme cases, an individual would be sentenced to death and "relaxed to the secular arm" for carrying out of the sentence, because the inquisition was not allowed to carry out executions. This was the case in Seville in February 1481, when the six *conversos* burned at the stake at an auto-da-fé had the unfortunate distinction of being the first to be executed by the Spanish Inquisition. On the whole, however, the Spanish Inquisition acted with considerable restraint in imposing the death penalty, especially in comparison with other secular tribunals at the time.[20] During the entire 354 years of its existence, there would be no more than 5,000 documented inquisition executions, or 2 percent of those accused. During the same period elsewhere in Europe, there would be approximately 150,000 documented witch burnings in Protestant and Catholic regions.

Initially, Jews cooperated with the inquisition in Spain, all too happy to point fingers at their former co-religionists who had abandoned their Judaism. The Jews themselves, as unbaptized, were exempt from the jurisdiction of the inquisition, except in cases where they had blasphemed Christianity, proselytized among Christians, or had rendered assistance to a relapsed Jewish convert to Christianity.

Beyond Rome

In February 1482, the rapidly expanding scope of the Castilian Inquisition led to papal appointment of seven more inquisitors, including Tomás de Torquemada (1420–1498), the prior of the Dominican friary in Segovia. The pope, however, accompanied the appointment of the new inquisitors with a stern admonition to Ferdinand to treat the *conversos* fairly. Then, *without* papal approval, Ferdinand revived the inquisition in Aragón from two hundred years earlier and tied it directly to the crown rather than to the episcopacy or Rome. Alarmed, Pope Sixtus IV tried in a papal bull to suspend the powers of the

Aragón Inquisition, complaining that it was moved "not by zeal for the faith and salvation of souls, but by lust for wealth . . . many true and faithful Christians, on the testimony of enemies, rivals, slaves and other lower and even less proper persons, have without any legitimate proof been thrust into secular prisons, tortured and condemned as relapsed heretics, deprived of their goods and property and handed over to the secular arm to be executed, to the peril of souls, setting a pernicious example, and causing disgust to many."[21]

Not only did Ferdinand ignore the papal objections, but he combined the Aragón Inquisition with that of Castile, thereby creating the *Consejo de la Suprema y General Inquisición*—the Supreme Council of the General Inquisition. Torquemada was appointed Grand Inquisitor and president of the council. What had started as a modest, local effort in Castile to put an end to friction between Jews and *conversos* now was one of five state councils in Spain. It was the single national entity in Spain under the direct authority of the crown and could claim both civil and canonical jurisdiction.[22] For its part, the papacy recognized the canonical and juridical nature of the inquisition but denied the authority of the Supreme Council of the Inquisition, which the papacy rightly regarded as a secular institution.

This, however, mattered little to Ferdinand or Isabella. As did most monarchs throughout the Middle Ages, Ferdinand and Isabella regarded kingship as divinely instituted, based on the model of King David in the Old Testament. As such, they saw themselves as legitimately and ultimately responsible for the affairs of the church *within their realm*. Why did the papacy tolerate this assumed autonomy and regionalization of a Catholicism that was supposed to be universal? It was a vexing dilemma. Were the pope to insist on complete authority over the church in Spain, or any other kingdom for that matter, he risked the very real possibility of that kingdom choosing schism from Rome, thus forfeiting even a semblance of universality. Thus, papal acquiescence to Catholic rulers was all too common.

Conflict between Jews and *conversos* continued, and, in 1483, Ferdinand ordered the Jews of Saragossa to wear a red patch on their clothing, perhaps using the decree of the Fourth Lateran Council as his inspiration. There is no evidence that the order was ever carried out, or that it was designed as a punitive or anti-Semitic measure.[23] Rather, it was more likely a clumsy and distasteful attempt to keep Jews, *conversos,* and Christians separate from each other in order to avoid further conflict. Then, in 1485, there was a significant turning-point in the position of *conversos* in Spain.

Pedro Arbués (1441–1485), the Dominican inquisitor of Aragón, wore chain mail under his habit and a steel cap on his head as he knelt in prayer in the cathedral in Saragossa, conscious of the threats against him. But his precautions were not enough. Eight assassins with knives struck him down, and when the conspirators were arrested, it was alleged that they had been hired by *conversos,* who were fearful of the escalating inquisition campaign against them in Aragón. The very foolishness of the conspiracy raises doubts about whether *conversos* were really involved, but a number of *conversos* were convicted and executed by an intentionally drawn-out and brutal method, and for the next fifty years, *conversos* would be the object of unbridled revenge by the Inquisition in Spain.[24] For his unhappy part in the drama, Pedro Arbués would be canonized by Pope Pius IX (1846–1878).

Ferdinand and Isabella continued to protect Jews during the heightened persecution of *conversos* in the aftermath of the Arbués assassination, and though difficult, life even as a *converso* was not impossible. A large number of leading aristocratic families had *converso* blood and continued to be an integral part of Spanish society. No less than four Catholic bishops under Ferdinand and Isabella were *conversos,* and court officials were also frequently from *converso* families, including Grand Inquisitor Torquemada. *Conversos* would later be some of the largest financiers of Columbus's voyage, and Jews and *conversos* would form a significant part of the crew. Most noteworthy of all, King Ferdinand himself had a *converso* background.[25]

Conflict between Jews and *conversos,* however, continued. In 1490, Torquemada convinced the monarchs that even the inquisition was insufficient to solve the conflict, and recommended complete separation of Jews and *conversos.* Accordingly, Ferdinand and Isabella in March of 1492 announced total expulsion of the 80,000 Jews in Spain at the time.

The edict bemoaned the presence in Spain of "wicked Christians," that is, those *conversos* who judaized and apostatized from the Catholic faith and seduced other Christians away from true belief. This, they said, was caused by interaction between *conversos* and Jews, which twelve years of attempted separation and inquisition sentences had failed to stop. Thus, Ferdinand and Isabella concluded that all Jews must leave Spain at the end of six months, never to return, under penalty of death and the confiscation of all property. The only implicit alternative to expulsion or death was baptism.[26] Until the July 1492 departure deadline, all Jews were to be under the direct protection of the crown, during which time they could arrange for the shipping of their goods out of the country, as long as they did not export any gold or silver. It was fortunate that the monarchs at least had the foresight to extend this protection, for the anti-Jewish feelings stirred up by the edict were widespread and heated.

Although undeniably an indefensibly drastic and inhumane measure, the Edict of Expulsion was neither for ethnic nor for financial reasons, but was only for religious reasons insofar as it was an attempt to prevent the further blurring of the lines of division between Judaism and Christianity. The negative financial impact of expulsion was in fact potentially quite significant for the kingdom, and it is likely that the monarchs expected mass conversions rather than emigration, which it was hoped would ameliorate the conflict between Jews and *conversos*. But the majority of Jews simply left. Many went to Portugal, Rome, and northern Italy, although, in 1497, Portugal would follow suit and expel all its Jews. Ironically, many Jews who went into exile found themselves neighbors with *conversos* who had fled Spain during earlier persecutions but had remained steadfast in their Catholicism.[27]

In the aftermath of the expulsion, there was now an even greater *converso* problem in Spain, but of a different sort. *Conversos* from before the edict now turned on new *conversos* and vigorously denounced them as judaizers, in retaliation for what had been done to them. Judaizing had been the most common charge since the inception of the inquisition in Spain and usually entailed celebrating Jewish feasts, not observing the requirements of the church (mass, confession, abstinence, etc.), and abusing sacred objects. In addition, accusations of judaizing often led to what were regarded as the related offenses of usury and atheism. A number of accused individuals were in fact sincere Christians attempting to preserve innocuous Jewish customs, while others naively sought to combine the two religions. Yet, the reality was that in the aftermath of the 1492 edict there was also a large number of Jews who had in fact overtly converted to Christianity but covertly continued to practice their Jewish faith, referred to in Hebrew as the *Anussim*.[28]

The inquisition now found itself very busy, since those now accused of judaizing had been baptized and were thus under the full jurisdiction of the tribunal. Some insisted that baptism under duress was invalid, but the inquisition countered with the semantically correct but theologically questionable response that these individuals had still *chosen* baptism rather than exile or death. Furthermore, the inquisition in Spain was now able to operate with even less interference from Rome, since the Spaniard Rodrigo Borgia had just been elected Pope Alexander VI (1492–1503).[29] Known more for his questionable morals and rumored bribes in obtaining the papacy than for apostolic zeal, Alexander VI would turn a blind eye to the operation of the inquisition in Spain for the duration of his pontificate.

In addition to removing Jews from Spain, Ferdinand and Isabella also took steps to reduce the Muslim population. The 1492 defeat of the Muslim Kingdom of Granada in Andalusia meant that Muslims were no longer a nation in Spain but rather a minority of *Mudéjares* living under Christian rule, and, by 1501, the last of these *Mudéjares* had been forced to convert and were thereafter referred to as *Moriscos*. Isabella then offered the Muslims of Castile, who up until that point had been left their freedom of religion, the "opportunity" to be baptized. Although initially resistant, most complied after 1504, when a *mufti* in Orán in North Africa issued a *fatwa*, or edict, that proclaimed it acceptable for Muslims to conform outwardly to all requirements of Christianity if they had no other option. Yet the well-intended edict now created a cloud of suspicion over Muslim converts, since they had essentially been given official approval to deceive. It is curious, however, that the meticulously kept inquisition records reveal that Muslim converts to Christianity, at least at this point, received nowhere near the attention Jewish converts had received. In Valencia from 1484–1530, 91.6 percent of the individuals tried were Jewish *conversos,* while from 1488–1505, 99.3 percent of those tried in Barcelona and 95.9 percent of those tried in Catalonia were Jewish *conversos.*[30]

The Inquisition and Church Reform

When Isabella died in 1504, followed by Ferdinand in 1516, the Kingdom of Spain passed to their grandson, Charles of Burgundy (1500–1558), who was already in possession of the Netherlands from the Hapsburg part of his family. When Charles was also elected Holy Roman Emperor Charles V in 1519, the nineteen-year-old had jurisdiction over Spain, the Netherlands, Germany, Northern Italy, and Austria and, in the tradition of Constantine, was in a high-profile position to enforce religious orthodoxy for much of Christendom. Yet there were renewed concerns in Rome about inquisitorial abuse. In 1519, Pope Leo X (1513–1521) penned letters to the new emperor, the Inquisitor General, and the tribunal of Saragossa, suspending all previous special privileges granted to the inquisition in Spain and insisting that it adhere to the norms of Canon Law. Charles, however ignored the efforts of the pope on behalf of the people of Aragón and refused even to allow the papal letters to be published. The inquisition had become constitutionally almost invulnerable in Spain.[31]

The first concern of Charles V was to eliminate Islam in Aragón, where it had remained intact for thirty years and was the last vestige of any significant Muslim presence in Spain. Following the example of his grandmother Isabella, he ordered all *Mudéjares* to become Christians and, by 1526, Islam would no longer exist officially in either Aragón or the rest of Spain, although there would still be isolated pockets of Islam throughout Spain.[32] But when Pope Leo X excommunicated Martin Luther in 1521, inquisitorial attention in Spain shifted abruptly from judaizing and Muslims to what was perceived as a new three-headed threat to religious orthodoxy in Spain—illuminism, Erasmus, and Martin Luther.

The origins of *alumbradismo*, or "illuminism," are not completely clear. Always a term of accusation only, it initially referred to individuals who espoused three essential stages of spirituality: (1) *recogimiento* (recollection), that is, a gathering of the senses toward God; (2) a period of meditation on God; and (3) *dejamiento*—abandonment to God in a passive union with him. In addition, some advocates of this threefold spirituality assembled in prayer groups and made frequent use of scripture in the vernacular. While it shared many traits of medieval Christian mysticism, *alumbradismo,* it was argued, had its roots in the Franciscan recollect spirituality of early-sixteenth-century Spain. Although there was nothing intrinsically unorthodox about *alumbradismo*, mysticism of any kind had always been regarded with suspicion by the church, since many felt that the notion of a direct union with God rendered irrelevant the mediation of the institutional church. Furthermore, the inquisition in Spain saw in the so-called *alumbrados* a direct link with the spiritual practices of the medieval Beghard heresy.[33]

The Franciscan tertiary Isabel de la Cruz is credited with giving shape to *alumbradismo*, based on her experiences in the convent. She was of *converso* descent, as were her early followers Pedro Ruiz de Alcaraz and María de Cazalla. All three were first denounced to the inquisition in 1519 by Mari Núñez, an individual of questionable motive and morals, but the first arrests did not occur until 1524. Ironically, these as well as several other leading *alumbrados* had emulated devotional literature and practices approved and encouraged by Cardinal Francisco Ximenes de Cisneros (1436–1517), who had been the most moderate of inquisitors in Spain and had in fact done much to foster intellectual and spiritual innovation. Over the next fifteen years, there would be a long series of arrests, mostly on the basis of wild accusations by Mari Núñez. De la Cruz, Alcaraz, and de Cazalla were tortured. Alcaraz was flogged and de Cazalla was paraded through the streets. They both had their property confiscated and were sentenced to lifelong confinement in a religious house, as well as to wearing the *sanbenito* for life, though these last two punishments were later reduced.[34]

After de la Cruz and her followers had been dealt with, charges of *alumbradismo* were increasingly leveled against individuals whose spirituality seemed in *any* way innovative. In April 1527, a young ex-soldier named Ignatius Loyola (1491–1556) was arrested and briefly imprisoned by the inquisition on suspicion of illuminism. Four years later, in 1531, John of Avila (1500– 1569), from a *converso* family and future spiritual advisor to Teresa of Avila (1515–1582), was arrested by the inquisition on the same charges. Besides alleged illuminism, inquisitors were greatly concerned about the large following of pious women associated with both Ignatius Loyola and John of Avila.[35]

Emphasis on a more directly Gospel-based Catholic spirituality found eloquent expression in the *Dialogue of Christian Doctrine* (1529) of Juan de Valdés (1500–1541). It also caught the attention of the inquisition, which suspected him of illuminism, so Valdés fled Spain in 1530 and ironically found refuge in Rome, working in the papal court. Eventually, he moved on to Naples, where he influenced a number of high-ranking church leaders in his evangelistic approach, including cardinals Reginald Pole (1500–1558), Gasparo Contarini (1483–1542), and Giovanni Morone (1509–1580), all of whom in different ways would later be instrumental in advancing the cause of Catholic reform at the Council of Trent.[36]

Ten years after his scrape with the inquisition, Ignatius was encouraged by cardinals Pole and Contarini to seek formal papal approval of the Society of Jesus, which was eventually given by Pope Paul III (1534–1549) in 1540. Ignatius then began to openly oppose the anti-*converso,* anti-Jewish mentality that had gained ground in Spain, remarking that he would consider it an honor to be a Jew. He referred to the *limpieza de sangre* mentality as "the joke of the Spanish king and his court" and, much to the consternation of the inquisition, even allowed *conversos* to become Jesuits, although he encouraged them to join in Italy in order to avoid difficulties with Spanish authorities. In 1553, the *Spiritual Exercises* of Ignatius were examined by the inquisition and declared to be heavily influenced by *alumbradismo.* But no action was taken against Ignatius, and, after his death in 1556, Diego Laínez (1512–1565), from a *converso* family, succeeded him as general of the order. Along with other Jesuits, Laínez worked vigorously to combat anti-*converso* and anti-Semitic thinking and policies in Spain.[37]

Early on, the inquisition saw a Lutheran inspiration behind illuminism. To be sure, the emphasis on abandonment to God in illuminism *resembled* Lutheranism, insofar as Luther insisted that there was nothing one could do to bring about God's grace and that one must therefore simply live by faith. Lutheran connections were further suspected when Pedro Ruiz de Alcaraz contended that works were a *sign* of God's grace rather than something that would bring about God's grace.[38] But that is where the similarities ended. Nevertheless, accusations of *alumbradismo* began to be used as part of a strategy to ensnare individuals with suspected Protestant leanings.

The inquisition in Spain also saw connections between Lutheranism and the Dutch priest and scholar Desiderius Erasmus (1469–1536), who became an early target in the growing anti-Lutheran atmosphere. Known for his expertise in biblical languages, the church fathers, and satire, Erasmus had espoused a Christian humanism in which reform was based on the model of the early church and scripture. He portrayed this vision in his *Enchiridion Militis Christiani* (1503), or *Handbook of the Christian Soldier,* and in 1516 he wrote as a companion piece his *Institutio Principis Christiani* or *Education of a Christian Prince,* specifically for the new king of Spain, Charles. Both books had been quite popular in Spain, and the Christian humanism of Erasmus was quite popular in the emperor's court.[39]

As Erasmus began to sharpen his satirical critiques of abuse within the Catholic Church, inquisitors insisted that he was no different from Luther. Although a strong critic of church abuse, Erasmus had in fact engaged in a heated literary exchange with Luther in 1524 because of the latter's views on grace and free will. Furthermore, Erasmus never deviated from Catholic doctrine and died a priest in good standing, after having been on good terms with all the popes of the Reformation; he even even politely declined Paul III's offer to make him a cardinal. Nevertheless, Erasmus's edition of the New Testament, along with most of his other works, were attacked, and in 1528, the first arrest for "Erasmianism" occurred. Even one of Charles V's own preachers was convicted of Erasmianism and spent four years in confinement, before Charles V was able to get a papal annulment of the sentence and appoint the "errant preacher" bishop to the Canary Islands. Other arrests for Erasmianism followed, including the rector of the University of Alcalá and the vice-rector of the Trilingual College of Alcalá, both of whom, along with their institutions, had been supportive of Erasmus's vision of Catholic reform.[40]

By the middle of the sixteenth century, the Spanish Inquisition seemed invincible. Since Ferdinand also ruled Sicily, he had appointed inquisitors there, who were particularly harsh against *conversos*. In 1535, Juan de Zumárraga (1468–1548), first bishop of Mexico City, also had become the first inquisitor in the New World, concerned not with Jews but rather with the question of whether Indian converts had truly given up their pagan ways.

Other than in Castile, however, support for the inquisition seemed to be eroding. The Spanish aristocracy, often at odds with the monarchy, generally supported church reformers, albeit only those who were orthodox. Many were even keen on the evangelistic spirit that underlay many new spiritualities and were unclear as to exactly what was unorthodox about *alumbradismo*.[41] The inquisition grudgingly fell into line behind the aristocracy, allowing that *alumbradismo* was something new and hard to define, and that many accused of it were simply individuals whose spiritual fervor had led them to misguided methods. As a result, accused illuminists were shown greater leniency when their cases came before the inquisition.

Such leniency, however, did not extend to accused Lutherans. Although a small number of Luther's works had circulated in Spain as early as 1521, there had been few cases of formal Lutheranism brought before the inquisition, due largely to the instructions of the otherwise reform-minded Dutch pope Adrian

VI (1522–1523) that Luther's works should be burned. Then, in 1558, approximately two hundred individuals were accused of full-blown Lutheranism.[42] Some of the accused were influential Spaniards, but many were foreigners; the accusations had to do with Spain's xenophobia as much as anything else, since all countries outside Spain were referred to by the inquisition as *tierras de herejes,* or "heretical lands."

Two years earlier, Charles V had abdicated and retired to the monastery of Yuste in Extremadura, leaving his son Philip II (1556–1598) to rule Spain and the Netherlands, while Charles's brother Ferdinand (1558–1564) became Holy Roman emperor. This did not, however, stop the former ruler from weighing in on the Spanish Lutheran matter in a letter, in which he advocated a hardline approach. After struggling unsuccessfully for forty years in Germany to prevent political disintegration as a result of religious disunity, Charles was fearful that the same thing would now play itself out in Spain.[43] Many agreed, and tragically, fifty-nine of the two hundred accused eventually were burned at the stake in Seville and Valladolid.

The Spanish Inquisition formally identified seven main signs of what made one Protestant, and, contrary to previous papal attempts to lessen the authority of the Spanish Inquisition, the new hardline policy found a sympathetic ear in Paul IV (1555–1559), formerly a cardinal-inquisitor of the Roman Inquisition. Arguably the most theologically narrow-minded pope of the sixteenth century, Paul IV saw heresy everywhere, once even remarking that he would carry the wood to the fire himself if his own father were accused of heresy. A founding member of the Theatine religious order, Paul IV made noises about "absorbing" the Society of Jesus into the much smaller Theatine order, but the plan never came to fruition, much to the relief of Ignatius Loyola. Convinced that heresy threatened to invade the very hierarchy of the church, the pontiff summoned Cardinal Pole to appear before the Roman Inquisition, though Pole died before he could comply. He also imprisoned Cardinal Morone, who would later be vindicated by Paul IV's successor and eventually preside over some of the sessions of the Council of Trent.

In this overzealous anti-Lutheran atmosphere of 1559, Paul IV granted the request of the Spanish Inquisition for a two-year waiver of episcopal exemption from inquisitorial prosecution, and Bartolomé de Carranza, Dominican archbishop of Toledo (1558–1576) and primate of the church in Spain, was quickly arrested and accused of Lutheran beliefs. Although Paul IV wanted Carranza sent to Rome for trial, Philip II refused to concede Roman jurisdiction in the case and kept Carranza imprisoned in Spain for seven years.[44] Clearly a pawn in the power struggle between Spain and Rome, Carranza was finally sent to Rome and spent another nine years imprisoned, until his release by Pope

Gregory XIII (1572–1585) in 1576. Carranza died eighteen days after his release.

In the anti-Lutheran fervor of 1560, the Spanish Inquisition expanded the Index of Forbidden Books, in an effort to prevent further outbreaks of heresy. The list included all works by heretics, all those written by people condemned by the inquisition, all works written about Jews and Muslims that had an anti-Catholic bias, all "heretical" translations of the Bible, all vernacular translations of the Bible (even Catholic ones), all devotional literature in the vernacular, and all books written between Catholics and Protestants, even if the former were attempting to point out the doctrinal errors of the latter. Even vernacular versions of the *Spiritual Exercises* of Ignatius Loyola were ordered to be delivered over to the inquisition.

Teresa of Avila (1515–1582) expressed shock at seeing the names of so many of those she admired on the Index of Forbidden Books. Yet she herself would not escape its suspicions. From a *converso* family, her grandfather had been penanced by the inquisition in 1485 for alleged judaizing, which in the inquisitorial mindset made Teresa herself suspect. Teresa had initially not taken seriously rumors of inquisition concerns about her: "people came to me in great alarm, saying that these were difficult times, that some charge might be raised against me, and that I might have to appear before the inquisitors. But this merely amused me and made me laugh. I never had any fear on that score." Then, in 1574, she was formally denounced to the inquisition in Cordova, which frowned on the accessibility of her meditation, the emphasis on feeling, and the talk of a personal, mystical union with God. In addition, her *Libro de la Vida*, or autobiography, was examined and deemed not worthy of publication.[45] Although not formally convicted of anything, inquisition interest in Teresa did not end until five years later, in 1579, when the case against her was dropped. The autobiography of the future saint and doctor of the church, however, was still not allowed to be published until after her death, and, even then, there were those who continued to question her orthodoxy.

In addition to concerns of orthodoxy, the inquisition once again turned to the question of the *Moriscos*. In 1560, half the population of Granada was Moriscos, and the inquisition was reluctant to prosecute them, because it felt that proper religious instruction had not really taken place. Moreover, the inquisition was under pressure from the Spanish aristocracy, who did not want interference with their Morisco vassals. The Morisco revolt in Granada of 1568, however, hardened the attitude of the inquisition. In the brutal conflict, thousands died, and both Christians and Muslims were guilty of atrocities. The Moriscos were now the chief subject of prosecution by the inquisition, though surprisingly, they were now treated as infidels rather than heretics.[46] Over 80,000 were expelled from Granada, and between 1609 and 1614, 300,000 of the 320,000 Moriscos remaining in Spain were expelled.

From the later 1560s on, neither Judaism nor Protestantism was considered a major threat. The inquisition in Spain did, however, remain active in its ongoing efforts to supervise the moral conduct of both clergy and laity. In particular, it aggressively prosecuted cases of clergy accused of solicitation of penitents during confession, which the inquisition treated as a type of heresy. The high incidence of this infraction was attributable in part to the fact that the anonymous confessional was unknown in Spain during this period. At the same time, the inquisition also delved into the personal conduct of lay Catholics, prosecuting blasphemy, homosexuality, bestiality, bigamy, and sexual relations outside of marriage.[47]

But as the decades passed, the inquisition in Spain became less and less feared, and the overwhelming reality was that most everyday Spaniards, for whose lives the institution was largely marginal, met it with indifference. Some towns would only see the inquisition every ten years, if at all, and in rural Spain, it was almost unknown. In those areas where it did operate, it was accepted as a fact of life, but, although there was passive popular support for it, it was never loved. It was seen as a Castilian creation that reflected an "Old Christian" mentality, and the mostly Castilian inquisitors seldom spoke the local language. As such, the inquisition was generally regarded outside of Castile as a foreign, punitive body, and the further removed from Castile it was, the less support one found.[48] Outside of Spain entirely, far removed from the mundane realities of the inquisition, the institution would become exactly what the opponents of Spain and Catholicism wanted it to be.

Inventing *The Inquisition*

The seminal moment came almost one hundred years after the Spanish Inquisition was established, when Protestant forces in the Netherlands, fearful that strict anti-Lutheran laws put in place in the Netherlands by Charles V in 1522 would lead to the establishment of the inquisition in the Netherlands, rebelled against Spanish rule. The revolt was unsuccessful, but it inspired a 1567 anti-Spanish pamphlet entitled "A Discovery and Plaine Declaration of Sundry Subtill Practices of the Holy Inquisition of Spain." Supposedly written by Reginaldus Montanus, an alleged inquisition victim, the work is now widely believed to have been written by two Spanish Protestant exiles. Translated into

English, French, Dutch, and German, the work was even well received in Catholic France, which was a long-standing enemy of Spain and the Hapsburgs. It also fueled anti-Spanish feelings in Italy, where there was resentment against Charles V's rule over Sicily, Naples, and Milan.[49]

A number of other similar pamphlets followed, all claiming firsthand experience with the Spanish Inquisition, but all clearly derived from Montanus. Of particular importance was the *Apologie of William of Orange*, written by the French Calvinist Pierre Loyseleur de Villiers (1530–1590) in 1581. Largely a distillation of all anti-Spanish treatises of the previous forty years, it portrayed Spain and Philip II as intrinsically and hopelessly inimical to political liberty and religious freedom. Such sentiments found a particularly sympathetic audience in the Huguenot areas of France as well as in Protestant Elizabethan England, especially in the aftermath of the failed 1588 Spanish Armada, which had attempted to unseat Elizabeth I as monarch.[50] Spain became synonymous with backwardness, repression, intolerance, intellectual decay, superstition, and brutality, and the Spanish Inquisition neatly reinforced this idea for the critics of Spain. *La Leyenda Negra*—the Black Legend—had been born.

A central component in the legend was the conviction that Protestant reformers and their beliefs represented a continuity with the "purity" of the early church and the persecuted Christians of antiquity, while the Latin church was seen as the heir to the persecuting pagan Roman authorities of antiquity. It was in this vein that Foxe's *Book of Martyrs* appeared in 1563, which catalogued the martyrdoms of the early church as well as the suffering of Protestants at the hands of Catholic authorities in the sixteenth century. The reality, however, was that the various inquisitions of the Catholic Church had no exclusive claim to coercion, torture, and execution for those accused of heresy. Luther insisted that civil authorities could punish blasphemy and remarked that peasants involved in the great revolt of 1525 in Germany should be "cut down like dogs." His co-religionist Philip Melanchthon (1497–1560) supported the execution of Anabaptists, and the great reformer John Calvin (1509–1564) not only supported but openly exulted in the burning at the stake of the anti-trinitarian Michael Servetus (1511–1533), the first person executed for heresy under the auspices of Protestant authorities. In Zürich, the reformer Ulrich Zwingli (1484–1531) approved the execution of Anabaptists, and Elizabethan England would become well known for its vigorous torture and execution of "renegade" Catholics.[51]

The execution in Italy in 1600 of Giordano Bruno (1548–1600) and the trial in 1633 of Galileo Galilei (1564–1642) were natural springboards for Enlightenment thinkers who saw an intrinsic incompatibility between institutional religion and science. Consequently, the growing popularity of *The Inqui-*

sition myth became the natural and widely accepted counterpoint for Enlightenment thinkers and French *Philosophes* advocating religious toleration and intellectual freedom.[52]

The Spanish Inquisition received harsh treatment from Voltaire (1694–1778) in his work *Candide,* which was mirrored in the artistic realm by the Spanish painter Francisco de Goya (1746–1828), who portrayed the Spanish Inquisition in dark, secular terms. In the nineteenth century, *Les raisons du Momotombo* of Victor Hugo (1802–1885) and *The Brothers Karamazov* of Fyodor Dostoyevsky (1821–1881) continued to portray the Black Legend. Described as one of the greatest propagators of *The Inquisition* myth, Dostoyevsky's grand inquisitor, with his "withered face and sunken eyes," patrols the streets of Seville and orders the arrest of Jesus himself, with the words "Tomorrow I shall condemn thee and burn thee at the stake as the worst of heretics." Among Anglophone writers, *The Pit and the Pendulum* of Edgar Allen Poe (1809–1849) continued to portray the sinister *Inquisition* of myth as historical reality. Nineteenth-century gothic novels, aimed at a more popular audience, mirrored this more serious literature but with the added innovation of the "erotic inquisitor" who coerced and tortured his mostly female victims for deviant purposes. This notion spilled over into fanciful artistic renditions of inquisition scenes, in which scantily clad women were tormented by menacing inquisitors. In this vein, the above-mentioned *converso*-hired murderers of Pedro Arbués were recast as a vengeful woman who strikes down Arbués after being tormented and ravaged by him during the inquisitorial process.[53]

Until the nineteenth century, portrayals of the Spanish Inquisition in historical writing were usually indistinguishable from *The Inquisition* of literary myth. Then, spurred to a large extent by American scholar Henry Charles Lea (1825–1909), a steady progression of historians began to utilize the actual meticulous and comprehensive records that had been kept by the inquisition. The result was that for the first time since its inception, the Spanish Inquisition was placed within the context of historical reality rather than literary myth. At least for serious scholars, the grossly inaccurate amalgamation of the various inquisitions of the fourteenth and fifteenth century into an omnipresent, sinister *Inquisition* which was foe to all manifestations of religious and intellectual freedom was finally gone, so that "the inquisitions now belonged primarily to historians."[54]

One cannot play down the *actual* activities of the inquisition in Spain, or suggest that it was simply misunderstood, and that it was in reality the friend of free-thinking individuals. For the purpose of avoiding religious discord, the government of Ferdinand and Isabella took a papally authorized local tribunal and turned it into an arm of the Spanish government that had jurisdiction throughout Spain and eventually its colonies in the New World. Then, when discord continued, the monarchs made a fateful bid to preserve social stability through the elimination of cultural pluralism, which ultimately resulted in the polarization of Spanish society.[55] Torture, coercion, and execution were sometimes used, and there is no question that at least in some larger cities, spiritual and intellectual freedom were constrained by the fear of inquisitorial prosecution.

Yet, in spite of what the modern mind rightly regards as an unnecessary, indeed destructive, attempt by the Spanish crown to create bureaucratic tools for the enforcement of religious orthodoxy, it would be a huge leap to transform the Spanish experience into a Christendom-wide juggernaut of religious oppression and cruelty, somehow synonymous with Roman Catholicism. Such power would not be possible for an institution that even at the height of its activity never had more than fifty inquisitors at work in all of Spain and suffered a perennial lack of both financial resources and full cooperation from local authorities. Furthermore, one cannot ignore the attempts by popes Sixtus IV and Innocent VIII, albeit unsuccessful, to scale back the power of the Spanish Inquisition. Yet in spite of the best efforts of historians, the indelible images of the myth will undoubtedly live on in popular genres, such as film, comedy, and confessional polemic. It is hoped that the informed individual will at least know the difference between the myth and the reality.

Questions for Reflection and Discussion

1. What has generally been your reaction to the term "inquisition," and how have you yourself used this term?

2. Can you think of other instances in which a monarch, national leader, or government has appropriated religious institutions to further its own agenda?

3. How does the Catholic Church, or any other church or religious body, maintain a balance between religious and intellectual freedom and the need to maintain its doctrinal and spiritual identity, without resorting to the repressive means used by the Spanish Inquisition?

4

A Squabble among Friars

The Excommunication of Martin Luther

The excommunication of Martin Luther in 1517 is the traditional starting point of the Protestant Reformation. A heroic Luther is portrayed as confidently nailing his 95 Theses to the door of the Wittenberg cathedral, and never looking back. The traditional Catholic perspective of Luther is that of the arch-heretic, bent on the willful destruction of the Catholic Church. Yet Luther vacillated over a two-year period and was frequently wracked with anxiety about the possibililty of excommunication. At the same time, representatives of the Catholic Church sought to appease Luther, in spite of his doctrinal challenges, in order to shape the course of political events in Europe.

————◄○►————

I will not follow the steps of Luther, whose judgment I esteem very little; and yet he and his disciples be not so wicked and foolish that in all things they err. Heretics be not in all things heretics. Therefore I will not so abhor their heresy, that for the hate thereof, I will fly from the truth.
—Cardinal Reginald Pole of England, 1535

No doctrine is defined until it is violated.
—Cardinal John Henry Newman, 1878

On the eighteenth of February 1546, at 2:45 A.M., Martin Luther (1483–1546) took his last breath. Formally excommunicated twenty-five years earlier—the only Protestant reformer to which this was ever done—Luther died in utter certitude of the righteousness of his cause and firm in the

71

belief of his commitment to Christ and the Gospels. He had set the church on the right path, and it would now be up to his followers throughout Germany to carry on his work. From the standpoint of the papacy, a troublesome heresiarch had finally been silenced, but not before he had rent the very fabric of Christendom through his public rejection of some of the most fundamental elements of Roman Catholicism and his subsequent efforts to establish a church in Germany fully independent of Rome. How had such a chasm occurred between this former Augustinian monk and the papacy, and how are we to understand it today in the context of post-Vatican II ecumenism? One must first look to the German political and religious context of what has come to be called the Protestant Reformation.

Unlike most other European countries, Germany in the sixteenth century had not yet achieved national unification, but instead was composed of three hundred semi-autonomous principalities under the nominal control of the Holy Roman emperor—at that time Maximilian I (1493–1519) of the Hapsburg family. After a failed attempt to unify Germany in order to strengthen his powerbase, Maximilian instead opted to enhance his power by marrying his children into other dynastic families of Europe and by taking over northern Italy, which for obvious reasons angered the papacy. Maximilian supported the notion of a national church in Germany, Catholic but autonomous, and toyed with the idea of becoming an antipope with the support of the German clergy. At one point he even thought about succeeding an ailing Julius II (1503–1513) as legitimate pope, but the pontiff had the temerity to recover from his illness.

As for the church in Germany, it would be wrong to accept the stereotype of widespread religious decay inevitably leading to Luther and the Protestant Reformation. To be sure, the bishops of Germany, as was the case in most other parts of Christendom, were often more princely than spiritual, and the clergy in general lacked sufficient education. There was also financial and moral abuse, which several ecumenical councils in the fifteenth and early sixteenth centuries had unsuccessfully attempted to eradicate. Yet there were also positive religious currents flowing in pre-Reformation Germany. Rhineland mysticism emphasized cultivation of the individual's relationship with God, while the Dutch Brethren of the Common Life stressed a more interior religion and living a life of virtue and morality. The blending of Italian humanism and Christian humanism championed the acquisition of linguistic and exegetical skills in order to better understand sacred scripture and early Christian writers.

All of these currents converged to some extent in Luther. That he valued mysticism is clearly shown by his editorship and publication in 1516 of the *Theologia Germanica*, a recently discovered treatise on mysticism by an anonymous German priest who had clear connections with mystics such as Johann

Tauler (c. 1300–1361), the Friends of God, and Meister Eckhart (c. 1260–1327). Though Luther is not traditionally described as a mystic, one must take seriously his statement that next to the Bible and the writings of St. Augustine, no other book had exercised such a profound influence on him as the *Theologia Germanica*. This connection with mysticism also does much to explain Luther's intense focus on the individual and his relationship with God.[1] Though Luther would voice little use for the new phenomenon of Christian humanism, there can be no denying that he benefited from this new world of Christian scholarship, which provided him with Greek skills, the ability to do superb exegesis, and a particular love for the Pauline letters. Furthermore, his primary education at Brethren of the Common Life schools exposed him at a young age to an emphasis on virtue, strong personal piety, and the development of an interior spirituality.

Luther's Early Years

Luther was born on November 10, 1483, in Eisleben, Saxony, to Hans and Margaretha Luther, and named for St. Martin of Tours. Luther's father took the family from peasantry to modest prosperity after becoming part-owner of a copper mine in Mansfeld, where he moved the family. Luther attended a variety of primary schools in and near Mansfeld, but his family life was harsh. Both parents were stern disciplinarians, and on more than one occasion, he was whipped until, in his words, "the blood flowed." Indeed, Luther's dominant, judging, and wrathful father has led psychologist Erik Erikson, in his groundbreaking *Young Man Luther: A Study in Psychoanalysis and History*, to theorize that this was at the basis of Luther's pre-Reformation fearful image of a wrathful, punishing God.[2]

In 1501, he entered the University of Erfurt to begin studies in the traditional curriculum of Aristotelian logic, natural philosophy, and ethics, and by 1505, had completed both the Bachelor of Arts and the Master of Arts degrees. Pressed by his father, Luther reluctantly began law studies at Erfurt, but matters quickly took a very different course. While returning to Erfurt in 1505 after a visit home, he was caught in a particularly violent thunder and lightning storm, and in fear of his life, vowed to St. Anne that he would become a monk if she protected him. Two weeks later, Luther entered the Augustinian monastery at Erfurt and professed his vows fourteen months later.

This story of Luther's vocation, first told by him sixteen years after the fact, prompted him to insist that his decision for monastic life had been made under duress and was the reason that he could not adequately fulfill the requirements of religious life. Many scholars, however, have questioned this, since Luther had shown inclinations toward religious life prior to 1505 and was regarded by his fellow Augustinians as an exemplary, pious friar. Ordained priest in 1507, Luther began advanced studies at the newly established University of Wittenberg, where he also taught Aristotelian ethics.

In 1510, Luther traveled to Rome as a representative of the German Augustinians, who sought permission to mandate monastic reform on all Augustinian monasteries in Germany. He stayed for a month and undertook the usual pilgrim practices, including ascending the *scala sancta* (holy stairs) on his knees, which at the time were located in the Church of St. John Lateran, the cathedral church of the bishop of Rome.

Andreas Karlstadt (1480–1541), dean of the faculty at Wittenberg, conferred the doctorate on Luther in 1512, who then began to deliver a major course of lectures on sacred scripture. What one sees at this early stage in his theological evolution is the overall theme of Christ and Christian experience. Against the backdrop of Christ crucified, Luther stresses ruthless self-accusation, radical obedience, and a commitment to grow spiritually.

His *Lectures on the Psalter* (1513) emphasized the appropriation of redemption through one's life of faith, which was intimately connected to an authentic humility. In this humility, one had to strive continually for holiness:

> We are always in motion, and we who are righteous need always to be made righteous. From this it comes that every righteousness for the present moment is sin with regard to that which must be added in the next moment. For blessed Bernard [St. Bernard of Clairvaux] says truly, "when you cease wanting to become better, you stop being good, for there is no stopping place on God's way. Delay is itself sin." Hence he who in the present moment trusts that he is righteous and stands in that opinion has already lost righteousness.

True conversion, as Luther explains it in his *Lectures on Romans* (1516), is the shift from satisfaction over one's spiritual state to a recognition of one's utter sinfulness. One must make oneself captive to the cross in self-denial and make oneself open to receive God's healing grace. To think that one could love God above all things by his own powers is insanity, according to Luther. One cannot perform works pleasing to God unless one is *already* in a state of grace. In his *Lectures on Hebrews* (1517–18), Luther stressed the importance of the personal dimension of one's encounter with Christ. Faith brings forgiveness *for the individual,* and good works flow forth spontaneously from one's faith.

Luther became engulfed by his scripture lectures but found philosophy unimportant. As early as 1509, he had referred to Aristotle's philosophy as "rancid" and now began to voice serious objections to the traditional scholastic method of theology, which relied so heavily on Aristotle. By February 1517, Aristotle was the "chief of all charlatans," and in mid-year, when lecturing on the Bible and St. Augustine increased in popularity, Luther quipped that "Aristotle is gradually falling from his throne, and his final doom is only a matter of time."[3] Then, in September 1517, Luther penned his *Disputation against Scholastic Theology,* sometimes referred to as the *97 Theses against Scholastic Theology.* A rejection of scholasticism, however, does not make one a heretic. One must turn for that scenario to a series of events that began in Mainz in 1514.

Conflict with Rome and the 95 Theses

The archdiocese of Mainz, as the primatial see in Germany, was the most powerful see, especially since the archbishop of Mainz was also *ex officio* the head of the seven imperial electors who chose the Holy Roman emperor. The archdiocese, however, had been vacant for four years, and in 1514 Albrecht von Brandenburg (1490–1545) decided that he desperately wanted the job. He was faced with a number of hurdles. He was already the bishop of Magdeburg, and church practice at the time did not allow a bishop of one diocese to be transferred to another. Furthermore, Albrecht was under the required canonical age of twenty-five. Undaunted, he secured the appropriate dispensations from Rome for these difficulties, but there was still one major problem. There were back taxes, or *annates*, which had accrued during the four years that the archbishopric had been vacant, and which would now need to be paid in full by the new bishop. Albrecht agreed to do so but had no money; so he turned to the renowned Fugger Bank for a loan. In order to insure repayment, the Fugger family arranged with some curial officials for Albrecht to keep half the proceeds from a proposed fundraising drive in his archdiocese, the other half going to Rome for the rebuilding of St. Peter's Basilica.

The funds were to be raised through the sale of indulgences. The theology of indulgences at the time was based on the belief that the grace of Christ and the exemplary lives of the saints had created a treasury of merits in heaven that could be drawn upon by a penitent for the remission of punishment for sins. In the correct form of an indulgence, pious works were needed to make it effective. The practice, however, was often far different. There had been numerous abuses of the doctrine prior to Luther, and indulgence certificates were sometimes even used in lieu of cash for the most nefarious of transactions. "The solemn offering of extraordinary papal indulgences," in the words of one Catholic scholar, "grew into a special evil." Yet anyone who doubted the efficacy of indulgences was said to be in grave sin.[4]

An enthusiastic Archbishop Albrecht hired the Dominican Johannes Tetzel (1465–1519), whose skill at preaching indulgences was renowned. Albrecht made it clear, however, that he expected results, giving instructions to Tetzel that "are immediately repulsive to any religious man. In a cold-blooded commercial manner the indulgences were proclaimed according to an exact catalogue in the parish churches."[5] With the catchy rhyme "when a coin in the coffer rings, a soul from purgatory does spring," Tetzel assured his audience that they could save dead relatives from purgatory through the purchase of an indulgence. They did not need to demonstrate contrition, and the certificates of indulgence were even valid for *future* sins.

Luther was rightly appalled at what Tetzel preached, and in October 1517 wrote his *Disputation on the Power and Efficacy of Indulgences,* more commonly know as the *95 Theses.*[6] Yet the importance of the *95 Theses* as marking a definitive break between Luther and Roman Catholicism has historically been overstated.

First, although there were various points in the *95 Theses* to which Catholic theologians objected, the document was far from being a comprehensive attack against the Catholic Church. It in fact accepted the doctrine of indulgences but objected to the numerous *abuses* of the doctrine exemplified most recently by Tetzel, especially the notion that there was no need for contrition and ongoing virtue on the part of the sinner in order for an indulgence to be effective. Almost at the same time in the Catholic diocese of Constance in southern Germany, the vicar-general of the diocese launched an effort that successfully expelled an Italian preacher of indulgences from the diocese who had been operating in a manner very similar to that of Tetzel.

Second, the *95 Theses* were not a summation of everything that Luther believed wholeheartedly but were rather intended to serve as the basis for a public debate, which Luther himself makes very clear in the preface. Such public disputations were common and acceptable in the sixteenth century in the case of theological or academic grievances and provided an opportunity for the relative merits of an individual's propositions to be debated, particularly if it involved areas of doctrine that had not been clearly defined by the church. The fact that the *95 Theses* were written in Latin rather than German supports the notion that Luther intended an academic debate rather than a popular revolt. It is likely that Luther expected the same low-key reaction to his *95 Theses* as that which greeted the publication of his *Disputation against Scholastic Theology* the previous month.

Public disputations were normally held under the auspices of the local cathedral. This was why Luther sent the *95 Theses* to the cathedral at Witten-berg, but he *never nailed them to the doors of the cathedral.* This popular iconic myth began in 1617, when designers of a commemorative medallion for the centenary of the Lutheran Reformation created a convenient and compact visual graphic that would symbolically illustrate Luther's challenge to the Catholic Church.[7] Furthermore, the respectful and nonconfrontational tone of the explanatory letter to Archbishop Albrecht which Luther included with the *95 Theses* would hardly have been consistent with an angry challenge nailed to the doors of the local cathedral.[8]

Events, however, took a dramatically different course when, within a few days, the *95 Theses* had been translated into German and published by someone whose identity is still unclear. What *is* clear is that the brief document was an immediate hit with the German populace. Luther seems not to have been responsible and was in fact put out at the popular circulation of the *95 Theses.* The previously obscure German Augustinian friar known for his piety, his learning, and his scrupulous conscience had quickly become a national figure. It was a role, however, for which Luther was not completely ready, and he would spend the next two years vacillating between fearful compliance with and auda-cious taunting of Rome.

Just six months after the publication of the *95 Theses,* Luther completed his *Explanations of the 95 Theses* (May 1518), in which he sought to clarify any mis-understandings. Throughout the *Explanations,* it is clear that Luther in no way had rejected Roman Catholicism; he was, in fact, experiencing a great degree of inner turmoil. He reiterated his objection to the misuse and misunderstanding of indulgences, but not to the theology of indulgences, nor even to the notion of the "treasury of merit" of the church. He now asserted that "one must yield to the papal authority in everything." Perhaps most tellingly, Luther sent a copy of his *Explanations* to a friend and asked that he forward it to the pope, remark-ing that "Christ is the judge whose verdict I am seeking through the Roman See."[9]

Luther was unaware that Pope Leo X (1513–1521), the second son of the powerful Lorenzo de Medici (1449–1492) of Florence, had already begun canonical proceedings against him. Initially, the pontiff had dismissed the Luther affair as a "squabble among friars," but, amidst growing pressure from Maximilian I and some church officials in Germany, he decided to take formal action. However, somewhat overconfident in implicit acceptance of papal authority, Leo X still had opted only to make the case a simple matter of disci-pline, which ruled out any discussion. Accordingly, what Leo X expected was Luther's compliant recantation and, to this end, summoned him to Rome. Dominican Cardinal Cajetan (1469–1534), who had been in Germany as papal legate since April 1518, was given the task of ensuring that Luther complied with the papal instructions.

Upon learning of his summons to Rome, however, Luther immediately sought the help of Frederick the Wise (1463–1525), one of the above-mentioned three hundred princes of Germany, who had taken an early interest in Luther and would emerge as his staunchest ally and protector. At the time, Frederick the Wise and Cardinal Cajetan were both present at the imperial Diet of Augsburg, convened at the request of Emperor Maximilian I in order to garner support for a campaign to turn back the Turkish advance and to secure assurances from the imperial electors that his grandson Charles would succeed him as Holy Roman emperor. The diet, however, would soon turn into something very different.

This question of the imperial succession was the trump card that Luther needed. The potential election of Maximilian's grandson Charles of Burgundy was looked on unfavorably by the Florentine Leo X, since another Hapsburg emperor would mean continued imperial control of northern Italy. Already at the diet, papal legate Cajetan had elevated Archbishop Albrecht of Mainz, head of the seven electors, to the rank of cardinal in order to gain his support in any future election. Frederick the Wise, also one of the imperial electors, indicated to Cardinal Cajetan that he and the imperial elector of Trier might also look unfavorably on the candidacy of Charles if Luther were allowed to appear before church authorities in Germany rather than in Rome. After consultation by letter with Leo X, Cajetan offered to meet with Luther at the diet in Augsburg, though the cardinal had been instructed by the pontiff not to engage in a debate with Luther. The pope also dispatched papal nuncio Karl von Miltitz (1490–1529) to Augsburg to confer on Frederick the Wise the rarely awarded papal Golden Rose—a practice observed even today.

Luther arrived in Augsburg on October 7, 1518, and five days later had the first of several meetings with Cajetan. Even Luther admitted to the low-key, fatherly manner employed by the scholarly cardinal, who was in fact committed to ecclesiastical reform as long as it did not involve doctrinal challenges. An impasse resulted, however, when besides refusing to debate with Luther, Cajetan made it clear that only a thorough recantation would suffice. Luther responded that only an ecumenical church council could judge him, and for the next three days, both he and Cajetan argued in circles. By his own later admission, Luther lost his temper and responded *irreverently* on several occasions with the cardinal, though the patience of the latter was also beginning to wear thin. With no resolution in sight, it was agreed that Cajetan would make a list of specific points that Luther was to recant, along with a proper statement of the correct belief on these particular points. It was likely a stall by Luther, who then abruptly departed Augsburg, though not before his religious superior convinced him to write a letter of apology to Cajetan.

The tone of Luther's apology was conciliatory and deferential: "I have thrown myself and all that is mine at the feet of His Holiness. I have demonstrated that I am ready to accept whatever would seem good to His Holiness, be it condemnation or be it approval."[10] Luther, however, was likely disingenuous, since two weeks later he wrote to a friend that Cajetan "offered to handle everything in a most fatherly manner. No doubt he would have done so had I only been willing to recant my statements, for the whole case was tied up in that knot."[11] Luther went on to insist that it was only because of his belief that Cajetan was intent on nothing less than recantation that he had now appealed his case beyond Augsburg to an ecumenical council.

Cajetan, on the other hand, after the failed meeting at Augsburg, now insisted to Frederick the Wise that Luther be turned over to church authorities. Perhaps in response, and certainly against the advice of Frederick the Wise, Luther published his own account of what had transpired at Augsburg, describing himself as simply an "inquiring disputant," and imprudently compared his meeting with Cajetan to the encounter between Jesus and Caiaphas. Luther then used the narrative largely as an opportunity to engage in the debate that Cajetan had denied him at Augsburg. He knew that he was pushing himself to the precipice with regard to church authorities. Just weeks later, he remarked to a friend, "I daily expect the condemnation from the city of Rome."[12]

There is evidence that Luther became anxious about possible excommunication. In early January, accompanied by Frederick the Wise, Luther met with papal nuncio Karl von Miltitz, who accused Luther of committing "offense and outrage" against the Catholic Church. Luther offered his willingness to be silent in the future about his theological propositions if his opponents would also drop the matter. He offered to write to Leo X and "submit myself with greatest humility. I wanted to confess that I had been too passionate and sharp, yet that I did not intend to disparage the Holy Roman Church with this tone." Luther also offered to issue a pamphlet in which he would urge everyone to submit to, obey, and respect the Roman Catholic Church, and would admit that he had written his theological propositions in an imprudent and untimely manner. However, all of this hinged on Luther's final request that his case be transferred from Roman jurisdiction to the jurisdiction of the cardinal-archbishop of Salzburg, Matthäus Lang (1468–1540).[13]

Though von Miltitz felt that Luther's proposals would not be sufficient, Luther nevertheless drafted the letter to Pope Leo X, who Luther now insisted truly stood in the place of Christ: "I cannot bear the power of your wrath, and I do not know of any means to escape it," Luther wrote. He reiterated to Leo X the same steps that he had told von Miltitz he would undertake but omitted his request that the matter be transferred to the cardinal-archbishop of Salzburg and insisted that his only purpose in all that he had written was to prevent people from preferring indulgences to works of love. In closing his letter, Luther assured the pontiff, "If I can do anything else, or if I discover that there is something else I can do, I will certainly be most ready to do it."[14]

Luther knew his options were exhausted, and there was little Frederick the Wise could do to stop a papal excommunication. Then, on January 12, 1519, Luther's fortunes took a sudden upward swing. The emperor Maximilian I had died, and so Pope Leo X now lobbied heavily for the election of Frederick the Wise himself to be the new Holy Roman emperor in order to block the election of Charles. The pope knew that in order to curry further favor with Frederick, he would have to be more lenient with Luther, so canonical proceedings against Luther were suspended. Luther reveled in his new-found freedom and almost mockingly remarked that "Rome is burning to destroy me, but I coolly laugh at her. I am told that in the Campo di Fiore a Martin-in-effigy has been publicly burned, cursed, and execrated. I am ready for their rage."[15]

The respite from canonical proceedings allowed Luther to attend to a long-simmering feud between his Wittenberg friend and fellow reformer Andreas Karlstadt and Catholic theologian Johannes Eck (1486–1543). Eck had been an early opponent of Luther's *95 Theses* and had also taken exception to the theology of Karlstadt, against whom Eck planned to debate publicly in Leipzig. Luther felt that Eck, whom he termed "a little glory-hungry beast," was really trying to use Karlstadt as a proxy for a debate with him.[16] If that was the case, then Luther took the bait. The debate between Eck and Karlstadt began on June 27 in Leipzig and continued for seven days, until on July 4, Luther showed up and entered the fray. Luther would perhaps not have made the journey had he known that on June 28, in spite of all efforts to the contrary, Charles of Burgundy had become Holy Roman Emperor Charles V. The papacy no longer had a need to appease Frederick the Wise or Luther, so canonical proceedings against him would soon be reactivated.

Eck and Luther mostly debated church authority, and Eck, known more for his theological acumen than for tact, shrewdly asked Luther whether the ecumenical Council of Constance (1414–1418) had been correct when it had condemned to death the Czech priest Jan Hus (1369–1415) because of alleged heresy. Luther let his guard down, and replied that both popes and councils could, and indeed *had*, erred. Eck seized on it, and immediately declared Luther to be a Hussite. Although untrue, Luther's appeal at Augsburg to an ecumenical council was now untenable, and in his own account of the Leipzig Disputation, he speaks disparagingly of the fawning attention showered on Eck by the people of Leipzig after his victorious debate.[17] Luther returned to Wittenberg, but he had not heard the last of Eck.

It is not surprising that when Luther published his *Lectures on Galatians* three months after Leipzig, it contained a dismissal of the authority of ecumenical councils. Instead, Luther now insisted that true doctrinal certainty could only be found in "the most solid rock of Divine Scripture" and that one must not "believe rashly any, whoever they may be, who speak, decide, or act contrary to its authority." He had laid the groundwork for his belief that doctrine was determined *sola scriptura*—by scripture alone, and had now made it clear that he believed in neither the divine origin of the papacy nor the authority of ecumenical councils. From the Catholic standpoint, Luther had thus separated theology from the church and made doctrine a matter of personal confession.

A Tower Experience

Also in 1519 Luther wrote treatises on penance, the eucharist, and absolution, but it was a non-literary event of that year which would be most significant for his theological development. According to Luther, while in the tower of his monastery at Wittenberg, he had a major theological breakthrough—the so-named tower experience—while pondering Romans 1:17: "For in it the justice of God is revealed through faith for faith; as it is written, 'The one who is just will live by faith.'" Luther remarked, "I hated that word, 'justice of God,' which, by the use and custom of all my teachers, I had been taught to understand philosophically as referring to formal or active justice, as they call it." He hated it because if God's justice was an *active* process whereby he judged, or *justified* us according to our works, then it seemed up to the individual rather than God to achieve certitude of one's salvation. In late medieval theology, this thinking was expressed through the axiom *facientibus quod in se est, deus non denegat suam gratiam*—"to those doing what is in them, God will not deny his grace." This led to Luther's obsessive scrupulosity over whether he had sufficiently appeased God and ongoing anxiety about his salvation: "I did not love, no, rather I hated the just God who punishes sinners."

Luther's tower insight, however, was that God's justice was a *passive* justice and a gift, which was revealed through the Gospel and which justifies us through our *faith*, regardless of good works. This was for Luther a sort of "road to Damascus" experience: "I exalted this sweetest word of mine, 'the justice of

God,' with as much love as before I had hated it with hate. This phrase of Paul was for me the very gate of paradise."[18] Henceforward, Luther regarded earlier teachings on justification as Pelagian, that is, the early church heresy which held that one could help bring about God's grace through his own actions. Faith alone (*sola fide*) now became everything for Luther. Man was helpless in the face of God. There was still grace, but no free will, no spark of goodness, and no need for mediation of an institutional church. Luther's new understanding of justification—a doctrine that had not at that point been defined by the Catholic Church—would henceforth be the cornerstone for all of his later theological assertions. It would lead his critics, however, to assert that he had "traded the pope of Rome for the pope of justification."

Historians debate about whether there was a true "tower experience." Some who argue in its favor even push back the date of this theological breakthrough to 1512, while others point out that Luther himself, who does not even write of the event for the first time until 1545, attributes it to 1519. If one accepts Luther's own dating as accurate, in combination with a cursory examination of his above-mentioned university lectures between 1512 and 1518, it strongly suggests that he had been *gradually* shifting from the notion of a God of divine judgment to one of God's consoling word of forgiving mercy. This is supported by a letter written in 1516 in which Luther clearly indicates that it was his rejection of scholasticism and Aristotelianism that had *necessarily* led him to discount any kind of earned justification: "For we are not, as Aristotle believes, made righteous by the doing of just deeds, unless we deceive ourselves; but rather—if I may say so—in becoming and being righteous people we do just deeds." Works, Luther concludes, do not earn righteousness, but are rather a *sign* of one's righteousness, predicated upon one's faith, for fulfillment of God's law "without faith in Christ . . . no more resembles righteousness than sorb apples resemble figs."[19]

Attendance at the University of Wittenberg swelled in 1519 as students were drawn to Luther's ideas, as well as to the lectures of his supporters Philip Melanchthon (1497–1560) and Karlstadt. Melanchthon, though not a priest, had been teaching Greek at the University of Wittenberg since 1518 and was noted for his conciliatory and peaceful temperament. Luther's university popularity, however, was a matter of great concern to church authorities. Throughout the Middle Ages and even into the early sixteenth century, universities were considered an important part of the *magisterium* of the church. Complex theological matters would be sorted out by these institutions and their decisions utilized by the church in the formulation of doctrine. Pope John XXII (1249–1334) was even sanctioned by the theology faculty of the University of Paris for his errant views on the Beatific Vision. Thus, with Luther spreading his ideas in a university setting, his theology had the very clear potential to spread to other academic institutions and threaten one of the very mechanisms by which the church maintained orthodoxy.

Luther's literary activity in 1520 also intensified. His *Treatise on Good Works* (March 1520) reflected his tower-experience belief that living one's faith rather than undertaking good works was the best way to observe God's commandments, while *On the Papacy in Rome* (May, 1520) argued that the church was a spiritual entity under the leadership of Christ rather than the pope. This was all too much for Rome. In June 1520, one year after the election of Charles V and almost three years since the writing of the *95 Theses,* the papal bull *Exsurge Domine,* prepared with the help of Luther's nemesis, Johannes Eck, was promulgated in Rome. Contrary to popular belief, however, *Exsurge Domine* did not excommunicate Luther but rather condemned forty-one of his propositions and *threatened* excommunication if he did not recant within sixty days.

Unfazed, Luther continued to write. His *To the Christian Nobility of the Germany Nation Concerning the Reform of Christendom* (June 23, 1520) appealed directly to the German princes to act on the basis of their priestly baptism and boldly reform the church: "We must compel the Romanists to follow not their own interpretation [of scripture] but the better one." Over four thousand copies were sold within weeks of publication and helped solidify Luther's place as a national leader. For the German princes, Luther had provided them theological support for ecclesial autonomy from both the Holy Roman Empire and from Rome. In the aftermath of the success of his book and presumed support from the territorial princes, Luther felt confident enough to remark, "I am not afraid of censures and force, since in the midst of Germany I can now be safe."[20]

Then, at the end of August 1520 as the sixty-day period was about to expire, Luther seemed once again to have doubts. He wrote to Charles V himself, and in language that was both self-deprecating and obsequious, he implored the emperor to intervene on his behalf to prevent ecclesiastical censure: "It will be the remembered glory of your age if Your Most Sacred majesty will not allow the unjust to crush and swallow him who is more just. . . ."[21]

Five weeks later, however, Luther's confidence returned. His *Pagan Servitude of the Church,* more commonly known as *The Babylonian Captivity of the Church* (October 6, 1520), was the most comprehensive challenge to traditional Catholic doctrine to date. In it, Luther rejected as objective sacraments confirmation, marriage, ordination, and anointing of the sick. Confession remained a sort of "semi-sacrament" for Luther in that it helped bring people to a deeper sense of their faith in Christ, though Luther made it a point to discount the value of imposed penances as having any value for one's salvation. Communion was to be given under the species of both bread and wine, and the term *transubstantiation* was rejected as an Aristotelian creation. Luther substituted *consubstantiation,* insisting that Christ was bodily present *with* the bread and wine, though Luther would continue vehemently to adhere to a belief in the Real Presence. Eucharistic sacrifice was also rejected, but it must be borne in mind that it had never been formally defined by the church and what Luther specifically rejected was largely an incorrect understanding of eucharistic sacrifice which had become widely accepted in the later Middle Ages.

The publication of *The Babylonian Captivity* became for Luther the crossing of a theological Rubicon. The famed Christian humanist Erasmus (1469–1536), previously on friendly terms with Luther, now wanted nothing to do with him. King Henry VIII (1509–1547) of England, still in the good graces of the Catholic Church, was outraged at Luther's book, and responded (probably with Thomas More as ghost writer) with his *Defense of the Seven Sacraments,* for which the pope awarded him the title "Defender of the Faith." Luther's own religious superior withdrew support from him, and the University of Paris, long a major arbiter of theological disputes, now began an in-depth examination of Luther's theology. Even more ominously, Eck and papal envoy Jerome Aleander (1480–1542) traveled throughout Germany to spread the promulgation of *Exsurge Domine.*

Luther again wavered. Papal nuncio von Miltitz, who genuinely wanted to resolve Luther's situation and who in fact had upbraided the indulgence preacher Tetzel the previous year, convinced Luther to write a conciliatory pamphlet on Christian faith, in order to curry favor with Leo X. To this end, Luther published in November 1520 *The Freedom of a Christian Man,* which showcased his new understanding of how God's passive justice fit into the life of the everyday Christian. If Luther's purpose was to appease, his words were not well chosen. In the dedicatory letter to Leo X, Luther spoke of him as though a peer, and brazenly assured the pontiff that his book "contains the whole of Christian life in a brief form, provided you grasp its meaning."[22]

Behind the scenes, Luther assured his friends that "the papal bull has in no way frightened me. I intend to preach, lecture, and write in spite of it."[23] And this he did with a vengeance. In late November, Luther published *Against the Accursed Bull of the Anti-christ,* and in December, accompanied by a group of Wittenberg students, publicly burned a copy of *Exsurge Domine,* along with various books of Catholic theology. It is not surprising that on January 3, 1521, the papal bull *Decet Romanum Pontificem* formally and officially excommunicated Martin Luther.

Imperial Intervention

Charles V, however, if he desired any kind of political unity in Germany, could not afford to alienate the growing faction of both princes and common people who supported Luther, and so against the wishes of Rome, he attempted to mediate the dispute at the upcoming Imperial Diet of Worms, in 1521. Luther readily agreed, remarking, "I am called by the Lord if the emperor summons."[24] Luther, however, would not have likely been so compliant, had he known that papal nuncio Aleander insisted that the diet only give him an opportunity to recant his errors. Furthermore, Luther became seriously ill during the three hundred-mile journey to Worms, to the point that he required medicine and medical bloodletting.

When Luther appeared before the diet and the emperor on April 17, 1521, he was simply asked to renounce his books. Surprised, Luther asked if he could give his answer the following day, to which the diet agreed. The next day, he again stood before the diet and refused to recant, insisting that he would only be convinced of his errors by sacred scripture and not by "fallible councils or popes." There is no record, however, of Luther ever having uttered the now-famous phrase, "Here I Stand. I can do no other." On April 26, Luther was allowed to return to Wittenberg, on the condition that he not preach, write, or do anything to stir up the populace on his way home. Luther agreed, but he did *not* return home. Frederick the Wise, with Luther's complicity, "kidnapped" him during his return journey and secreted him away at the Wartburg castle in Eisenach. Now in hiding, Luther took the name Junker Jörg (Knight George), and let his hair and beard grow to disguise his appearance.

On May 26, the Edict of Worms declared Luther an outlaw of the empire and made it illegal to print, sell, read, or purchase his writings. This was essential if the spread of Luther's ideas was to be stopped, for the relatively recent invention of movable type by German printer Johannes Gutenberg (1400–1468) meant that books could now be produced by the thousands, fairly inexpensively, and in a short period of time. For Luther, as well as for other writers of his time, this meant an effective and rapid conduit to a much wider audience.

Initially at the Wartburg castle Luther declared, "I am sitting here all day, drunk with leisure."[25] This would soon change, as he began to suffer from depression, severe constipation, and what he described as attacks from the devil. Though attributing psychological and emotional distress to demonic forces was quite common in sixteenth-century Germany, there is no evidence to support the popular story that Luther threw an inkwell at a demonic apparition. Nevertheless, visitors to his room at the Wartburg today are proudly shown the "mark" on the wall.

The Wartburg became for Luther *my Patmos* and *my wilderness*, and to buoy his spirits, he wrote. His *Explanation of the Magnificat* demonstrated a traditional Marian theology, in which Mary was both Mother of God and spiritual mother of all Christians. He followed commentaries on Psalms 37 and 68 with his *Judgment on Monastic Vows*, which dismissed religious vows as worthless because they allegedly put works before faith. In a lengthy dedicatory letter to his father, Luther maintained that Christ had absolved him from his monastic vows anyway, though one senses anxiety throughout the letter that somehow his father would not accept him as an excommunicated ex-monk.[26] Luther also penned his *Abrogating the Private Mass* and *The Misuse of the Mass,* in which he spelled out the liturgical implications of his eucharistic theology.

But the most significant literary achievement during Luther's seclusion was his translation of the New Testament into German. It daunted Luther, who remarked, "I have here shouldered a burden beyond my power. Now I realize what it means to translate, and why no one has previously undertaken it who would disclose his name."[27] Nevertheless, he finished in just eleven weeks. The commentaries at the beginning of each book helped to spread his theology, and the fact that the Bible was now in German, though not for the first time, would exercise a profound role in the standardization of the German language. But Luther encountered one major problem in his translation—the Letter of James: "You see that a person is justified by works and not by faith alone.... For just as the body without the spirit is dead, so faith without works is also dead" (James 2:14–26). No matter how Luther translated it, the passage from James clashed headlong with his rejection of "works righteousness." Finally, he resolved the dilemma by dismissing the Letter of James as an "epistle of straw" which "contains nothing evangelical," and relegated it to the back of his Bible among the apocryphal books.

While Luther hid at the Wartburg, trouble began in Wittenberg when a group of apocalyptic Anabaptists known as the Zwickau Prophets began to spread their ideas among the townspeople and students. After a brief secret visit to Wittenberg at the beginning of December 1521, Luther remarked, "I am highly suspicious of their boastings that they have conversations with God in his majesty."[28] Even worse, Karlstadt was enamored of the strange new group and took church reform in Wittenberg in a radical direction that Luther had never envisioned. Karlstadt immediately offered a simplified form of the Mass in German rather than Latin and began to preach a kind of iconoclasm that led to the destruction of statues, paintings, and other religious art, as well as to attacks against "non-reformed" clergy. When the town council made many of the changes law, Luther became even more alarmed, since he felt that reform should not be mandated but should rather result from one's inner conversion to the saving Word of Christ.

Frederick the Wise, under pressure from imperial authorities to stop what was happening in Wittenberg, turned to Melanchthon and Luther for advice. Luther needed little convincing. Remarking that "Satan has intruded into my fold at Wittenberg," he hurried back to the town in early 1522, in spite of the objections of Frederick the Wise, who as a Roman Catholic in good standing was concerned about the reaction of imperial authorities to the public presence of the excommunicated outlaw. Luther began a series of homilies that set a more moderate course of what he regarded as authentic reform: "Nothing is more disgusting to me than our mob of people here who have abandoned Word, faith, and love and can only boast that they are Christians because . . . they can eat meat, eggs, and milk, receive the Lord's Supper in both kinds, and neither fast nor pray."[29]

The new ecclesiology that Luther envisioned for Wittenberg as well as for the church at large was based on an invisible congregation of the justified, which could be outwardly recognized by two norms: (1) where the Word of God is preached purely; and (2) where baptism and the "Lord's Supper" are celebrated. Yet when imperial authorities in 1523 decreed the confiscation of Luther's German New Testament, he realized that this invisible ecclesial community of the justified would have to coexist with the real world of rulers, authority, and society. Therefore, he published *Temporal Authority: To What Extent It Should Be Obeyed* (1523), which although insisting that for those who are justified through the inner transforming power of grace, externals were unnecessary and even potentially harmful, nevertheless allowed that the Christian, out of love for neighbor, should live by external laws, even if this meant obeying a tyrannical ruler. German psychotherapist Eric Fromm (1900–1980) would later argue that this "ethic of obedience" was a contributing factor to the success of Nazism.

Luther also found that his Christian message could be misunderstood, as was the case in 1525 when the German peasantry rebelled against religious oppression and serfdom and pointed to Luther's message of Gospel liberty as their inspiration. The response of Luther, shocking to the standards of today, was *Against the Robbing and Murdering Hordes of the Peasants* (1525), in which he suggested that the peasants be "cut down like dogs." Luther's support of the civil authorities to put down religious dissent is something that would become commonplace, particularly with the later repression and execution of Anabaptists in Germany.

The death of Frederick the Wise on May 5, 1525, meant Luther had lost his greatest protector and ally. The reality, however, was that Luther no longer *needed* the protection. After initial fears of excommunication, trial, exile, and even frequently voiced concerns that he might be put to death, he had survived. Now firmly ensconced in Wittenberg, he lived openly.

On June 27, 1525, Luther married twenty-six-year-old Katharina von Bora (1499–1552), one of nine Cistercian nuns for whom Luther had helped provide refuge in Wittenberg two years earlier after they fled their convent. Luther had suggested a suitor for von Bora, but in spite of the sixteen-year age difference, she declared her love for him. For his part, Luther says he undertook the marriage to silence gossip about him, as well as to fulfill his father's wish of progeny. Though he believed that it was God's will that he marry, he remarked candidly to a friend, "I feel neither passionate love nor burning for my spouse, but I cherish her."[30] Whatever the degree of their passion, Luther would have six children with von Bora and would make his home with her at the Augustinian monastery at Wittenberg, after it had been taken over by the state.

A new phase in the campaign to stop Luther had begun with the papal election of Dutchman Adrian VI (1522–1523)—the last non-Italian pope until 1978 and the last pope to retain his given name. Adrian VI was no stranger to the Hapsburgs. He had tutored Charles V as a youth and, along with Cardinal Jiménez de Cisneros (1436–1517), had served as co-regent of Spain until Charles had reached the age of accession. Pope Adrian, whose candidacy for the papacy had been supported by Cardinal Cajetan, was committed to an internal reform of the Catholic Church, which he insisted must begin at the top with the pope and cardinals. At the same time, he was no fan of Luther and recognized that Luther's *theology* rather than Luther himself needed to be addressed. To this end, Pope Adrian enlisted the aid of numerous Catholic theological writers to refute Luther's theology point by point. The work of these theologians was challenging. Many of the areas of doctrine to which Luther had objected had never been formally defined by the church or had been sometimes misunderstood. Undaunted, these Catholic theologians would utilize a variety of sources in their writing in order to come up with provisional definitions of doctrine.[31]

Further Political Developments

The untimely death of Adrian VI in 1523 and the accession of Pope Clement VII (1523–1534) were huge setbacks for Charles V, who faced a serious military crisis. The Ottoman Turks, who had overrun the Byzantine Empire in the previous century, would soon be at the gates of Vienna. At the same time, intermittent wars with King Francis I of France (1515–1547) meant that Charles V desperately needed a religiously unified Germany if he were to raise an army to turn back the Turkish advance while still keeping the French in check. France in fact exploited the religious division in Germany by entering into alliances with Lutheran-leaning territorial princes, the Italian states of northern Italy, and even with the Ottoman Turks. When France also entered an alliance with Clement VII, who shared the pro-French and anti-Hapsburg sentiments of his cousin, Pope Leo X, and uncle, Lorenzo de Medici, Charles knew he would find little support for efforts to stem the deteriorating religious situation in the Holy Roman Empire. Yet, he still needed the help of *all* the German territorial princes, Lutherans included, so in defiance of Rome, the imperial Diet at Speyer in 1526 suspended the Edict of Worms and decreed that each German prince would be allowed to determine the type of religious practices in his realm. Religious orthodoxy had yielded to political pragmatism.

It was not difficult for German territorial princes to realize that if they embraced Luther's theology, they would have virtual control over the church in their realms, particularly since Luther had maintained that all external elements of the church should fall under secular authority. Ironically, the religious tolerance shown by Charles V at the Diet of Speyer contributed to both the spread of the Lutheran reform as well as to the marginalization of Luther as a major figure of influence. As territorial princes began to take the helm in religious affairs in their regions, most of Luther's activities from 1526 to his death in 1546 would be limited to continued exegetical work as well as to efforts to preserve Protestant orthodoxy in the face of challenges from the more radical wing of the Protestant reformation, particularly with regard to eucharistic issues.

Charles V, however, would find that religion still mattered. In 1527, a contingent of Spanish, German, and Italian troops of the Holy Roman Empire in Northern Italy made a detour to Rome, sacked the city, and took anti-Hapsburg Pope Clement VII hostage. Charles V had not given orders for this and tried to head them off, but to no avail. Many of the troops, though politically loyal to Charles V, were in fact Lutheran, and one anonymous individual even scribbled the name "Luther" on one of the paintings in the Sistine Chapel, and both Clement VII and Cardinal Cajetan had to ransom themselves at enormous financial cost. Chastened by the sack of Rome, Pope Clement VII reconciled with Charles V and implored him to put an end to religious concessions in Germany. The details of their reconciliation are not known, but what happened afterward strongly suggests a deal had been made. Charles V convoked yet another Diet of Speyer (1529), but this time *withdrew* the concessions made to Lutherans three years earlier. When Luther supporters at the diet "protested" against the withdrawal, the name *protestants* thereafter became associated with the reformers. The following year, troops of Charles V laid siege to Florence and restored to power the Medici family of Clement VII.

Initially, Lutherans appeared to have been bested by what had happened at Speyer and hoped to use the upcoming imperial diet at Augsburg in 1530 to regain some ground. The Augsburg Confession of faith was prepared through the efforts of Philip Melanchthon, but with Luther's approval, and stated Lutheran beliefs in a somewhat conciliatory manner. It was the first authoritative and comprehensive statement of Lutheran belief, but the official Catholic response was harsh and uncompromising, and in 1531 the Lutheran princes of Germany reacted with the formation of the Schmalkaldic League. Luther approved of this formidable political block, because he felt that Charles V's rejection of the Augsburg Confession was an attempt to stand in the way of the gospel. For the next fifteen years, Protestantism flourished, as Charles V once again became engrossed in wars with France and could no longer rely on Lutheran princes for support.

At the funeral for Luther in 1546, his friend Johann Bugenhagen (1485–1558) concluded his homily with what were said by Luther's physician to have been the reformer's last words: "Pestis eram vivus, moriens tua mors ero Papa—Pope, when I lived, I was your pestilence. When I die, I will be your death." Yet the papacy, which Luther maintained had been "founded by the devil," did not die, and Paul III himself, to whom Luther referred in writing as *Your Hellishness*, would outlive Luther by three years. More importantly, Paul III had already set in motion the ecumenical Council of Trent (1545–1563), which during its three separate sessions over eighteen years would emerge not only as a major tool for Catholic reform but would also be the main vehicle for providing a comprehensive condemnation of Luther's theology, though neither Luther nor any other reformer is ever mentioned by name in the decrees of the council. Relying to a large extant on the theological writings of the early respondents to Luther, the council would also clarify, and in some cases formulate for the first time, key areas of Catholic doctrine.

Only the death of Francis I in 1547 finally gave Charles V a free hand to deal with Lutheranism, but it was too late. The best he could hope for now was a way for Catholics and Lutherans to coexist in Germany. To this end, the Augsburg Interim of 1548 allowed clerical marriage and communion in both kinds in Germany, in spite of strong objections from Rome. The definitive solution to the Lutheran dilemma finally came in 1555, when Charles V and his brother Ferdinand I negotiated the Peace of Augsburg with the imperial electors. It was essentially a restoration of the concessions of the Diet of Speyer in 1526 and was embodied in the Latin phrase *cuius regio eius religio* (whoever's principality, his religion). In other words, if a territorial prince had embraced Lutheranism, then

Lutheranism would be the official religion throughout his realm. If a prince were Catholic, the principality would remain Catholic. Lutherans who happened to live in a Catholic principality could be given permission to continue living as such, though it was not reciprocal for Catholics in Lutheran principalities. Imperial cities, which by definition belonged to no prince but rather to the Holy Roman Emperor, were to allow both Catholicism and Lutheranism, if both religions were already established. Thus, the visitor today to the Catholic cathedral in Augsburg will notice an architecturally distinct Lutheran side chapel, added in accordance with the Peace of Augsburg. For all the efforts of Charles V, all he was able to accomplish in terms of dealing with Lutheranism was on the surface imperial religious toleration, which was in reality a grudging recognition of the *status quo*.

Conflicting Images of Luther

Though the statement has been made that "there are as many Luthers as there are books about Luther,"[32] this obvious hyperbole holds true only for the modern period. Prior to the twentieth century, there were essentially two ways in which he was viewed. Protestant historians understandably portrayed Luther in a glowingly positive light, while Catholic writers painted a picture of a narcissistic expounder of heresy, who had little regard for the Catholic Church. An in-depth survey of literature on Luther over the centuries is beyond our scope here, but it is important to have at least a general sense of how the Catholic view of Luther has evolved.

The demonization of Luther by contemporary Catholic theologian Johannes Cochlaeus (1479–1552) in his inflammatory and polemical book *The Seven-Headed Luther* created a negative image that would reach down into the twentieth century, even as historical scholarship was becoming more meticulous and seemingly objective. The biography of Luther by Austrian Dominican Heinrich Denifle (1844–1905) was scholarly and well researched, but unfortunately it was also replete with subjectivism and *ad hominem* attacks and reinforced Catholic scholarly hostility toward the German reformer.[33] A similar assessment of Luther was found in Denifle's contemporary, German Jesuit Hartman Grisar (1845–1935), whose vast three-volume biography of Luther, though full of important facts, found little good to say about him. Unfortunately, the works of Denifle and Grisar became the standard Catholic assessments of Luther in the early twentieth century and are still regarded in some circles as the best, and certainly *safest* books for Catholics interested in knowing more about Luther.

Papal comments in the twentieth century about Luther have generally mirrored the negative scholarship of Denifle and Grisar. When Pius X condemned modernism in *Pascendi Dominici Gregis* (1907), he spoke of modernists who "feel no horror at treading in the footsteps of Luther." In *Mediator Dei* (1947), which concerned liturgical matters, Pius XII felt the need to single out the "new and false opinion of Luther" with regard to private masses as explained in his *Abrogating the Private Mass* (1521).

Pioneering work in counterbalancing the harshly negative view of Luther in Catholic circles was undertaken by Catholic priest and scholar Josef Lortz (1887–1975), whose *Die Reformation in Deutschland* (1939) took great pains not only to portray objectively the deficiencies of Roman Catholicism on the eve of Luther's reforms but also to assess and understand Luther within the context of the theological confusion of his time. This led Lortz to his provocative and famous conclusion that "Luther wrestled with and overthrew a Catholicism that was not Catholic."[34] Fully aware, as Lortz himself states, that "with Luther as with no one else, it is easy to sketch distortedly,"[35] he nevertheless offered a portrait of Luther that, though not uncritical, highlighted his catholicity, even after his excommunication.

The work of Lortz was a turning point toward a more positive assessment of Luther in Roman Catholic scholarly circles, which helped lay the groundwork for the *Decree on Ecumenism* of the Second Vatican Council two decades later. The council stated the desire of the Catholic Church to work toward the restoration of unity among all Christians and, in language of which Luther would have approved heartily, declared that "all who have been justified by faith in Baptism are members of Christ's body, and have a right to be called Christian." The *Decree on Ecumenism* called for experts from different ecclesial communities to establish dialogue meetings, at which representatives from each tradition, in a religious spirit, could present an in-depth explanation of what their respective communion believes.

This was the starting-point for the Lutheran–Catholic dialogue, which over the last forty years has made great strides in finding common ground between the Lutheran and Catholic Churches.[36] Fundamental to the success of the dialogue has been its ability to reexamine their respective doctrines *outside* of the polemical context of the sixteenth century. In so doing, *listening* to each other has replaced the extreme language previously employed, which had obscured the basic substance of what each side actually believed. This process of toned-down polemic and rhetoric has led to the discovery that in many areas, Lutherans and Catholics are not in disagreement after all, even concerning the vexing question of justification. It is a slow process, and differences remain, but when one looks at the content of the Augsburg Confession and the decrees of the Council of Trent, one no longer sees an insurmountable chasm but rather a substantial bridge under construction. Just as theologians from both sides during the sixteenth century furthered the Lutheran–Catholic rift, so too are theologians now trying to put things back together.

In addition to the work of the Lutheran–Catholic dialogue, Pope John Paul II has done more to reach out to Lutherans than any pope in history. On June 25, 1980, in a speech in recognition of the 450th anniversary of the Augsburg Confession, he spoke of the honorable intentions of all those who participated in the formulation of the Augsburg Confession and their earnest desire to give holy and catholic witness, and praised the years-long intensive efforts by the Lutheran–Catholic dialogue to uncover common doctrinal ground between the two churches.

On November 5, 1983, in a letter commemorating the 500th anniversary of Luther's birth, John Paul II remarked: "One must be enlightened by the convincing manner of the proud religious spirit of Martin Luther, animated by a burning passion for the question of eternal salvation."

The following month, on December 11, in a Liturgy of the Word at an Evangelical Lutheran church in Rome, the pope remarked:

> During this five hundredth anniversary of the birth of Martin Luther, we seem to see rise in the distance like the dawn the advent of a restoration of our unity and of our community. This unity is the fruit of the renewal, of the daily conversion and penance of all Christians in the light of the eternal Word of God. It is also the best preparation for the advent of God in our world.

John Paul II reiterated in his encyclical *Ut Unum Sint* (1995) the commitment of the Catholic Church to the restoration of unity. It is for him an irrevocable commitment, the ultimate goal of which is "full visible unity among all the baptized." In impassioned words that just as easily could have come from Luther himself, the pope identifies a common belief in the new life and transforming power of the Cross of Christ as a fundamental starting point for true ecumenism. For John Paul II, the tragedy of the sixteenth-century Lutheran–Catholic division was the blindness on both sides: "intolerant polemics and controversies have made incompatible assertions out of what was really the result of two different ways of looking at the same reality."

At an ecumenical meeting in 1996 in Paderborn, Germany, the pope praised Luther's desire for church reform and bemoaned the missed opportunity in the sixteenth century to appreciate positive elements of his theology. Acknowledging that the Catholic Church was partially responsible for the sixteenth-century division, he reiterated his earnest hope for a greater degree of unity between Lutherans and Catholics. But perhaps most remarkable of all was the general audience of John Paul II on March 21, 2001, during which the pontiff both praised and quoted from Luther's *Explanation of the Magnificat.* It would no doubt have been impossible for Luther to have envisioned such an event as he sat writing his commentary 480 years earlier, exiled and excommunicated.

Numerous doctrinal challenges have occurred within the Christian church, most of them confined to the first few centuries, and few were successful in establishing a large-scale viable ecclesial community outside of either Greek Orthodoxy or Roman Catholicism. This was not the case with Luther's reform movement. In less than thirty years, he had changed the religious and political face of western Europe and shaken Roman Catholicism to its foundations. Though the Catholic Church emerged from this trial stronger and clearer about what it believed, there would be no turning back the clock to the Middle Ages, where one was simply Catholic, Jewish, or Muslim. The principle of Christian pluralism had been irrevocably established.

Questions for Reflection and Discussion

1. How much do you think the inner spiritual struggles and the personality of Martin Luther influenced his excommunication and eventual emergence as a major leader of the Protestant Reformation?

2. If you were Pope Leo X, how would you have handled the Luther case?

3. Do you think that the excommunication of Martin Luther was inevitable?

5

First Contact

Colonization and Evangelization
in the Sixteenth Century

The cultural damage done by Western missionaries in their efforts in the sixteenth century to evangelize the non-European world, particularly in those areas where a strong colonial government was established, is well known. Yet, the notion of eliminating indigenous culture and replacing it with a European-based form of Christianity is only half the story. There were, in fact, groundbreaking efforts in the sixteenth century to adapt Christianity to indigenous cultures to an extraordinary degree, with results that have in some cases stood the test of time.

———◄○►———

Who can deny that the use of gunpowder against pagans is the burning of incense to Our Lord?

—Fernández de Oviedo, conquistador and
governor of Hispaniola (1526)

A fundamental challenge faced the Catholic Church when, in the fifteenth and sixteenth centuries, Spanish and Portuguese exploration led to large-scale overseas colonization for the first time in history. How did one establish Catholicism in a culture that is different, sometimes radically, from the European world? Two diametrically opposed strategies emerged: (1) the *tabula rasa* (clean slate) approach, in which local culture, which was considered desolate and inferior to European culture, was eradicated as much as possible; (2) the implan-

95

tation, or inculturation of Christianity *within* each new-found culture. Though Spain generally employed the former and Portugal the latter, there would be exceptions to this based on individual personalities, particular culture, and religious order.

Fundamental to understanding this process is an awareness of the high degree of competition between Portugal and Spain, and of the shifting intervention of the papacy. Portugal had gotten a significant head start in exploration with the inspiration of Prince Henry the Navigator (1390–1460), Grand Master of the Military Order of Christ, who sponsored numerous expeditions along the western African coast. This led a series of pro-Portuguese popes to grant Portugal the right of royal patronage, which meant that they could convert, govern, and establish churches in those discovered lands in which there was not already a Christian king.

This papal favoritism, however, came to an abrupt end in 1492, with the election of the Spaniard Rodrigo Borgia as Alexander VI, whose personal moral failings are well known. The Spanish were fearful that Portuguese domination and privilege in exploration would hamper their ability to lay claim to any land discovered by Christopher Columbus (1451–1506), who, though an Italian, had sailed on behalf of Spain. Columbus was not a visionary, nor was he trying to prove the world was round, since this well-known fact had been believed since antiquity.[1] Rather, he was simply trying to find a better route to India.

Columbus returned to Spain in May 1493 and claimed to have achieved his objective, though it now seems that he may in fact have intentionally concealed his failure. Alexander VI acted immediately to protect Spanish interests. The papal bull *Inter Caetera Divinae* of May 3, 1493, granted to Spain the rights to the new-world discoveries of Columbus, and an addendum to the bull the following day took the remarkable and unprecedented step of dividing the world in half between Portugal and Spain.

A year later after much quarreling between the Portuguese and the Spanish, the Treaty of Tordesillas (June 7, 1494) adjusted the north-south line of demarcation to 46° 37′. This meant that an imaginary line ran from Greenland in the north through the eastern half of South America. Everything to the east of this line, which included Africa, India, and western China, belonged to Portugal. Everything west, which included the Americas (except present-day Brazil), Japan, the Philippines, and eastern China, belonged to Spain. In 1529, however, the Treaty of Saragossa adjusted the ante-meridian so that all of Asia belonged to Portugal, though the Portuguese unwisely relinquished the Philippines to Spain in the mistaken belief that it would not be profitable. The stage had been set.

Spanish Missionary Debates

The first missionary work in the Americas was done in the context of the conquest and colonization of Hispaniola and the greater Caribbean, which Columbus had claimed for Spain in 1493 on his second voyage to the New World. The Spaniards established the feudalistic *encomienda* (commendation) system, in which a colonist, or *encomendero*, would be granted a number of natives from a specific geographical region. Though the *encomendero* would not own the land from which the natives came, he could require their labor for his own lands in return for provision of minimal material needs and instruction in Christian doctrine. Though clearly unjust, few Spaniards in Hispaniola were troubled by the system, and some doubted whether natives even possessed souls.

One Spaniard, however, was very troubled. Bartolomé de las Casas (1474–1566), a friend of Columbus and editor of his sea journals, arrived in Hispaniola in 1502 initially as an *encomendero* himself but, in 1512, became the first person ordained to the priesthood in the Americas. As a priest, de las Casas witnessed first-hand the mistreatment of the native peoples of Hispaniola. He also accompanied the Cuban conquest expedition of Diego Velasquez (1465–1524), who held the license from the crown to explore and conquer. Such licenses were the main source of control the Spanish crown wielded over New Spain and gave to the holder the title of captain-general or governor over those areas he conquered.

During the Cuban expedition, de las Casas was appalled at the violence toward native Cubans, including the burning alive of their leaders. He began to speak out on behalf of the natives when he returned to Hispaniola, and, though already a diocesan priest, he eventually joined the Dominicans. Over a forty-year period, he would make five trips to Spain in order to argue the case for better treatment of New World natives and to wrest from the Spanish crown legal concessions aimed at improving their lot.

The principal opponent of de las Casas in Spain was philosopher and theologian Juan de Sepúlveda (1494–1573), who insisted that the conquest was justified and fair, since New World natives were in his opinion "wild and cruel barbarians, as different from men as apes."[2] De las Casas, however, prevailed. He went on to serve as bishop of Chiapas in southern Mexico, a region known even today for conflict between the government and indigenous peoples, and then retired to Spain, where without ecclesiastical permission, he published his famous *Destruction of the Indies* (1552).

The *conquistador* Hernando Cortés (1485–1547) knew de las Casas well.

They had arrived in Hispaniola around the same time, and Cortés had also taken part in the Cuban conquest led by Velasquez. The two men, however, could not have been more different. While the Cuban expedition had led de las Casas to take up the defense of native peoples, it seemed to have whetted Cortés's appetite for more conquest. A paradox of a man, the greedy, debauched, and unscrupulous Cortés attended Mass daily, carried an image of the Virgin Mary on him at all times, and marched under a personal banner that read "friends, let us follow the Cross, and if we have faith, we will truly be victorious under this sign."[3]

In 1518, Velasquez sent Cortés from Cuba as his fourth choice to undertake the conquest of Mexico on his behalf, but had second thoughts and sent an expedition to retrieve him. It was too late. Cortés landed near Vera Cruz on Good Friday, April 21, 1519, already planning to bypass Velasquez and apply directly to the King of Spain for a license to explore. Immediately, Cortés scuttled all but one of his ships, which was run aground so that none of his men could return to Cuba and betray his plans to Velasquez.

Who were the men who accompanied Cortés? Contrary to popular belief, Spain sent no armies to conquer the Americas. The *conquistadores* were in fact fortune seekers—*armed entrepreneurs,* as one historian calls them—who hoped that wealth and status might come to them not in the form of gold or silver but in the grant of an *encomienda*.[4] The average *conquistador* was in his late twenties and was only semiliterate. The largest number (30 percent) came from the southern Spanish kingdom of Andalusia, only recently retaken from the Muslims, from which one can infer that these *conquistadores* were especially imbued with the tools and the spirit of conquest.

Seldom mentioned either in contemporary or modern accounts of the Spanish conquest was the large number of Africans who accompanied Cortés. Originally brought as slaves to the Spanish sugar plantations of the Caribbean, they functioned as armed servants to the *conquistadores*. Many, however, quickly won their freedom, and some even became full-fledged *conquistadores*, such as Juan Valiente, who later took part in the conquest of Peru, and Juan Garrido (1480–1547), who participated with Cortés in the capture of Tenochtitlán. So strong was the African participation in the conquest of New Spain that by 1537 there would be 10,000 Africans in Mexico City.[5]

Cortés was neither tactical genius nor innovator, but he followed a methodical formula for conquest that had been developed and proven successful in Hispaniola and the greater Caribbean.

First, the *requiremento* (requirement) was read aloud in Spanish to the local population, though at times not actually within their earshot. Largely a legalistic maneuver, it stated that the natives were now subjects of the crown and, if they resisted, would be regarded as treasonous rebels against whom war would be waged (with the help of God). This would be their fault and not that of the *conquistadores* or the crown. De las Casas remarked about the *requiremento* that he did not know "whether to laugh or cry at the absurdity of it."[6]

Second, the *conquistadores* would claim the land in the name of the king of Spain, and third, a town would be founded so that it could serve as a legal entity of the crown. In the case of Cortés, he chose his landing site of Vera Cruz for this purpose.

The fourth element of conquest strategy was the establishment of native alliances, which proved easy for Cortés. Though the term *Aztec* referred to all of the Náhuatl-speaking tribes in the valley of Mexico, it by no means meant a *unified* Aztec empire. One of these various Aztec tribes was the Mexica, of which the Tenochcas were a subtribe who had settled on an island in Lake Texcoco, which they named Tenochtitlán (Mexico City). By the time of the Tenochca ruler Moctezuma, whose name means "he who rules with rage," Tenochtitlán dominated other Aztec tribes, which was deeply resented. Thus, Cortés found ready native Aztec allies, who saw the Spaniards as deliverers from Tenochca oppression.

The fifth strategic element was to find an interpreter. Cortés settled on an Aztec teenage noblewoman known to history as both La Malinche (1505–1529) and Doña Maria, who, in addition to her native Náhuatl, was fluent in Mayan after living as a captive among them for several years. Initially she knew no Spanish, so Cortés devised a cumbersome solution. He had just rescued the shipwrecked Spaniard Geronimo de Aguilar, who had also lived among the Yucatan Maya for seven years, so de Aguilar translated Spanish to Mayan, which La Malinche translated into Náhuatl.

The final component was the displaying of violence, which was meant to shock and intimidate. This could involve the severing of hands or arms, the execution of women, the mutilation or burning alive of individuals, setting huge mastiffs against them, a large massacre, the disruption of an important religious festival, or the seizure and execution of an important leader.

Cortés wasted no time. He and his men were welcomed with hospitality to the city of Cholula and, with the help of Tlaxcalan allies, thanked their Cholulan hosts by massacring several thousand men, women, and children, including the leaders of the city. Though the Spaniards later claimed it was in self-defense, de las Casas would later criticize Cortés heavily for this in his *Destruction of the Indies*. Yet as horrific as the massacre was, it must be understood as strategic rather than genocidal. The tragic reality is that the *conquistadores* ultimately needed a thriving native population, whose taxes and tithes would be an important source of support for the colonial enterprise.[7]

The Cholula massacre had achieved its objective. Word of what had happened had already reached Tenochtitlán when, in November 1519, Cortés and his men arrived and gazed at the surreal scene of canals, islands, and temples. Moctezuma (1466–1520) greeted Cortés on the causeway that linked Tenochtitlán to the mainland, and the myth arose that he believed Cortés to be the god Quetzalcoatl and handed the empire over to him.[8] The reality was that important nuances of Moctezuma's speech were lost in the difficult Spanish-Mayan-Náhuatl chain of translation, and a courteous welcome was initially misunderstood to mean much more. Nevertheless, this apotheosis of Cortés would be vigorously perpetuated by the Spaniards in an effort to underscore what they believed to be the ignorant, childlike, and credulous nature of the native population.

A few months later, again following standard strategy, Cortés took his host Moctezuma captive and disrupted the celebration of one of the most important Aztec religious festivals. The Tenochcans revolted, and when the Spanish-engineered appearance of Moctezuma on the balcony of his palace to stop the uprising failed, Cortés and his men killed him, along with a large number of other Tenochcan nobility. [9]

Moctezuma's brother Cuitláhuac led the outraged Tenochcans in driving the *conquistadores* from the city on July 1, 1520. Known as *La Noche Triste* (the Night of Sorrow), more than four hundred *conquistadores* were killed, along with several thousand of their Indian allies. Cuitláhuac, however, died three months later of smallpox and was succeeded by his nephew Cuauhtémoc, who was unable to fend off the counterattack of Spaniards and their native allies, estimated to be as many as 100,000, which took place from August to April 1521. Tenochtitlán fell and Cuauhtémoc was taken captive; he was eventually to be executed by Cortés on suspicion of treason.

Much to the fury of Velasquez in Cuba, Charles V of Spain in 1522 granted Cortés a license to explore, which allowed him to serve as captain general and governor of New Spain from 1523 to 1526. He shared his house in Tenochtitlán with his Spanish wife, his interpreter La Malinche, who soon bore him a child, and three of Moctezuma's daughters, one of whom also bore Cortés a child. These children of Cortés are often regarded as the "first *mestizos*" in New Spain, but native women had accompanied the *conquistadores* from the beginning as cooks, and thus there was already a substantial number of *mestizos* by this time.

After Cortés retired to Spain in 1526, the *audiencia,* which was the royal court of justice in Spain and its colonies, became the governing body in New Spain. It answered to the Council of the Indies in Spain, which in turn answered to the monarch. It did not work well in Mexico, however, where the first *audiencia* (1528–1530) has been described as "the most cynically despotic, dishonest, and vicious government that colonial Mexico ever suffered."[10] Though the second *audiencia* (1531–1535) was an improvement, it was only the arrival in 1535 of Antonio de Mendoza (1480–1552) as first viceroy of Mexico that colonial government improved significantly.

Varying Practices and Beliefs

Missionary work in New Spain between 1523 and 1572 was undertaken almost entirely by mendicants and, initially, almost exclusively by the Franciscans, who in 1521 had been granted by Pope Adrian VI all the administrative powers of a bishop in those areas of New Spain where the closest bishop was more than a two-day ride away. This would greatly facilitate the process of evangelization in the most remote of areas of Mexico.[11]

Like the early Christians, the Franciscans saw an opportunity to take the Christian message to peoples who had never before heard it and to place themselves in harm's way for a potential opportunity to be martyred. Evangelization of the New World was also seen by the Franciscans in the context of millennial beliefs, in which the conversion of all humanity would be the harbinger of the Second Coming. The conquest itself was thus justified, and the entire endeavor was the divine providence of God, for which they, Columbus, Cortés, and the Spanish crown were simply the agents. Indeed, the Franciscans helped perpetuate the belief that the Aztecs had regarded Cortés as divine, since it implied recognition on the part of the natives that the *conquistadores* were a part of God's providential purpose.[12]

All the Franciscans were either Spanish or Flemish, because Hapsburg Spain did not allow religious from other countries to work in its colonies. One of the earliest and most well-known Franciscans was Peter of Ghent (1480–1572), nephew of Holy Roman Emperor Charles V, who arrived in New Spain in 1523 and as Pedro de Gante remained there the rest of his life. With the arrival of twelve Spanish Franciscans the year after Peter of Ghent systematic evangelization began in New Spain.

The Franciscan practice of moving natives from remote areas into created towns, or *doctrinas*, in order to facilitate evangelization was similar to the *encomienda* system but without the required labor. The Franciscans in general were not very adept at parish administration, for papal decrees in Europe had excluded them from this work for several centuries, and they were thus found initially ill-prepared to run the *doctrinas*. As one historian writes, governing the Indians in these villages "had given some religious a taste for, and the habit of, domination; their absolute government of the native villages gave them a redoubtable temporal power."[13]

Some believed that in some circumstances force was justified if it served to protect the missionaries and help to further evangelization. Indians were often compelled to attend sermons, and though the Mexican bishops in 1539 disallowed the practice of beating with wooden rods or imprisonment for uncooperative Indians, as late as 1570, there were still occurrences of it.[14] In general, however, the Franciscans were quite protective of the natives, albeit in a paternalistic way, and because of their simple lifestyle, they established an easy rapport with poorer segments of Aztec society. Pedro de Gante, in particular, advocated a peaceful conversion of the Aztecs and was regarded as the "great protector" of the natives.

In addition to the creation of *doctrinas*, there was experimentation in the establishment of Christian utopian communities of natives, inspired largely by the well-known *Utopia* (1516) written by St. Thomas More (1478–1535). Former colonial judge and bishop of Michoacán, Vasco de Quiroga (1470–1565), established a series of such communities in the context of hospital republics, which practiced a kind of monastic collectivism and were far more than simple health facilities. Bartolomé de las Casas also attempted to establish a utopian community in a remote area of present-day Venezuela.[15]

Contrary to popular belief, there was no effort to force the Spanish language on the natives. Nevertheless, the ten major native languages spoken in Mexico at the time made communication a challenge for the Franciscans, who ultimately decided to adopt the more widely spoken Náhuatl. Initially, Franciscans had to rely on Aztec assistants for preaching, which was usually of the "hellfire and damnation" type. Music, pictures, and sacred drama were also used to explain the essentials of the Christian faith—a methodology that had been used successfully to indoctrinate the illiterate in medieval Europe. One overzealous Franciscan, however, went too far with visual aids when he adopted the practice of throwing live cats and dogs into a portable oven so that their cries could illustrate the pains of hell.[16]

In 1525, Tlaxcala became the first diocese in New Spain, which perhaps coincidentally was the city in which Cortés had found his first native allies. This was followed by the dioceses of Mexico City (1528), Oaxaca (1535), Mihoacán (1538), and New Galicia (1548). But with the establishment of the traditional diocesan structure, there also arose tension, sometimes fierce, between the diocesan clergy and the religious orders. The most difficult work now done, the bishops and their diocesan clergy wanted to incorporate the Franciscan *doctrinas* into the colonial church and tithe the natives, but the friars

objected to both plans.[17] It was a battle that the diocesan bishops would ultimately win, though not without considerable mudslinging on both sides.

As in the case of most other missions in the first half of the sixteenth century, baptism took place fairly quickly, though some felt that natives did not pos-
sess sufficient reason to accept this sacrament.[18] The Franciscans, however, felt
that the natives possessed a natural state of innocence which *predisposed* them to
the Christian faith, and found an ally in the Dominican bishop of Tlaxcala,
Julián Garcés (1452–1542), who petitioned Pope Paul III for support.

The pope responded with the landmark decree *Sublimis Deus* (June 1537),
in which he states forcefully, almost angrily, that "all are capable of receiving the
doctrines of the faith," and that it is the "enemy of the human race" who argues
that Indians "should be treated as dumb brutes created for our service, pretend-
ing that they are incapable of receiving the Catholic Faith." No Indians, even
those yet to be discovered or non-Christian, are to be deprived of their property
or their liberty, "nor should they be in any way enslaved; should the contrary
happen, it shall be null and have no effect." The document, however, was
ignored in Spain and its colonies, where papal communications were considered advisory and could only be published with royal permission.

The reception of communion also became an issue. In Europe at the time,
infrequent communion was quite common, but there were some missionaries
who felt that baptized Indians should either be denied communion *altogether*
or at least for a period of four to five years so that there would be certainty of
their understanding of the Christian faith.[19]

The missionaries had a unique opportunity to implant their beliefs in the
soil of various Aztec religious practices which had at least superficial similarities
to aspects of Christianity. For example, though polytheistic and totemistic, the
Aztecs believed in an eternal afterlife of heaven or hell, depending on the circumstances of one's death. They practiced something similar to the sign of the
cross, which was based on the four cardinal directions of the earth, and also
practiced a sort of baptism and confession. Twice a year, the Aztecs consumed
a small pastry that was meant to represent their god Huitzilopochtli, whom
they believed was born of a virgin.[20]

Unfortunately, in one of the greatest failures by both diocesan and religious
clergy, they categorically rejected *all* Aztec religious practices as inferior obstacles to Christian faith. The Franciscans, including even Pedro de Gante, spent a
good deal of time destroying idols, which were regarded not just as tools of idolatry but also as symbols of political independence for the natives.[21] There were
raids on temples, or *teocallis,* often built at the top of pyramids, which would
then become the site for a church or monastery. Though perhaps exaggerating,

the first bishop of Mexico City, the Franciscan Juan de Zumárraga (1468–1548), reported in a letter (1531) that he had destroyed over 500 temples and 20,000 pagan idols. In the process, countless Aztec monuments, works of art, and literary manuscripts were lost.

The Franciscan Bernardino de Sahagún (1499–1590) wrote his *General History of the Customs of New Spain* to help other missionaries recognize and eradicate indigenous cultural practices. He writes at the beginning of his book that a physician "would be unable to treat his patient properly unless he knew from the beginning the humor and causes of the disease . . . it is necessary for preachers and confessors, who are the true physicians of souls in spiritual sicknesses, to gain a knowledge of spiritual maladies and the medicines they require."[22] The history included a grammar and dictionary of Náhuatl, and though not actually published until 1829, it circulated in manuscript form among other Spanish missionaries.

Very likely in order to help bring about the pacification of the natives of New Spain, it was the desire of the Spanish crown that the sons of *caciques*, who were native leaders, be given a sound education. Almost immediately after his arrival, Pedro de Gante founded a rudimentary school in Texcoco for this purpose, and he eventually founded the famous school of San Francisco in Mexico City, which he would direct for forty years.

But the Franciscans also attempted to look beyond simple education, and in January 1536, they founded the College of Santiago Tlatelolco in Mexico City. Its primary purpose was in fact to educate sons of the *caciques* for eventual ordination to the priesthood. It was not a college in the modern sense but rather a simple stone residence in which students lived and received instruction. The curriculum, which was taught in Náhuatl, consisted of reading, writing, music, Latin, rhetoric, logic, philosophy, and Indian medicine. The native students by and large excelled in their learning and seemed to have had a particular ability with Latin.

In addition to clear papal support for a native clergy in New Spain, the college was welcomed by both Franciscan Bishop Zumárraga and his friend, Viceroy Antonio de Mendoza, who was unequivocal in how he felt about the Spanish diocesan clergy. In written instructions for his successor in 1551, as de Mendoza prepared to become viceroy of Peru, he remarked that the majority of the diocesan clergy in Mexico "are bad priests. They are all looking after their own interests, and if it were not that they are under orders from His Majesty, and administer baptism, the Indians would be better off without them."[23]

In spite of such seemingly strong support, however, opposition ran deep from the diocesan clergy, the Spanish colonists, the Dominicans, and even some

Franciscans. Alleged chronic drunkenness, intellectual deficiency, and an inability to observe celibacy were some of the more frequently given reasons which they felt rendered Indians unfit for priesthood. The Dominican Alfonso de Montúfar, (1489–1572), who in 1551 succeeded Zumárraga as bishop of Mexico City, was also cool to the idea. It is not surprising that a church synod in Mexico City in 1555 prohibited the ordination of Indians, *mestizos*, and blacks, and even disallowed their entry into non-ordained religious life. Consequently, the college died a slow but steady death and never produced a single Indian priest.

Ultimately, one of the most powerful factors that led to at least some sense of indigenization of Christianity for the natives of New Spain was belief in Our Lady of Guadalupe. According to tradition, she appeared several times to fifty-seven-year-old Indian convert Juan Diego Cuauhtlatoatzin (1474–1548), in December of 1531 in the hills near Mexico City. Cuauhtlatoatzin, who had been baptized by Pedro de Gante, requested a sign of her presence for Bishop Zumárraga and was told to pick all the flowers in the vicinity. When he unfolded his *tilma* (apron) and let the collected flowers spill forth in front of the bishop, the image of Mary was said to have been miraculously painted on it.

There was, however, Spanish resistance to the claimed apparition. The Dominicans paid little attention to it, and the Franciscans have been described as outright hostile to it.[24] There was almost a sense of resentment and competition among the Spanish, who had a long-established tradition of devotion to Our Lady of the Remedies. Even in 1575, forty-four years after the alleged apparition, Mexican viceroy Martín Enríquez de Almanza (1580–1583) pleaded with King Philip II of Spain not to allow the archbishop of Mexico City to build a parish and monastery at the site.

Peruvian Chaos

The Spanish colonization and evangelization of Peru, as well as for the rest of Latin America, followed much the same course as it did in Mexico, though the Peruvian endeavor was much more of a family enterprise and far more politically chaotic. The expedition in 1531 was comprised of the illiterate *conquistador* Francisco Pizarro (1478–1541), his brothers Juan (1511–1536), Gonzalo (1506–1548), and their half-brother Hernándo (1478–1575), who was the only one among them legitimately born and educated, and Dominican friar Vincent de Valverde (d. 1541), who was related to both Cortés and the Pizarros.

Francisco Pizarro, who had obtained a royal license to explore but had failed during two earlier attempts to conquer Peru, employed the standard methodology of conquest. The *conquistadores* marched inland to Cajamarca, where they were met hospitably by unarmed Inca leader Atahuallpa (1502–1533), whose father had already died of smallpox. Immediately, they imprisoned him, killed a large number of Incans, and then ransomed Atahuallpa for a large sum of gold. Then they baptized him and executed him.

Now as captain-general and governor of Peru, Pizarro sent a group of men to sack Pachacamac, perhaps the most important religious site of the Inca Empire.[25] Then, he installed Manco Inca Yupanqui (1516–1544) as a puppet emperor, and, in 1534, founded the city of Cuzco. Valverde became its first bishop, and land was set aside for the Franciscans, as well as for the Dominicans. There were still, however, too few priests. As in Mexico, the diocesan clergy in Peru were of a very low caliber, but the friars were not interested in a native clergy. The most frequent solution was the importation of friars from Mexico, because it was commonly believed that evangelization methods of the Mexican friars had proved successful.[26]

Pizarro, however, found that being governor of Peru in name was much easier than establishing a viable government. Manco Inca Yupanqui quickly abandoned the role as Spanish puppet and led an Incan uprising, which in 1536 laid siege to the city of Cuzco.[27] Though ultimately unsuccessful, Manco Inca Yupanqui would continue a bloody guerrilla war against the Spanish for the next eight years.

Then, in 1541, Diego de Almagro (1520–1542), whose father of the same name had conquered neighboring Chile and whose mother was a Panamanian Indian, assassinated Francisco Pizarro and laid claim to Cuzco. His followers proclaimed him governor of Peru, but his rebellion was put down, and he was executed. A number of the Spanish rebels found refuge with Manco Inca Yupanqui but repaid his two years of hospitality by murdering him in 1544.

A viceroy took over rule of Peru in place of the assassinated Francisco Pizarro, but Gonzalo Pizarro (1502–1548) rebelled in 1545 and executed him. He illegally declared himself to be the true ruler of Peru but was executed himself in 1548 by Spanish authorities, who suppressed the rebellion and installed a new viceroy.[28] As Spanish colonial rule over Peru normalized in the second half of the sixteenth century, so too did the establishment of the traditional diocesan church structure, and it would not be long before the church in other parts of Latin America bore a close resemblance to the church in Mexico.

As has been seen, there was little that was unique in the conquest by the opportunistic Cortés, who could not have accomplished the task without a significant amount of help from Africans and native allies. Furthermore, 1521 only marked victory against Tenochtitlán and Tenochca domination of other Aztecs. Throughout the sixteenth century, native communities continued to flourish, and the Spanish, in fact, had a very tenuous hold on New Spain. The Mayas in the Yucatan did not even regard the conquest as an event of major significance but simply as one of the many expected ups and downs of their history.[29]

There were also sporadic, though unsuccessful, signs of native resistance to Spanish colonialism. Don Carlos, known also by his Aztec name Chichimecatecuhtli, was a former student of the Franciscan College of Santiago Tlatelolco. In 1539, he was executed for alleged preaching of heresy, though the reality was that he had publicly rejected Spanish authority and insisted on indigenous sovereignty. In 1541, the Indians of New Galicia (Guadalajara) unsuccessfully rebelled in the Mixtón war, which was the first organized attempt to challenge Spanish colonization. In Peru, Túpac Amaru (1544–1572), son of Manco Inca Yupanqui, led a brief rebellion but was executed.[30]

In the end, the collapse of indigenous cultures in New Spain and Peru was due to disease more than anything else. By the end of the sixteenth century, there was a population decline of approximately forty million people in New Spain, or 90 percent of the indigenous population. This was by no means what had been envisioned or hoped for by the Spaniards, who needed the native population to sustain the colonial enterprise economically.

How, then, did the image of a larger-than-life Cortés and a handful of exceptional men bringing a cowering superstitious Moctezuma and the mighty Aztec empire to its knees become so ingrained? A royal contract for exploration and conquest had to be fulfilled before the *conquistador* could reap his four-fifths of revenue from his *encomienda*. Completion was recorded in a legal document known as a *probanza* in which the *conquistador* attested to thorough pacification of the native peoples and sufficient resources for the territory to be profitable. Anxious to reap the benefits, the *conquistadores* engaged in premature claims, exaggerations, and outright lies in the *probanzas*, which soon formed the basis for numerous chronicles of New Spain.[31]

Similarly, it became an accepted belief that the essential work of conversion had been completed early on in the missionary process and that indigenous religious and cultural practices had been eliminated. It is now recognized, however, that the Christianity of the natives was far more complex and was sometimes feigned. In some cases, idols were hidden under crosses or beneath altars so that one could surreptitiously continue pagan worship under the guise of Christian worship. In other cases, there was a sincere Christian faith that tried to incorporate prohibited elements of indigenous culture and religion.[32]

Portugal and Inculturation

Portuguese missionary work in Africa, India, and Brazil would be undertaken in two distinct phases, first by the Franciscans and second by the Jesuits, and overall would see a much greater effort at inculturation. Initially, this was not so much a fundamental difference in ideology or national character as it was the fact that Portugal had fewer resources and lacked the same mechanisms of conquest that Spain possessed and thus required a greater degree of cooperation and goodwill from the local populace to maintain its relatively fragile hold on its colonies.

In 1542, King João III gave to the Jesuits missionary responsibility for all Portuguese colonies, in part because his wife, Catherine of Hapsburg (1507–1578), sister of Holy Roman Emperor Charles V, was enamored of the new religious order and corresponded with Ignatius Loyola. This brought two important, and perhaps related, changes to Portuguese colonies. First, Jesuits from a variety of countries, especially Italy, now had the opportunity to operate freely in Portuguese territory—a prerogative that they did not enjoy in Spanish colonies. Second, as the Jesuits built on the work of the Franciscans in Africa, India, and Brazil, and began new work in Asia, there was an increasing, conscious commitment to inculturation.

The Portuguese laid claim to the Azores in 1439 and, by 1487 when Bartolomeu Dias (1457–1500) sailed around the Cape of Good Hope for the first time, had established forts and sugar-producing colonies on islands and the coastline along western Africa. When the voyage of Vasco da Gama (1469–1524) to India in 1498 proved that Columbus was wrong, the Portuguese took further steps to establish and fortify support outposts along the way of their new sea route to India.

Pope Pius II (1458–1464) in 1462 had ceded to the Franciscans responsibility for the evangelization of West Africa as far south as the mouth of the Congo River. The friars, however, had little impact initially. When Diego Cam (b. 1450) discovered the mouth of the Congo River in 1484, a friar baptized the chief of the Sogno tribe, and a handful of his tribe was then taken back to Portugal for baptism at the court of King João II. They returned to the Guinea Coast, where others requested baptism, but there were not enough Franciscans to achieve any long-term results.

More successful were Portuguese efforts in the Congo. The traditional view is that the Portuguese imposed Christianity on a passive indigenous population, whereas recent scholarship has argued that there was an indigenous church that blended Congolese religious practices with Catholicism and only shifted to a more Eurocentric model in the nineteenth century. The truth, however, lies somewhere in between.[33]

To be sure, the Franciscans did little in terms of inculturation, but it was a moot point anyway, since the *Manikongo* (king) Nzinga a Nkuwu (1482–1505) was so enamored of European culture. When he requested baptism in 1491, he took the Portuguese name João and declared himself King João I—a practice continued by each of his successors well into the twentieth century. A large number of his nobility followed suit, including his son Nzinga Mbemba (c. 1455–1543), who took the name Afonso.

Nzinga a Nkuwu imported carpenters, textiles, cattle, horses, and even two German printers along with their presses. The depth of his commitment to Christianity, however, was not as deep as his love of things European, and he eventually returned to indigenous religious practices before his death. His son Afonso, however, remained a stalwart Christian, and in 1505 he attributed his successful challenge for the kingship against his non-Christian brother Mpanzu to the intervention of Santiago Matamoros (St. James the Moorslayer).[34]

Christianity became a main feature of court life for Afonso I (1505–1543). In 1513 he even sent his son Don Henrique to Lisbon and Rome for a theological education, which led to his ordination to the priesthood in 1518 and consecration as a bishop by Leo X himself. The pope also issued a papal brief (*Exponi Nobis*) that authorized Portuguese bishops to ordain "other Ethiopians, Indians and Africans" to the priesthood.

Henrique, who would be the only sub-Saharan African bishop until 1939, was titular bishop of Utica (North Africa). His actual episcopal assignment, however, was as an auxiliary bishop to the recently created diocese of Funchal on the island of Madeira. Four hundred miles from the African coast and six-hundred miles southwest of Portugal, Funchal would be the mission diocese for *all* Portuguese colonies, whether in India, the Far East, or Brazil. Henrique was sent almost immediately back to the Congo where he served until 1531 as apostolic vicar. Though he would endure a great deal of resentment and hostility from Portuguese clergy, it must be remembered that he could not have become a bishop without the permission of King Manuel I of Portugal (1495–1521), which signals something of a commitment by the monarch to an indigenous Congolese church.

By 1534, the impracticality of Funchal had become apparent, so it was made an archdiocese, and a string of new island-dioceses down the African coast was created—Sān Tomé, Santiago de Cabo Verde, and São Salvador de Angra. These islands were already the site of Portuguese outposts, strategically important because they were far easier to defend than coastal settlements but were still in proximity to Africa proper.

The Jesuits did further work in the Congo and also brought Christianity to Angola and Mozambique. In 1560, the Jesuit Gonçalo da Silveira (1526–1561) traveled up the Zambezi River, along which Portuguese trading posts had been established in the 1530s, and converted the *monomotapa* (great chief) of the Makalanga tribe along with his entire court. Some, however, believed da Silveira to be a Portuguese spy, and he was soon killed. The death of da Silveira helped to convince the Jesuits of how imperative inculturation was, so as not to be regarded as outsiders.

Portuguese missions in Africa would ultimately be only partially successful for a variety of reasons. Jesuit efforts were aimed primarily at chiefs, who had great difficulty accepting monogamy, since polygamy was relied on to cement marriage alliances with neighboring tribes. Furthermore, Christian instruction of the general populace by both Jesuits and Franciscans was inadequate, which led new Christians to abandon their faith easily. In addition, there was a growing awareness of the Portuguese slave trade in West Africa. Perhaps most fundamental, however, was that the Portuguese regarded Africa more as an obstacle to their true object of desire—India, Japan, and China.

Looking East

In 1500, the first Franciscans arrived in India and expected to find Christians already there. Marco Polo (1251–1324) as well as earlier Franciscan friars returning from the Far East had mentioned Indian Christians, whom the Portuguese believed were part of the mythical kingdom of legendary eastern priest and king Prester (presbyter) John. So certain were they of this, that Vasco da Gama carried letters of introduction to the mythical king on his journey to India in 1498.[35]

The Malabar, or St. Thomas Christians, of southwest India maintained, however, that they had originally been evangelized by the apostle Thomas himself. According to local tradition as well as the apocryphal *Acts of Thomas*, Christianity had been taught at the court of the historical Indian king Gundaphorus in the first century, and there is evidence of Jewish diaspora communities in India at that time, which is noteworthy in light of the remark of the church historian Eusebius (260–341) that in the second century, Indians read the Gospel of Matthew in Hebrew. All that can by said with certainty, however, is that by the fourth century, Christian immigrants from Persia led to the establishment of a Syrian hierarchy and clergy in India.

The Franciscans built friaries in Goa, Cochin, and Bombay. The port of

Goa came under Portuguese control in 1510 and quickly became the center of colonial government, and by 1515, the trade route with India was well established.

The first area of missionary focus was along the Fishery Coast in Southern India among the Paravas, a Tamil-speaking caste of pearl divers. Long-persecuted by the Arabs for punishing an Arab who had allegedly raped a Parava woman, many Paravas saw in the adoption of Christianity the opportunity for at least nominal Portuguese protection. Approximately 20,000 were baptized but with almost no instruction in the Christian faith and no concern for inculturation. Furthermore, the behavior of many Portuguese colonists offered a poor example of what it meant to be Christian. Consequently, as the missionaries moved on, so too did the faith of the Paravas.

When Jesuit Francis Xavier (1506–1552) arrived in India in 1542 as both missionary and papal nuncio, he tried to provide the Paravas with a deeper understanding of Christianity and would spend three years in western India and Sri Lanka. Though opposed to the idea of a native clergy, he was overruled by Ignatius Loyola. The College of St. Paul in Goa began to admit Indians as well as a few Africans, and in 1560, the first Indians were admitted to the Society of Jesus.

Converts among the Hindu upper class, however, in particular the Brahmans, were few. The Portuguese were looked on as *harijans* (untouchables), since they ate meat, did not bathe regularly, married outside their caste, and were often promiscuous. In addition, most Indian converts at this point had come from the low-caste Paravas, which did not make Christianity attractive to a Brahman. No headway would be made until 1605, when Italian Jesuit Robert de Nobili (1577–1656) became proficient in Hindi and Hindu literature and conducted himself as if he were a "Brahman from the West."[36]

An accident of the Portuguese obsession with India was the discovery of Brazil. Portuguese navigator Pedro Alvares Cabral (1467–1520) set out on the second Portuguese expedition to India in 1500 with thirteen ships and 1,500 men but got blown off course. He named the area of his landfall Porto Seguro (safe port), claimed the land for Portugal, and on April 26, 1500, watched as the handful of diocesan priests and friars on the expedition celebrated the first mass in Brazil. After a week of exploration, the entire expedition continued on to India. The following year, Italian navigator Amerigo Vespucci (1451– 1512) continued the exploration of what he called Terra do Brasil, because of the preponderance of the tropical redwood *brasil*.

The Portuguese essentially ignored Brazil for the next few decades. Then, in 1530, after other European powers had begun to explore the Brazilian coast, the king of Portugal divided Brazil into autonomous colonial captaincies, which were to be hereditary fiefs, some of them even larger than Portugal. The head of each captaincy had absolute power, subject only to the monarch.

The first settlers arrived in 1532, and while many of the captaincies failed, Pernambuco became quite successful, largely because of sugar-cane production methods brought from Madeira and slave labor brought from West Africa. The appetite of Europe for imported sugar seemed insatiable, and in the course of three centuries, approximately 3.5 million African slaves would be brought to Brazil—six times the number brought to the United States and 40 percent of the estimated 9.5 million slaves transported to the New World.

At the time of the initial colonization of Brazil, only a handful of Franciscans had worked sporadically as missionaries in the area around Porto Seguro. When Porto Seguro was made a captaincy in 1538 and afforded greater colonial protection, Franciscan activity increased, but in 1548, King João III of Portugal (1521–1557) decided that the captaincy system had failed and repossessed them in order to establish a centralized colonial government.

Tomé de Sousa (1501–1573), the first governor general, arrived in 1549, accompanied by five Jesuits who had been asked to help out in the centralization and unification of Brazil. Manuel da Nóbrega (1517–1570), the Portuguese Jesuit who headed the group, was one of the earliest to join the Society of Jesus. He started out as a diocesan priest and aspiring academic until a persistent speech stammer put an end to his university career. As a missionary, however, he would excel.

The initial apostolate of the Jesuits was centered in Salvador, where they built a primitive church, established a school, and lived in mud huts. As in India, the task of evangelization was made more difficult because of the poor example of the Portuguese colonists, who had little regard for the indigenous peoples of Brazil and often killed them or used them as slave labor. As in Mexico, the diocesan clergy in Brazil also tended to be of a low quality, some of them little more than fortune-seeking adventurers who found an easy way to get to the New World.

Da Nóbrega and others begin to work among the Tupi, which must have been a strange first encounter for both. The Tupi wore little or no clothing, lived in longhouses in the rain forest with their extended maternal family, and subsisted largely on agriculture and fishing. They were pantheistic and animistic and looked to *feiticeiros* (shamans) for medicinal help and to communicate with demons and ghosts. Most troubling of all, however, was the fact that prisoners of the Tupi were usually roasted and eaten, as had happened to many of the first Franciscans in Brazil.

Language was the biggest practical hurdle they faced, and almost immediately, they began to work on grammars of the various Tupi dialects. Ultimately, however, as the Jesuits began to work among more distant tribes, they found it most efficient to speak a patois of Tupi, Guarani, Latin, and Portuguese known as the *lingua geral.*

Tupan was the Tupi mythical hero, who controlled thunder and lightning, and the Jesuits equated him with God, though later they found they would simply have to adopt *Dio* as a more appropriate term. They began to baptize the Tupi, though it would be a long time before any large-scale conversions took place, since the decentralized nature of Tupi society meant that there were few chiefs to serve as examples.

In addition to his work among the Tupi, da Nóbrega traveled extensively to tend to the needs of the growing number of Jesuits in Brazil, and soon, Ignatius Loyola appointed him provincial of the newly created Jesuit province of Brazil, a post that da Nóbrega would try unsuccessfully to relinquish for the rest of his life. It quickly became clear to da Nóbrega, however, that a bishop was needed for Brazil.

In response to da Nóbrega's request, Bishop Pedro Fernandes Sardinha (1497–1556) arrived in Bahia in June 1552, along with more diocesan priests and canons, and established São Salvador as Brazil's first diocese. Sardinha, however, was not really up to the task, made even more difficult by the insubordination of his own priests. He left for Europe four years later, but his ship ran aground, and he was eaten by some hostile Tupi.

Ultimately, the work of the Jesuits in Brazil would be successful, in no small measure because of the assistance of Jesuit José de Anchieta (1534–1597), who arrived in Brazil in 1553. The following year, he and da Nóbrega opened the College of São Paulo dos Campos de Piratininga, which would eventually grow into the huge city of São Paulo. A master of language, de Anchieta compiled a dictionary and grammar of the Tupi language and also wrote dramatic literature. The Jesuits, however, did not seek to ordain native Brazilians, and attempts at an indigenized Christianity were minimal. It would be in Japan where the promotion of an indigenized Christianity would find fuller expression.

Mission to Japan and "The Christian Century"

The great visionary of the Japan mission was Francis Xavier, who arrived in Kagoshima on the southern island of Kyushu on August 15, 1549, accompanied by Jesuit priest Cosme de Torres (1510–1570), Jesuit brother Juan Fernández (d. 1567), three Japanese interpreters, and two servants—one Indian, the other Chinese. Chief among the interpreters was the exiled samurai Yajiro (Anjiro), whom Xavier had met in Malaysia and had sent to the College of St. Paul in Goa to learn Portuguese and Christian doctrine.[37]

Xavier came to Japan in part because he believed that Portuguese colonial mistreatment of Indians had undermined the missions, and he felt that Japan offered a more fruitful atmosphere. His plan for Japan was bold. Consonant with the admonition in the *Constitutions* of the Society of Jesus to convert persons of power so that their subjects would quickly follow, Xavier intended no less than to convert the emperor in Kyoto.

Once in the ancient capital, however, he quickly discovered that the emperor, whom he was never allowed to meet, was in fact a weak figurehead. Decades of civil war had left real power in the hands of the military rule of the *shōgun* (general), controlled at the time by the Ashikaga family. Further discord was caused by the approximately 150 different *daimyos* (warlords), who constantly did battle and plotted against each other in an effort to become dominant enough to take over the *shōgunate*.

The political instability would ultimately work to the advantage of the Jesuits, as was first demonstrated by the *daimyo* Shimazu Takahisa (1514–1571). In the midst of a major campaign to reclaim and unite three contiguous provinces on the southern tip of Kyushu, Takahisa actively sought good relations with foreign countries in order to enhance his position and thus welcomed the presence of Xavier and his companions. Even more important, in 1549 Takahisa granted permission for any vassals in his territories on Kyushu to convert to Christianity, if that was their desire. This gave the Jesuits an important base of operations from which to further evangelize Japan.

How did the Buddhist *bonzes* (priests) react to the presence of the Jesuits? Initially, they gave the missionaries a cordial reception, believing Christianity to be simply a branch of Buddhism with which they were not familiar. After all, Xavier had come from India, the birthplace of Buddhism. Additionally, Shingon Buddhism bore a number of liturgical similarities to Christianity, perhaps because of the possible presence in Japan of Nestorian Christianity from China a thousand years earlier.

After baptizing some members of Yajiro's family in Kagoshima, Xavier began to cast his net wider but soon encountered linguistic difficulties. Though he would never learn to speak Japanese, he could rely on Yajiro to speak for him. The difficulty was to convey Christian doctrine in a language that had no vocabulary for these concepts. Yajiro had been a Shingon Buddhist and opted to adapt Buddhist terminology. Thus, the pantheistic deity *Dainichi* became "God," *jōdo* was "paradise," *jigoku* was "hell," and *tennin* were "angels." It proved far more difficult than anticipated, however, to erase Buddhist associations with this terminology, particularly in the case of references to *Dainichi*, so Xavier decided instead to refer to God simply as *Deus*.

Relations between Xavier and the *bonzes* began to sour, in part because in his public preaching he began to accuse them of immorality, but also because they served as political advisors to the *daimyos* and felt increasingly supplanted by the popularity of the Jesuits. The *bonzes* began publicly to discredit Christianity. They frequently referred to *Deus* as *Daiuso* (Great Lie) and convinced many Japanese that Buddhist terminology had been used in order to dupe them into becoming Christians.

Nevertheless, Xavier brimmed with enthusiasm about the Japanese, whom he referred to as the "delight of my heart," and he believed that no culture the Jesuits had encountered to date had been as sophisticated and able to receive and understand the Christian message. There were only, however, approximately one thousand Christians after two years of work, and Xavier concluded that inculturation was essential and that there should eventually be a native Japanese clergy. Xavier was also convinced that if China became Christian, so too would Japan. Therefore, he left Japan in November 1551 but died a year later on the island of Sancian (Shang-ch'uan), within sight of the Chinese mainland.[38]

Cosme de Torres became the new head of the mission, and he worked tirelessly for twenty-one years to advance the work that he and Xavier had started. Resources, however, were limited. An indispensable role was played by the *dojuku* (catechist), which was modeled after the *jisha* (teaching assistant) in Zen Buddhism. The *dojuku*, acting as sacristan, homilist, and interpreter, would go out in teams with Jesuit priests and brothers. After fifteen to twenty days of instruction followed by baptism, the priest would move on, leaving behind a *dojuku* for further instruction. Few priests meant infrequent mass. Instead, the *dojuku* would preach, lead group prayers, and prepare Christians for confession, so that when a priest did visit, confessions and mass could be conducted more expeditiously. Christian hymns were sung in Japanese; the rosary was recited daily; and funerals were held with great solemnity, perhaps in keeping with a similar solemn emphasis in the Buddhist tradition.

De Torres continued to attempt conversion of influential individuals and baptized the *daimyos* Omura Sumitada (1533–1587) and Otomo Yoshishige (1539–1587). Both would, in fact, become strong and sincere supporters of the mission rather than mere political pragmatists. In 1580, Omura would cede perpetual control of Nagasaki to the Jesuits, and Otomo took the baptismal name *Francesco*, to honor Xavier whom he had met in 1551.[39]

The goal of residence and evangelization in Kyoto on the central island of Honshu became reality in 1559, when the *shōgun* Yoshiteru Ashikaga (1546–1565) quite literally shared the same cup of wine with Jesuit Gaspar Vilela

(1525–1575) and gave his permission. Six years later, the *shōgun* was assassinated, and the *daimyo* Oda Nobunaga (1534–1582) seized Kyoto. Nobunaga, however, continued good relations with the Jesuits, not out of personal religious conviction but because of his interest in Western technology, especially firearms, and his intense hatred of the political power of the *bonzes*. These motives were likely not lost on the Jesuits, but their overriding concern was the firm support of the virtual ruler of Japan.

The Jesuit window of opportunity in Japan, however, was almost closed by the heavily Eurocentric Portuguese Jesuit Francisco Cabral (1529–1609), superior of the Japan mission from 1570–1581. Cabral disallowed the Jesuit practice of wearing traditional Japanese silk clothing and insisted on a return to the black cassock. He also ended Jesuit involvement in the silk trade, which had been the mainstay of the Japan mission, but he provided no alternate means of support. Most important, however, Cabral balked at Xavier's insistence on the need for Japanese priests and only allowed five Japanese to enter the Society of Jesus during his eleven-year leadership.

The arrival in Japan in 1579 of Italian Jesuit Alessandro Valignano (1539–1606), who was making the first of three lengthy stays as visitor general of the Orient, set the Japanese mission back on course. Firm in his commitment to inculturation, Valignano's *Code of Behavior* (1581) for missionaries contained rules of Japanese etiquette, encouraged the adoption of Japanese dress, and required all Jesuits new to Japan to spend two years in intensive language study. Valignano also insisted that Japanese were suitable for both religious life and priestly ordination and began admitting them as seminarians.[40] When Cabral opposed him, Valignano replaced him with a new superior, Gaspar Coelho (d. 1590).

Valignano reinforced good relations with Oda Nobunaga through an exchange of gifts in Kyoto, and in 1582 in Nagasaki, he held a Jesuit conference in which he spelled out five elements necessary for their future success: (1) a Japanese clergy; (2) assurances that the Japan mission would be exclusively Jesuit, since only uniform methodology and a deep awareness of Japanese culture would succeed; (3) a bishop for Japan, which had first been under the diocese of Goa, and since 1575, under the diocese of Macao; (4) increased training and use of Japanese aides to support the fifty-five Jesuit brothers and twenty-three Jesuit priests who served a Christian population that now numbered 100,000; (5) much-needed financial support for the mission.

In 1582, Valignano dispatched four teenage Japanese seminary students to Rome, officially as representatives of the Christian *daimyos* Omura Sumitada, Otomo Yoshishige, and Arima Harunobu (d. 1612). The reality, however, was that Valignano intended them to garner support for the Japan mission, as well as to serve as a two-way cultural bridge between Japan and Europe. Valignano intended to accompany the envoys, but he was forced to remain behind in Goa, where he had just been appointed the new Jesuit provincial for India. When the envoys reached Europe in 1584, they met King Philip II of Spain, Pope Gregory XIII (1572–1585), and Pope Sixtus V (1585–1590), whose installation they attended. The trip paid off. Before his death, Gregory XIII declared the Japan mission to be the specific domain of the Jesuits and pledged money for support. Pope Sixtus V also pledged money, and in 1588 designated Funai on the island of Kyushu as the first Japanese diocese, though its first bishop, the Jesuit Pedro Martins (1542–1598), would not arrive until 1596.

Valignano rejoined the envoys in Goa on their return journey in 1587 but bore distressing news. Oda Nobunaga had been killed just after they left Japan, and just months earlier, the Christian *daimyos* Otomo Yoshishige and Omura Sumitada, whom the envoys had been representing, had also died. More ominous news greeted them when they finally reached Japan in 1590. Nobunaga's leading general, Toyotomi Hideyoshi (1536–1598), had seized power and had been given the title *taikosama* (regent) of Japan, the highest rank one could have next to that of emperor. Even worse, aware of how Spain had colonized Mexico and the Philippines, Hideyoshi had issued a 1587 edict that ordered all missionaries to leave Japan within twenty days.

The situation, however, was not as bad as it seemed. Valignano was given a cordial welcome by Hideyoshi, who apparently did little to enforce the edict. Still quite desirous of trade with the Portuguese, Hideyoshi hoped to raise money for a planned invasion of Korea, which ultimately would prove disastrous. Relieved about the continued tolerant atmosphere, Valignano set up Japan's first movable-type printing press, which for the next eighteen years would produce books in both Latin and Japanese, including devotional literature as well as a Japanese translation of *Aesop's Fables*. Most important, however, was the production of the Japanese grammar and Portuguese–Japanese dictionary of Portuguese Jesuit interpreter João Rodriguez (1558–1633), whose Japanese fluency was unequaled.

A new concern of the Jesuits, however, was the cordial reception Hideyoshi also gave in 1593 to an embassy of three Spanish Franciscans from Manila who had been sent by the King of Spain in the hope of establishing trade with Japan. Hideyoshi gave them permission to reside and evangelize in Kyoto, and the Jesuits were not in a position to object. The crowns of Spain and Portugal had been united since 1580, so the papal division of the world was now meaningless. And though Gregory XIII (1572–1585) had granted exclusive mission rights in Japan to the Jesuits, his successor Sixtus V (1585–1590), a Franciscan, had granted permission for the friars to work in the *regio sinorum* (region of the Chinese), which they had loosely interpreted to include Japan.

The Franciscans established themselves in Kyoto quickly, where they identified completely with the poor. Franciscan Jeronimo de Jesus, in fact, expressed disdain for the Jesuit strategy of converting the influential: "we should take the way opposite to the way of the Jesuit fathers ... they have sought after those who stood above, because once the head is caught, then his followers will be caught as well."[41] An act of nature, however, would soon lead to a most unfortunate turn of events for the Franciscans.

On October 19, 1596, the Spanish vessel San Felipe from Manila, heavily laden with 1.5 million silver pesos, ran aground off Shikoku Island. Spanish Franciscans from Kyoto convinced the captain to seek protection of the cargo from Hideyoshi, but in a foolish display of bravado, the captain boasted to Hideyoshi that Christian missionaries served also as an advanced guard for the inevitable arrival of Spanish conquerors. Certain that his deepest concerns had been confirmed, Hideyoshi confiscated the entire cargo. On February 5, 1597, in Nagasaki, six Spanish Franciscans, seventeen Japanese Franciscan novices, and three Japanese Jesuit brothers (possibly included by accident), were executed as alleged lawbreakers and disturbers of the public peace. The Jesuit interpreter João Rodriguez was an eyewitness, having been allowed to be present to comfort the condemned.

In the aftermath of the twenty-six deaths, charges flew fast and furious that the Jesuits had somehow conspired with Hideyoshi against the Spanish Franciscans and had even encouraged him to confiscate the cargo of the San Felipe. The Jesuit bishop Pedro Martins, who had been welcomed to Japan only months earlier by Hideyoshi, vehemently denied this, and in fact there is no evidence to support Spanish accusations.[42]

As for Hideyoshi, he regarded the affair as a political and military matter that was over and done with, offered to return the cargo of the San Felipe to the Philippines, and signaled a continued interested in trade. By the time of his death in 1598, the situation of the mission had normalized to the point that Jesuit bishop Luis Cerqueira (1552–1614) was able to succeed Pedro Martins as bishop of Japan. This was followed by the ordinations in 1601 of the first two Japanese Jesuits and the first Japanese diocesan priest in 1604—a milestone in Valignano's policy of inculturation.

In 1603, five years after the death of Hideyoshi, the opportunistic *daimyo* Tokugawa Ieyasu (1543–1616) became *shōgun* and moved the capital from Kyoto to Edo (Tokyo), beginning a family dynasty that would last 265 years. Ieyasu initially was tolerant of Christianity, since he also desired continued trade with the Portuguese and Spanish. Catholic missionaries, however, became irrelevant to Ieyasu when the Dutch and English arrived and offered the same trade opportunities without any desire to evangelize. Thus, in 1614, Tokugawa Ieyasu issued a nationwide ban on Christianity, which though it would take time to implement, proved in the long term to be a fatal blow to the mission.

Ironically, the Jesuit attempt to establish an indigenous Christianity in Japan had begun to take hold, evidenced by the presence of a growing number of Japanese priests and a Christian population estimated at 300,000. Now it would succumb to the political vicissitudes of Tokugawa Japan. Although many clergy left the country, approximately forty-two priests, twenty-nine of them Jesuits and the rest a mix of Franciscans, Dominicans, and Augustinians, defied the order and went underground. Persecutions intensified under the rule of Ieyasu's son and grandson. Though the actual number is probably much higher, 2,128 Christians are known to have been executed between 1614 and 1650, including two of the four young envoys from the 1582 voyage, both of whom had been ordained to the priesthood. By 1650, there were no known priests left in Japan, and the country would be closed to foreigners until 1853. What has often been called the Christian Century in Japan had come to a close.[43]

Matteo Ricci and the Mission to China

Valignano, like Xavier, was convinced that China was the key to the conversion of Japan. Though he was incorrect, Valignano stepped up Jesuit missionary efforts to penetrate China and insisted that Jesuits enter China legitimately and operate along the same mission principles he had established for Japan. It was in China that the inculturation policy of Valignano would be most successful and find its most eloquent expression in the person of the Italian Jesuit Matteo Ricci (1552–1610).

Christianity was not altogether new to China. During the T'ang dynasty (618–877), Nestorian Christianity had established itself on a limited and temporary basis, and Franciscan missionaries during the Mongol Yuan dynasty (1275–1368) built a modest church in Beijing, which disappeared with the fall of the Yuan dynasty. Travel to China in the sixteenth century, however, had become more difficult. The Ming dynasty (1368–1644), concerned that Chinese culture had become "diluted" by the Yuan dynasty and fearful of the growing strength of the Manchu in northeastern China, had essentially closed the borders of China. Nevertheless, Jorge Álvares reached China in 1514, and in 1520, the Portuguese diplomat Tomé Pires traveled to Beijing and made the first official contact with China.

In 1557, the Chinese gave Macao to the Portuguese as a trading post in return for aid in ridding South China of a particularly vexing pirate leader. Though this was intended by the Chinese to keep the foreigners contained in the small peninsular city, Macao would become a critical center of training and embarkation for the approximately twenty-five missionaries, mostly Jesuits, who traveled to China between 1552 and 1583. All had hopes of residing permanently, but all would be sent home after only a few months.[44]

Valignano put out a call for Jesuits to come to Macao, where they would learn the Chinese language, customs, and etiquette, before being sent to China. First to respond was Italian Jesuit Michele Ruggieri (1543–1607), who arrived from Goa in 1579. In addition to language study, Ruggieri composed a Chinese catechism with the help of Chinese interpreters and studied Confucianism. Ruggieri's preparations, however, were regarded with disdain by many of the other Macao Jesuits, who felt there were more pressing apostolic needs. This negative atmosphere quickly changed when Valignano replaced the superior in Macao in 1582, with the instructions that Jesuits preparing for China were to be left alone.[45]

Beginning in 1580, Ruggieri made regular forays into China, paying strict attention to Chinese customs and protocol. Finally, in 1582, he received a formal invitation from the prefect of Zhaoqing to take up residence there. At the request of Ruggieri, Valignano sent Matteo Ricci from Goa to join him in Zhaoqing in September 1583. Born in central Italy in 1552, Ricci had studied law, but became a Jesuit, against his father's wishes. After studies at the Roman College under famed German Jesuit mathematician and astronomer Christopher Clavius (1537–1612) and Jesuit theologian and future cardinal Robert Bellarmine (1542–1621), Ricci left for India, where he was ordained to the priesthood. After four years teaching theology in Goa and some disillusionment about India, Ricci did not hesitate when his former novice master Valignano summoned him to China.[46]

From the very beginning in Zhaoqing, Ricci and Ruggieri adopted Chinese dress, ate Chinese food, and were highly attentive to Chinese etiquette. They adopted the attire and manner of Buddhist *bonzes* and patterned their daily life in accordance with Zen monastic regulations. But inculturation for Ricci was not just a matter of dress, policy, or behavior. It was an *attitude*. He quickly improved the rudimentary Chinese language skills he had acquired in Macao and began an intensive study of Mandarin, the language of the Confucian scholars. Then, in 1584, with Chinese help, Ricci produced *A True Account of God and the Sacred Religion* (*T'ien-chu sheng-chiao shih-lu*), a revision of a basic catechism he had written three years earlier.

The mission seemed to be going well. They were joined in 1585 by the Jesuits Duarte de Sande (1547–1599) and Antonio d'Almeida (1556–1591). Though there had been initial hostility toward the Westerners, it was mitigated by the fact that the Jesuit residence became a sort of curiosity shop in which to view items such as Western art, prisms, clocks, and solar quadrants. In 1588, Valignano ordered Ruggieri to Rome for the purpose of stepping up papal support for the China mission. De Sande had already returned to Macao, so Ricci and d'Almeida were left alone in Zhaoqing; but they were soon expelled after a run-in with some local Mandarins. As for Ruggieri, he fell into poor health and never returned to China.

In August of 1589, Ricci and d'Almeida headed north to Shaozhou, where they bought land and built a house and church. It was here that the well-connected young scholar Qu Rukui sought out Ricci because of rumors that Jesuits could perform alchemy. Rukui quickly became intrigued by Ricci's knowledge of mathematics, astronomy, and general science, and was particularly fascinated by Ricci's *Map of the World* (*Mappamondo*), which was the first map in China to depict the Americas. Rukui convinced Ricci to reproduce it with Chinese place names, and as copies of the map spread, so did Ricci's reputation.

Though the widower Rukui accepted the Christian faith, he would defer baptism for fourteen years, unwilling either to dismiss or marry his concubine, who was from a lower social order. Nevertheless, he and Ricci remained close friends, and Rukui soon offered advice that would transform the Jesuit mission. They should abandon the role of Buddhist monks and adopt the role of Confucian scholars, who commanded the highest degree of respect in China. Ricci, however, was not content just to dress like a Confucian scholar. He would *become* one.

In 1591, Ricci began a Latin translation of the Confucian *Four Books* (*Ssu-shu*), which were the synthesis of classical Confucian texts and commentaries from the Song dynasty (960–1279) and would become required reading for China-bound Jesuits.[47] He felt they were written "in the moral vein of Seneca" but soon discovered that because the *Four Books* had been compiled 1,500 years after the death of Confucius (551-479 B.C.E.), they were regarded by true Confucian scholars as neo-Confucianism, tainted by Taoism and Buddhism. Ricci began to study classical Confucianism and found in it strong moral tenets and a sense of God's goodness and omnipotence in the face of evil. Thus, he decided to use classical Confucianism in the service of Christianity, just as Thomas Aquinas had used Aristotle.

Ricci attempted to move even further north to Nanjing in 1595 but was unable to do so because of Chinese nervousness about the presence of foreign-

ers in light of Hideyoshi's invasion of nearby Korea. Fortunately, Chinese officials seemed unaware of the presence of Jesuit chaplains to the many Japanese
Christians who were part of Hideyoshi's army. Ricci opted instead to settle further south in the provincial capital of Nanchang, where aspiring scholars came
every year to take the rigorous ten-day civil service examination.

Ricci became a much-sought-after person in Nanchang when it became
known that he had a special system of memorization that allowed him to recall
large amounts of information correctly, such as four hundred Chinese characters forward and backward, in the random order which they had been recited to
him. Aware of the attraction this had for young scholars, Ricci soon wrote *Western Memory Techniques* (*His-kuo chi-fa,* 1596), which explained his methods in
detail and furthered his reputation as a scholar of great wisdom.[48]

In Nanchang, Ricci also met the famous Confucian scholar Chang Huang
(1526–1608), who introduced him to the budding societies of scholars committed to "making friends by means of literature" and changing society for the
better. These scholars were heartened by Ricci's emphasis on classical Confucianism and were especially receptive to Ricci's *Treatise on Friendship* (*Chiao-yu
lun,* 1595), which was his first composition directly in Chinese. Though modeled largely on Cicero's *On Friendship,* it demonstrated the compatibility of
Christian love with the classical Confucian concept of humanitarianism (*jen*).
The book gained notoriety for Ricci throughout China, and in his own words,
"has established our reputation as scholars of talent and virtue, and thus it is
read and received with great applause."[49]

In 1598, after Valignano had named him superior of the mission in China,
Ricci set out for Beijing, laden with Western presents for the Wan-li emperor
(1573–1620). He was forced, however, to retreat to Nanjing, again because of
Chinese nervousness over Hideyoshi's inroads in Korea. He made use of his
time there to build more friendships with scholars and imperial officials and
also utilized the exceptionally well-equipped astronomical observatory, which
had fallen into relative disuse during the Ming dynasty.

It had not been an easy eighteen years for Ricci, who, in a moment of dis-
couragement, remarked that the Chinese in "this sterile land" were the main
source of his preponderance of grey hair.[50] Yet in January 1601, he made one
more attempt to take up residence in Beijing. Accompanied by Spanish Jesuit
Diego de Pantoia (1571–1618) and Jesuit brother Chung Ming-jên, he was not
received cordially, in spite of numerous letters of introduction from high government officials. Caught in the midst of a power struggle between the Mandarin scholars and court eunuchs, the three were confined to a house owned by
a powerful eunuch.

Eventually, Ricci was able to convey to the emperor via messenger his academic skills and his willingness to put them at the emperor's disposal. He was soon allowed to present his numerous gifts by proxy, including a painting, a small harpsichord, and a clock. Though Ricci would never meet the emperor, he and Pantoia were summoned to the Forbidden City, where they resided for several days and taught the eunuchs how to wind and set the clock. Ricci also later composed eight songs for the harpsichord, each containing some elements of Christian doctrine, and taught the eunuchs how to play. Finally, in May 1601, three months after their arrival and in an unprecedented demonstration of trust toward foreigners, Ricci and the others were allowed to reside permanently in the capital.[51]

Now known to the Chinese as Li Madou (Ricci, Matteo) or Li Xitai (Ricci from the West), Ricci first published in Beijing *On the True Meaning of the Lord of Heaven* (*Tianzhu shiyi,* 1603), which was well received and even influenced a visiting group of Korean intellectuals. It had no impact, however, on the Wanli emperor, whom Ricci soon learned was a corrupt recluse who got most of his advice not from educated advisors but rather from the largely self-serving imperial court eunuchs. Consequently, Ricci realized that trying to convert him or convince him to issue an edict in support of Christianity would likely be counter-productive. Instead, Ricci decided to redouble his efforts to convert members of the scholarly class in Beijing.

The newly founded Tung-lin Academy, which sought to curb the undue influence of the court eunuchs and restore traditional ethics in the government and people, would prove to be the perfect venue for this. The Tung-lin were delighted to count Ricci among their friends, and there he met two of his greatest Beijing collaborators—Li Zhizao (1565–1630) and Xu Guangqi (1562–1633). Both studied geography, Western science, and Euclidian geometry with Ricci and assisted him in publishing books on these subjects. Like Rukui, Zhizao put off baptism for some time because of his concubine, but Ricci finally baptized him in 1610. Two months later, Ricci was dead.

Ricci was entombed in Beijing, with an epitaph from the imperial governor: "To one who loved righteousness and wrote illustrious books, to Li Madou, far Westerner." Indeed, Ricci had accomplished much through his "illustrious books." There were approximately two thousand Christians in China, and four chapels, all of them attached to the Jesuit residences Ricci had established in Zhaoqing, Shaozhou, Nanchang, and Nanjing. A fifth chapel was under construction in Beijing. He had thoroughly embedded Christianity among the Confucian scholars, which would be demonstrated by the subsequent strong leadership of Li Zhizao and Xu Guangqi.

The Legacy of the Sixteenth-Century Missions

Spanish cultural exclusivism and the failure to establish an indigenous Christianity would ultimately weaken the church in Mexico and Latin America. By the seventeenth century, the Spanish hold on Mexico and Latin America would become more tenuous in the face of strong competition from the English, French, and Dutch, which would in turn facilitate internal dissent.

In 1780 in Peru, Túpac Amaru's Jesuit-educated great-grandson, José Gabriel Condorcanqui (1738–1781), took the name Túpac Amaru II and attempted another indigenous uprising, but he was executed on the same spot as his great-grandfather. The name, however, still symbolizes Peruvian resistance to foreign rule, as evidenced by its rebirth in 1983 as the Marxist Túpac Amaru revolutionary movement. Furthermore, the heavy identification of the church with Spanish colonial rule made it a logical target during the Mexican War of Independence (1810–1821), which was heavily supported by natives and *mestizos*. A telling illustration of the changed position of the once-powerful colonial church in Mexico is the fact that until 1992, it was illegal for a priest in Mexico to wear clerical dress in public.

In China, some Jesuits after Ricci questioned whether he might have gone too far in his inculturation and opted for a more direct, heavy-handed approach, which led to a 1617 edict against Christianity. The edict, however, resulted in little more than petty harassment, and there were no instances of martyrdom. A committed return to Ricci's approach brought permission from Rome for a vernacular liturgy, a vernacular Bible, and for priests to wear the traditional headgear of a Confucian scholar while celebrating mass. Even some court eunuchs were converted and in turn led a number of women in the imperial court to baptism; by 1642, there was even a chapel *within* the imperial palace in the Forbidden City, serving approximately fifty Christians.

Because of Ricci, the Jesuits made a remarkable transition from unwelcome visitors to Beijing to trusted imperial advisors at the beginning of the Manchu dynasty (1644–1911). In 1692, the Kangxi emperor issued an Edict of Toleration of Christianity and declared it a Chinese religion, after having read Ricci's *On the True Meaning of the Lord of Heaven*. With the support of Chinese priests and bishops, conversions in the general population continued at a rate of approximately five thousand per year.

It would be Rome rather than secular Western powers or the Chinese who would deal a major setback to the China mission. Ricci had supported the practice of ancestor worship, so important to the Chinese, "since they do not recognize any divinity in these dead ones, nor do they ask or hope for anything from them, all this stands outside of idolatry."[52] But after a protracted struggle and pressure from the mendicant orders, Rome disallowed the practice in 1742. Though not a death blow, it unquestionably seriously hampered the cause of Christianity in China. Largely due to the inculturation policy of Valignano and the work of Ricci, however, Christianity would survive in China to the present.

In 1939, Rome would again allow ancestor worship for Asian Catholics, and Matteo Ricci's intimate understanding of true inculturation would be recognized by Pope John Paul II, who remarked in October 2001 that "Father Matteo Ricci made himself so 'Chinese with the Chinese' that he became an expert Sinologist, in the deepest cultural and spiritual sense of the term."[53] Ricci continues to be held in high regard in communist mainland China, and, in 1983, the Republic of China (Taiwan) issued a postage stamp with Ricci's image in commemoration of the 400th anniversary of his arrival in China. Ricci from the West had indeed embedded himself thoroughly in the cultural life of China.

It has often been said, and usually quite accurately, that the sign of a good missionary is one who knows when it is time to go home. Certainly it is clear that when the missionary endeavor is bound together with the secular goals of the colonial enterprise, a high price will eventually be paid in terms of credibility and depth of faith, even in countries that are today officially Catholic. Though inculturation is not a panacea for solving challenges of mission, it was tested in Japan and achieved its greatest degree of success in China, where there was virtually no colonial apparatus. Ultimately, it leaves one with a question for which some may find the answers uncomfortable: "How does one measure success in the evangelization of a new culture?"

Questions for Reflection and Discussion

1. Is the evangelization of new cultures an intrinsically destructive process?

2. What do you see as the signs of successful evangelization of a non-Western culture? Should the missionary always be concerned about the quality of conversion rather than the quantity?

3. What do you see as the predominant cultural context of your own religious beliefs and practices? Is this cultural context consistent with your actual ethnic and cultural heritage?

6

A Tragic Mutual Incomprehension

Galileo Galilei and His Conflict with the Church

The career and subsequent trial of Galileo Galilei has become an oft-repeated example of a fundamental intolerance on the part of the Catholic Church for science and reason. There is no question that Galileo was brilliant and that his case was tragic. Galileo indeed had many enemies in Rome, but often over-looked are the significant contributing factors of Galileo's abrupt personality, the ostensible betrayal of his friendship with Pope Urban, and the fact that Galileo, even by the standards of today, had not scientifically proven his hypothesis of a heliocentric universe.

—◀◉▶—

There is no sadder sight in the world than to see a beautiful theory killed by a brutal fact.
> —English biologist Thomas Henry Huxley (1825–1895)

One does not read in the Gospel that the Lord said: "I will send to you the Paraclete who will teach you about the course of the sun and moon. For he willed to make them Christians, not mathematicians.
> —St. Augustine of Hippo

The Galileo affair is generally, though incorrectly, seen as the paradigm that illustrates the intrinsic hostility of religion toward science and a fundamental opposition between faith and science. In this scenario, the brilliant scientific insights of Galileo with regard to a heliocentric, or sun-centered universe, obviously correct to anyone of reason, are immediately quashed by a Catholic Church hostile to the new science and to any semblance of individual or original thought. The reality, however, is far different. Over the course of forty-six years and six trips to Rome, which cumulatively numbered over five hundred days, a high drama would be played out, in which Galileo would struggle to convince the world of the correctness of his beliefs, sometimes on the basis of tentative, even *inaccurate* science. The whole affair, which would involve a large cast of characters, clashes of personalities, intellectual pride, hurt feelings, and bruised egos, began in Pisa, Italy.

Galileo was born into a noble, though not wealthy, family in Pisa, on February 15, 1564. His father, Vincenzio, a musician, found it difficult to support Galileo and his three siblings, so at age twelve Galileo was sent to the monastery of Vallombrosa near Florence to be educated. Two years later, however, when Galileo entered the novitiate for the order, his exasperated father removed him from religious life so he could continue his education. Galileo went to the University of Pisa in 1581, intending to get a liberal arts degree before continuing on with medicine. After four years, he left the university with no degree, although he had shown strong aptitude for mathematics and mechanics.

A Man of Many Gifts

An accomplished organist and lute player, Galileo also possessed considerable art skill, tried his hand at playwriting, and contemplated becoming a painter, but in the end he opted to continue with academic pursuits. This led in 1586 to his invention of a hydrostatic balance, which suddenly began to open doors for him. In 1587, at the age of twenty-three, he traveled to Rome for the first time, where he met famed German Jesuit mathematician Christopher Clavius (1537–1612). Impressed by Galileo, Clavius would thereafter maintain a friendship with him through regular, though not always frequent, correspondence.

The trip in 1587 also gave Galileo the unique opportunity to acquaint himself with other faculty members at the Roman College. Founded by Ignatius Loyola in 1551, it was the most prestigious university in the Christian world, and though the curriculum was heavily Aristotelian, it was not at all adverse to science, mathematics, and astronomy. Painstaking research of Galileo's notebooks from 1588–1589 has in fact demonstrated that his scientific views were heavily influenced by many of the leading Jesuits at the Roman College, particularly with regard to scientific method and theories about the application of knowledge.[1]

Before leaving Rome, Galileo met the influential patron of art and scholarship Cardinal Francesco del Monte (1549–1627), who along with Clavius, helped him obtain a professorship in mathematics at the University of Pisa. When Galileo took up his new professorship, in spite of having no degree, he perhaps realized for the first time the high value that patronage could play in the furtherance of his work and fame.

While at the university, Galileo was reputed to have dropped two bodies of different weight from the leaning tower of Pisa to challenge Aristotle's view that bodies of different weight will fall at a different velocity. In all likelihood, this never happened, but the popularity of the story is certainly indicative of Galileo's conviction that the common practice of unquestioned deference to Aristotle was unacceptable.[2]

After three years at Pisa, Galileo longed for change. In 1592, again with help from Clavius, he obtained a professorship at the University of Padua, in the Republic of Venice. It was here that Galileo eventually began an eleven-year relationship with Marina Gamba (1578–1619), fourteen years his junior. Though they would always maintain separate residences and never married, she would eventually bear Galileo three children—Virginia (1600–1634), Livia (1601–1659), and a son, Vincenzio (1606–1649).

But not all of Galileo's time in Padua was spent in amorous pursuits. He also began to focus his attention on astronomy, spurred largely by his observation in 1604 of a supernova. Galileo's calculations convinced him that this "new star" was beyond the moon, and so in 1605, he postulated in a series of public lectures that, contrary to Aristotle, the heavens were in fact changeable.

Then, in 1609, Galileo learned of the invention by Dutchman Hans Lippershey (1570–1619) of a type of spyglass that allowed far-away objects to appear much closer. Galileo obtained one of the devices, improved it with superior lenses, and then turned it to the heavens. He first looked at the moon, likely to confirm the hunch by Plutarch (A.D. 45–125) that there were mountains on the moon. Then, to his astonishment, he discovered four of Jupiter's moons, which he shrewdly named the Medician Stars in honor of Cosimo II de Medici (1590–1621), grand duke of Tuscany.

Ruled by the powerful Medici family in Florence, the Duchy of Tuscany comprised a large section of central Italy north of Rome and was a force to be reckoned with. Under Grand Duke Ferdinand I (1549–1609) and his wife, the grand duchess Christina of Lorraine (1565–1636), Tuscany had prospered. Galileo's birth town of Pisa had been annexed in 1509 to Tuscany, and he considered himself a proud citizen. Now, with Ferdinand's son Grand Duke Cosimo II de Medici in power since the previous year, Galileo had sensed an opportunity for patronage and was not disappointed. When Cosimo II heard of Galileo's naming of Jupiter's moons after his family, he rewarded him by appointing him for life as official court mathematician and philosopher of Tuscany.[3]

Galileo presented his astronomical observations in *The Starry Messenger* (March 13, 1610): "All these facts were observed and discovered by me not many days ago with the aid of a spyglass which I devised, after first being illuminated by divine grace." In it, he argued that the craters and irregular surface of the moon demonstrated that the heavens were not in fact perfect after all, that Jupiter's moons proved that not all heavenly bodies revolve around the earth, and that the greater number of stars he had observed demonstrated that the common wisdom about the universe was not correct.[4]

Although Galileo was not yet arguing explicitly for a heliocentric universe, he had challenged some fundamental elements of the long-accepted geocentric universe advocated by Aristotle (378–322 B.C.E.) and Ptolemy (150 B.C.E.), according to which the earth was motionless. Aristotle insisted that heavenly material and terrestrial material differed, and that the perfect and unchangeable heavens were governed by a set of physics very different from those that governed the earth. Ptolemy occupied himself with "saving the appearances," that is, explaining why the heavenly bodies appear the way they do rather than trying to explain how or why they move.

The first significant challenge to a geocentric universe had already been made by Polish astronomer Nicholas Copernicus (1473–1543). Orphaned at the age of ten and raised by his uncle, the bishop of Ermland, Copernicus studied at the universities of Cracow, Bologna, and Padua. After gaining expertise in the humanities, canon law, astronomy, mathematics, and medicine, Copernicus returned to Poland to care for his ailing uncle. Although never a priest, Copernicus did become a cathedral canon, which meant that he was a minor cleric.

His initial astronomical theories, like those of Ptolemy, were also designed to "save the appearances." Eventually, however, Copernicus began to advocate a heliocentric universe, and his astronomical theories won the approval even of Pope Clement VII (1523–1534). The Protestant reformers Martin Luther and Philip Melanchthon, on the other hand, ridiculed him as an "upstart astrologer" whose ideas were contrary to scripture, especially the passage "Joshua declaimed 'Sun, stand still over Gibeon' . . . and the sun stood still . . . till the people had vengeance on their enemies" (Joshua 10:12–13). Copernicus, however, persevered, and in 1543, his *On the Revolutions of the Heavenly Spheres* finally appeared, dedicated to Pope Paul III. Tragically, Copernicus was literally on his deathbed when he perused an advance copy and discovered that a preface had been surreptitiously inserted by the publisher. Written by the Lutheran theologian Andreas Osiander (1498–1552), the preface insisted that Copernicus intended his heliocentric theory to be used simply as a mathematical computing device rather than to represent any kind of physical reality. Too ill to protest, that is how the book went before the public.

How was it that Copernicus had been so bold as to challenge conventional wisdom about the universe in the first place? It must be remembered that the first half of the sixteenth century during which Copernicus lived was a time of great intellectual inquiry, eclecticism, and discovery. Renaissance humanists and Christian humanists, in their efforts to come to a greater understanding of classical antiquity, advocated what has been called an "authorization of the human intellect," and did not always feel bound by academic convention. A temporary casualty in this process was the implicit acceptance of the absolute priority of Aristotelianism and Thomism in intellectual matters. But by the end of the Council of Trent in 1563, Aristotelianism and Thomism had been re-affirmed, some would say almost dogmatized, as the official framework for intellectual inquiry, and the relatively free atmosphere of intellectual inquiry that had been a hallmark of Christian humanism receded into the background.

In September 1610, after eighteen years in Padua, Galileo moved to Florence to take up his post as official mathematician and philosopher at the Tuscan court. He took his daughters, Virginia and Livia, with him and sent for the young Vincenzio a few years later. Their mother, Marina Gamba, for reasons known perhaps only to her and Galileo, remained behind and married the Paduan Giovanni Bartoluzzi. After an apparently amiable parting of the ways, Galileo actually used some connections in Padua to find Bartoluzzi a job and remained in contact with the couple until Marina died in 1619. As for his daughters, Galileo soon followed a custom common at the time and entered them into religious life, where Virginia flourished as Sister Maria Celeste. Livia, on the other hand, found her life as Sister Arcangela quite difficult and seems to have suffered from what today would likely be called depression.[5]

In Florence, Galileo continued his astronomical observations, and in December 1610, he observed that just like the moon, Venus too had phases. This could only happen, he realized, if Venus were orbiting the sun rather than the earth. He also studied sunspots, already observed and recorded by English astronomer Thomas Harriot (1560–1621), and concluded that they offered further proof of the imperfection of the heavens.

Opposition and Acclaim

Not everyone, however, was enamored of Galileo's discoveries and theories. In April 1610, Czech mathematician Martin Horky had written to German Protestant astronomer Johannes Kepler (1571–1630) that "Galileo Galilei, the mathematician of Padua, came to us in Bologna and he brought with him that spyglass through which he sees four fictitious planets." Kepler, however, reacted by sending a letter of support to Galileo, published as *Conversation with the Starry Messenger*. Still determined to discredit Galileo, Horky then published *A Very Short Excursion against the Starry Messenger* (June 1610), while others asserted that Galileo's spyglass was actually *creating* illusions.

Florentine philosopher Ludovico delle Colombe (1565–1616) published *Against the Earth's Motion* (December 1610), which challenged Galileo's conclusions and alleged that they conflicted with sacred scripture: "You set the earth on its foundations, so that it shall never be shaken" (Psalm 104:5); "The world is firmly established; it shall never be moved" (1 Chronicles 16:30); "Who has ascended to heaven and come down?" (Proverbs 30:3); "The sun rises and the sun goes down, and hurries to the place where it rises" (Ecclesiastes 1:5). Rather than get into an exegetical argument with delle Colombe, Galileo wisely turned to Rome for authentication and found support in his old friend Christopher Clavius, chief mathematician at the Roman College. When Clavius wrote back that the Jesuits had acquired their own spyglass and had confirmed his discoveries, Galileo felt confident in traveling to Rome personally to argue his case with other academics.[6]

The second trip to Rome by the forty-seven-year-old Galileo on March 29, 1611, was almost triumphal in nature and would be a watershed event in his career. Word of his discoveries preceded him, and people of great influence clamored for time with him. Galileo traveled from banquet to banquet, setting up his spyglass for his fascinated guests.

At the Roman College, Galileo met Jesuit Cardinal Robert Bellarmine (1542–1621). A nephew of Pope Marcellus II (d. 1555), whose three-week papacy had been the shortest in the history of the church, Bellarmine was a force to be reckoned with. As a member of the Holy Office, he had been involved in the process against Giordano Bruno (1548–1600), a Dominican priest who had been burned at the stake eleven years earlier in Rome. Some argue that Bruno had been punished because of Copernican views, but the reality was that his sentence, albeit unjust, had to do with strictly theological matters, such as transubstantiation, the trinity, and the substantiality of the soul.[7] Bellarmine himself looked through Galileo's spyglass, and then quietly asked four Jesuit mathematics professors at the Roman College what they thought, not just about Galileo's discoveries but his *ideas*. The four, including Clavius, expressed cautious support for the *Starry Messenger*.[8]

Galileo was also well received by Pope Paul V (1605–1621), with whom he had a long audience. Even more important for Galileo professionally was his attendance at an elaborate dinner in his honor hosted by Prince Federico Cesi

(1585–1630), founder of the Accademia dei Lincei (Academy of the Lynx), dedicated to the study of mathematics and nature. Galileo set up his spyglass, which Cesi decided would henceforth be called a *telescope,* and after Cesi and his guests had taken their turn with it, he made Galileo a member of the academy. The simple device would continue to open many doors for Galileo in the ensuing years, as he gave them to notables of influence, never for money but only for the hope of possible patronage.

In April, the ever-cautious Bellarmine asked the Holy Office to ascertain whether Galileo had been named in a proceeding against Cesare Cremonini (1550–1631), an Aristotelian philosophy professor at the University of Pisa, with whom Galileo was on friendly terms. This inquiry, although innocuous and with negative results, was the first mention of Galileo in Holy Office records. Satisfied that Galileo was not involved in the case, the Roman College then officially confirmed Galileo's discoveries, though they were silent about Galileo's interpretation of the larger implications of those discoveries. The following month, the Jesuits at the Roman College arranged a reception for Galileo, upon whom they conferred what today would be called an honorary doctorate.[9]

Michelangelo Buonarroti (1568–1646), the great-nephew of the artist of the same name, had given a letter of recommendation to Galileo, which he now presented to Cardinal Maffeo Barberini (1568–1644). A friendship quickly followed, and, shortly after Galileo returned to Florence in June 1611, Barberini made clear in a letter his admiration and regard for him: "May God keep you, not only because outstanding persons, such as yourself, deserve a long life of public service, but because of the particular affection I have, and always will have for you."[10] Galileo's second Roman trip had been a huge success. He had made numerous important connections in Rome, especially Cardinal Barberini, and his reputation now seemed secure.

In 1612, using the pseudonym Apelles, Jesuit astronomer Christoph (1573–1650) argued incorrectly that sunspots were caused by some sort of satellites passing in front of the sun, and that in accordance with Aristotle, the sun, like the rest of the heavens, therefore remained unchangeable. It was too much for Galileo to resist.

In his *History and Demonstrations about Sunspots and Their Properties* (March 1613), published by the Academy of the Lynx, Galileo challenged Scheiner's theory and insisted that sunspots were some sort of cloud on the surface of the sun. More important, Galileo endorsed Copernicanism in print for the first time: "With absolute necessity we shall conclude, in agreement with the theories of Pythagoreans and Copernicus, that Venus revolves around the sun just as do all the other planets."[11] Yet it is important to note that even with this unequivocal endorsement of Copernicanism, ecclesiastical authorities in

Rome allowed publication of Galileo's response to Scheiner, which was well received by Cardinal Maffeo Barberini.

Then, in December 1613, a dinner conversation in Pisa, at which Galileo was not even present, led to a major escalation in tension between him and his critics. Benedetto Castelli (1577–1644), a Benedictine monk and chief mathematician at the University of Pisa as well as friend and follower of Galileo, was at a banquet hosted by the grand duchess Christina, who as mother of Grand Duke Cosimo II still exerted considerable influence. When the topic of Copernicanism came up, Castelli functioned as Galileo's impromptu proxy in defending it, while others purportedly whispered comments in the grand duchess's ear about inherent conflicts between Copernicanism and scripture.

When Castelli related the incident to Galileo, he responded with his *Letter to Castelli* (December 21, 1613), which explained his views on the relationship between scripture and science.[12] He told Castelli that it is true that sacred scripture can neither lie nor err, but that *interpreters* of scripture can, especially those who insist on always understanding the words of scripture in a literal sense. This would mean that one would have to attribute to God feet, hands, eyes, and human emotions. In cases of natural phenomena that contradict a literal interpretation of scripture, the truly wise interpreter should always defer to the natural explanation since two truths cannot contradict each other, and the laws of nature are inherently true and unchangeable. Anything less would be tantamount to saying that everything knowable is found in scripture, which would wrongly put limits on the human mind.

Galileo was not the first to argue for a nonliteral interpretation of scripture in the matter of heliocentrism. The Spanish Augustinian theologian Diego de Zuñiga (1536–1598) in his *Commentary on Job* (1584) had wrestled with the passage where God is described as he "who moves the earth out of its place and its pillars tremble" (Job 9:6) and concluded that the passage made sense only if one accepted a heliocentric universe. Zuñiga went on to declare the superiority of Copernicanism to the Aristotelian worldview and insisted that any passages that seemed to contradict Copernicanism had to be interpreted analogously.

Heightened Tensions

Galileo's *Letter to Castelli* outraged his critics. Tommaso Caccini (1574–1648), a Dominican friar and associate of Galileo's nemesis Ludovico delle Colombe, denounced Galileo from the pulpit in Florence in December 1614. Caccini told his audience that Galileo, the Copernican system, and all mathematicians were "enemies of the church and state." So sharp and unwarranted was Caccini's attack that his religious superior apologized to Galileo the following month. Then, in February 1615, the Dominican Niccoló Lorini filed a formal complaint about Galileo to the Holy Office and enclosed a copy of the *Letter to Castelli*.[13]

This was followed up by a personal deposition given by Caccini at the Holy Office, in which he maintained that the Academy of the Lynx to which Galileo belonged interacted with Germans—that is, Protestants. The growing number of individuals who supported delle Colombe in his efforts against Galileo led the latter to nickname them the League of Pigeons, which was a wordplay on colombe—"pigeons" in Italian.[14]

Galileo, however, was not without his supporters. The Carmelite friar Paolo Antonio Foscarini (1565–1616) came to his defense with *Letter on the Pythagorean and Copernican Opinion of the Earth's Motion and Sun's Rest* (March 1615), which argued that the Copernican system was compatible with sacred scripture. Foscarini's support was likely instrumental in convincing Galileo to insist that Copernicanism was no mere theory.[15] The following month, however, Cardinal Bellarmine admonished Foscarini and Galileo to treat Copernicanism as a theory rather than absolute truth: "It seems to me that your Reverence and Signor Galileo act prudently when you content yourselves with speaking hypothetically and not absolutely, as I have always understood that Copernicus spoke." Given that Bellarmine was unaware of the surreptitiously inserted preface in Copernicus's book, the request did not seem unreasonable, particularly when one considers that Galileo had *not* in fact proven Copernicanism conclusively.[16]

Bellarmine also reminded Foscarini and Galileo that "the Council of Trent forbids the interpretation of the Scriptures in a way contrary to the common opinion of the holy Fathers." The problem for Galileo was that the idea of a rotating earth orbiting a stationary sun *was* in fact in conflict with numerous passages from scripture, at least on a literal level: "The sun rises and the sun goes down; then it presses on to the place where it rises" (Ecclesiastes 1:5); "He has pitched a tent there for the sun, which comes forth like the groom from his bridal chamber and, like a giant, joyfully runs its course. At one end of the heavens it comes forth, and its course is to the other end" (Psalm 18:6-7); "The Lord is king… and he has made the world firm, not to be moved" (Psalm 92:1); "God fixed the earth upon its foundations, not to be moved forever" (Psalm 103:5)."

Galileo realized that acceptance of his contention that scripture could not always be interpreted literally when it came to matters of science was fundamental to acceptance of Copernicanism. To this end, he spent the summer of 1615 expanding and revising his *Letter to Castelli*, which he retitled *Letter to the Grand Duchess Christina*. Although it would not actually be published until

1636, the letter was circulated, copied, and widely read. In it, Galileo now adopted a much harsher tone toward his critics, who had made the "grave mistake of sprinkling" their writings "with passages taken from places in the Bible which they failed to understand properly." These critics had "resolved to fabricate a shield for their fallacies out of the mantle of pretended religion and the authority of the Bible," and because of their literalism, had been led to "conclusions that are repugnant to manifest reason and sense."

For Galileo, the Bible was designed to persuade men of those articles and propositions which, surpassing all human reasoning, could not be made credible by science, or by any other means than through the very mouth of the Holy Spirit. He cites Augustine in support of his belief that sacred scripture is concerned about teaching us things of salvation rather than things of nature, and also cites the remark of church historian Cardinal Cesare Baronius (1538–1607) that "the Bible was written to show us how to go to heaven, not how the heavens go."

As in the *Letter to Castelli,* Galileo is unequivocal in his support for Copernicanism: "as to the arrangement of the parts of the universe, I hold the sun to be situated motionless in the center of the revolution of the celestial orbs while the earth revolves about the sun." Because he had insisted that a properly understood Bible was inerrant, Galileo is led to conclude that anyone who maintains that the sun is inherently motionless and the earth movable takes an erroneous and heretical position. Clearly, Galileo had raised the stakes.

The tone of the *Letter to the Grand Duchess Christina* was in one sense not surprising. Even as a young faculty member at the University of Pisa, Galileo was known for his sarcasm and inflexibility in arguing with his opponents. While scholars today recognize Galileo's intellectual brilliance and quick wittedness, they also admit to his impatience, conceit, and scorn for any who disagreed with him. Galileo would even on occasion improve the objections of his critics, so as to be able to knock them down all the harder. As one scholar puts it bluntly but accurately, "Galileo never ceased to be enamored of the brilliance of his own wit."[17]

Galileo resolved to return to Rome, confident that his *Letter to the Grand Duchess Christina* would supply the exegetical approach necessary for acceptance of Copernicanism and would silence accusations that his scientific ideas were contrary to sacred scripture. Galileo was right. His opponents *had* misunderstood the correct meaning of scripture. Galileo, however, had grossly underestimated the residual fears the church had concerning personal interpretation of scripture in the aftermath of the Protestant Reformation, as well as the fact that he, like Luther, had challenged the authority of Aristotelianism. And in entering into the realm of theology and scripture, Galileo had now given his opponents the weapon they needed to fight back.

Galileo, now fifty-one, arrived in Rome for the third time on December 10, 1615, confident that he could get church authorities on his side, especially after finding out that the Holy Office had dismissed Caccini's complaint against him. In early January, he wrote a letter on his theory of the tides, which he wrongly believed were caused by the rotation of the earth on its axis in combination with its annual orbit around the sun, and boldly sent it to his patron, the Florentine Cardinal Alessandro Orsini (1592–1626). But Galileo was not as close to victory as he had thought. Though the accusations by Caccini and Lorini had been dismissed, the Holy Office decided to examine Galileo's *Letter on Sunspots,* most likely at the instigation of Cardinal Bellarmine.[18] The cardinal unfortunately had a tendency to see the "new science" as being from the same mold as Protestantism and perhaps became alarmed at Caccini's suggestion of Protestant influence on the members of the Academy of the Lynx.

Additionally, Galileo himself seems to have exacerbated the situation through his relentless quest to have others accept the validity of his position. The Tuscan ambassador remarked in a letter to Galileo's patron, the grand duke: "Galileo has relied more on his own counsel than on that of his friends. Cardinal del Monte and myself, and also several cardinals from the Holy Office, tried to persuade him to be quiet and not to go on irritating the issue. If he wanted to hold this Copernican opinion, he was told, let him hold it quietly and not spend so much effort in trying to have others share it."[19] But just as he was almost incapable of civil discourse with his opponents, so too was Galileo not good at keeping a "strategic silence."

Galileo and Bellarmine seemed incapable of seeing things from each other's perspectives. Unlike Galileo, Bellarmine felt that truth should not be expanded but rather simply defended. Furthermore, as a scholastic theologian, he was likely annoyed by Galileo's repudiation of Aristotelianism, still the predominant philosophical system and recently reaffirmed by the general of the Jesuits as the accepted system in Jesuit schools. But Bellarmine was neither petty nor inflexible. As stated earlier, he was willing to allow for Copernicanism as a superior hypothesis, but not as *fact.* Furthermore, he had even stated in his letter to Foscarini that if solid proof of heliocentrism were shown to him, then he would change his view. But unless Galileo could offer such proof, the scripture passages in question would have to be taken literally. And the reality was that Galileo had *not* offered conclusive proof of the validity of Copernicanism, nor would he do so in his lifetime. Bellarmine advised Galileo to stick to mathematics and physics and not tell theologians how to interpret the Bible.[20]

After consultants to the Holy Office in February deemed heliocentrism to be heretical and the notion of a moving earth erroneous, Pope Paul V directed Bellarmine to admonish Galileo to abandon Copernicanism. If he refused, he was to be ordered in the presence of a notary, not to teach, hold, or defend it. If he still refused, he was to be imprisoned. Accordingly, Bellarmine summoned Galileo to appear before a regular meeting of the Holy Office and conveyed the papal wishes to him, to which Galileo acquiesced. This relatively mild private admonition was due in large part to the intervention of Galileo's patrons, Prince Cesi, the Grand Duke Cosimo, and Cardinal Maffeo Barberini.[21]

Although the consultants of the Holy Office had referred to heliocentrism as heretical and the motion of the earth erroneous in the faith, the final say was with the Congregation of the Index of Forbidden Books, which now simply referred to both beliefs as "false and contrary to sacred scripture." Copernicanism could still be taught as a hypothesis, but on March 5, 1616, the congregation suspended until corrected the *Commentary on Job* (1584) of Diego Zuñiga and the *On the Revolutions of the Heavenly Spheres* of Copernicus. The Letter of Foscarini was prohibited altogether, though this was not necessarily the end of his career, since Bellarmine himself had seen his own *De Controversiis* designated for the Index in 1590 at the direction of the Franciscan pope Sixtus V.[22]

The strict secrecy of all Holy Office proceedings meant that no one except Galileo, Paul V, and Bellarmine and his immediate staff, would ever be aware of what had transpired. Even Cardinal Barberini seemed in the dark, though he did remark to a friend that although he admired Galileo highly, he "would like greater caution in not going beyond the arguments used by Ptolemy and Copernicus, and, finally, in not exceeding the limitations of physics and mathematics." Nevertheless, various cardinals continued to request and receive telescopes from Galileo, as well as copies of his books, and just one week after the Congregation of the Index decree against Copernicanism, Pope Paul V himself went for a forty-five minute walk with Galileo, who recounted later that the pope "assured me several times that he bore me the greatest goodwill and was ready to show his affection and favor towards me at all times."[23]

But precisely because of the absence of factual information, rumors began to circulate that Galileo had formally abjured his errors before Bellarmine and the Holy Office. Galileo turned to Bellarmine himself for help, who provided a declaration of clarification, which because of its critical later importance is quoted in full:

> We, Robert Cardinal Bellarmine, having heard that it is calumniously reported that Signor Galileo Galilei has in our hand abjured and has also been punished with salutary penance, and being requested to state the truth as to this, declare that the said Galileo has not abjured, either

in our hand or the hand of any other person here in Rome, or anywhere else, so far as we know, any opinion or doctrine held by him. Neither has any salutary penance been imposed on him; but that only the declaration made by the Holy Father and published by the Sacred Congregation of the Index was notified to him, which says that the doctrine attributed to Copernicus, that the earth moves around the sun, and that the sun is stationary in the center of the world and does not move from east to west, is contrary to the Holy Scriptures, and therefore cannot be defended or held. In witness whereof we have written and subscribed the present document with our own hand this twenty-sixth day of May, 1616.[24]

For all his talents, Galileo had not offered solid proof of the validity of the Copernican theory, and on an official level, had failed to win Rome over to his point of view with regard to the proper interpretation of scripture. Nevertheless, his reputation seemed intact. He had not been on trial; no charges had been brought against him; and the official proceedings of both the Holy Office and the Congregation of the Index in 1616 made "no mention whatsoever of him or his writings." Most important, he had a clear and unequivocal statement from Cardinal Bellarmine about the true course of events during his interview with the Holy Office. Though as an obedient Catholic he had acceded to the wishes of the Holy Office, Galileo left Rome for Florence on June 4, 1616, hopeful that somehow the prohibition of Copernicus would be reversed.

In the aftermath of his encounter with the Holy Office in 1616, Galileo had laid low, mindful of the admonition. When an oral dispute over Copernicanism with the priest and jurist Francesco Ingoli (1578–1649) led both to agree to state their points of view in writing, Galileo, contrary to his nature, backed off. His resolve, however, weakened in 1618, when three comets appeared and mathematicians began to proffer their theories about the nature of the astronomical displays.[25]

The Jesuit Orazio Grassi (1583–1654), a widely respected mathematician from the Roman College, correctly argued in a lecture in 1618 that comets were celestial bodies. When his lecture was published in early 1619, Galileo used his student Mario Guiducci (1585–1646) to deliver a public lecture entitled *A Discourse on Comets* in June 1619. It was a well-known secret that it had in fact been written by Galileo. Not known at the time was that Galileo's argument that comets were in fact optical phenomena and not celestial bodies was completely wrong. Grassi responded to Guiducci/Galileo in *The Astronomical Balance* (October 1619), under the pseudonym Lothario Sarsi. The stakes had been raised.

Galileo in turn began work on *The Assayer*, described as "one of the all-time masterpieces of sarcastic invective."[26] Written in the form of a letter to his friend Virginio Cesarini (1595–1624), Galileo relentlessly derided Sarsi/Grassi and continued to maintain that comets were optical illusions rather than celestial bodies. What is more important, Galileo now argued for the first time that knowledge of science was written *only* in mathematical language, which would mark the beginning of a gradual separation between philosophy and science.

New Popes and Changing Fortunes

In January 1621, while Galileo worked on *The Assayer*, Pope Paul V died and was succeeded by Gregory XV (1621–1623). Much to the delight of Galileo, the new pope appointed his close friends Giovanni Ciampoli (1589–1643) and Virginio Cesarini (1595–1624), both members of the Academy of the Lynx, to influential papal positions. Then, in February, Galileo's longtime protector and patron, Cosimo II de Medici, died, leaving the rule of Tuscany in the hands of his mother, the grand duchess Christina, until his eleven-year-old son, Ferdinand, was old enough to succeed him. For Galileo, this meant that patronal support from Florence would be uncertain at best. Finally, in August, Cardinal Robert Bellarmine died, just a few weeks short of his eightieth birthday.

Whether it was because he sensed the time was now opportune or just coincidental is uncertain, but the following month, Galileo submitted his manuscript of *The Assayer* to the Academy of the Lynx in Rome, to prepare it for publication. In early 1623, the censor of books in Rome granted it an *imprimatur*, on the recommendation of Dominican theological consultant Niccoló Riccardi (1585–1639). In addition, Riccardi, who because of his girth had been callously nicknamed "Father Monster" by King Philip III of Spain, also took the opportunity to give a glowing and unprecedented endorsement of the book, perhaps because it refuted the thinking of a member of the Society of Jesus.

In August 1623, while *The Assayer* was still at the printer, Gregory XV died suddenly after a pontificate of less than three years. Then, a stunned Galileo got the news that his friend Cardinal Maffeo Barberini had succeeded Gregory as Pope Urban VIII. Galileo called his friend's election a "marvelous conjuncture" and saw a door now wide open to acceptance of the new astronomy, remarking "we are about to see the most precious learning recalled from its long exile."[27] As pope, Urban VIII continued to see himself as a supportive patron of the intellectual world and soon promoted to cardinal his nephew Francesco Barberini (1597–1679), a member of the Academy of the Lynx and a close friend and supporter of Galileo. The great fear now among Galileo's critics was that his friendship with Urban would lead to the nullification of the censure against Copernicanism (1616), and he would then be unstoppable.

Hurriedly, Galileo added to *The Assayer* a dedication to Pope Urban VIII, who just three years earlier had written a poem in honor of Galileo and had referred to himself as "your brother." The pontiff reacted favorably to the book when it finally appeared. The Jesuits, however, were incensed that Galileo had attacked "one of their own." In addition, the Jesuit Christoph Scheiner assumed that Galileo had also attacked *him* in *The Assayer* and began laying plans for a response. The Jesuits must have also felt let down by Urban, who had been educated at the Roman College and, on the very day he was installed as pope, canonized Ignatius Loyola (1491–1556) as well as the great Jesuit missionary Francis Xavier (1506–1552). Galileo had underestimated Jesuit solidarity and had unwittingly begun the process of alienation from the Society of Jesus, which in the end would contribute significantly to his difficulties with church authorities.

In April 1624, sixty-year-old Galileo arrived in Rome for the fourth time, in the hopes of having the censure against Copernicanism lifted. Over the course of two months, he had six lengthy meetings with Urban, who assured Galileo that the church had not defined Copernicanism as heretical and would never do so. Galileo could thus write what he wanted about Copernicanism as long as it was presented as a theory rather than truth. Urban did, however, make clear his belief in God's boundless creativity in nature, as well as his conviction that the speculation of philosophers and mathematicians about the nature of the universe could lead to belief but never certitude, since this would presume to place limitations on the power of God.[28] Not an uncommon view at the time, Urban had seen confirmation of his position in the "story of the cicada" in Galileo's *Assayer* and almost certainly felt that Galileo would recognize it as such.

Before Galileo's departure in June 1624, the pope gave him silver and gold papal medallions, a painting, a promise of a church pension for his son, Vincenzio, who had been legitimized by the grand duke of Tuscany, and the promise of a new chaplain for the convent of Galileo's daughter, Sister Maria Celeste.[29] So confident now was Galileo of his position that he decided to take on Francesco Ingoli, who had attacked him five years earlier, in spite of the fact that Ingoli was now secretary of the Congregation for the Propagation of the Faith in Rome.

But though Galileo's old nemesis, Ludovico delle Colombe, was long dead, there were others who still sought ways to discredit him, and, in 1625, they thought they had found one. A recently discovered document shows that Galileo was anonymously denounced to the Holy Office in 1625 because of his acceptance of the atomic theory of matter in *The Assayer,* which the denunciation alleged was incompatible with the doctrine of transubstantiation. The consultor assigned to examine *The Assayer,* however, concluded that there was nothing heretical in it and that Galileo's treatment of the motion of the earth did not even merit concern. It seems plausible that the denunciation was perhaps made because of a desire to link Galileo to Giordano Bruno, whose condemnation in 1600 had in part been because of his views on transubstantiation.[30]

Cleared of all charges and bristling with confidence, Galileo began in 1625 to revise his essay on the tides (1616), but his critics became more vocal. In 1626, Orazio Grassi published a reply to *The Assayer,* and, in 1630, Christoph Scheiner attacked Galileo in *Rosa Ursina Sive Sol,* though at the same time he accepted Galileo's argument that sunspots are in fact on the surface of the sun.[31]

Galileo continued revision of his essay on tides, but poor health, in particular chronic rheumatism, dragged the project out over five years. It was finally completed in June 1630, with the new title *Dialogue concerning the Two Chief World Systems,* and was to have been published by the Academy of the Lynx, but then disaster struck. Galileo's friend and patron Prince Cesi died, destitute after so many years of supporting scholarship. Undaunted, Galileo pressed ahead and left for Rome to obtain permission to publish his work.

On May 3, 1630, Galileo arrived in Rome for the fifth time, where his protégé, Benedetto Castelli, an expert in hydraulics, was already residing as papal consultant concerning river flooding. Castelli informed Galileo that the *imprimatur* should go smoothly, since Niccoló Riccardi, who had recommended approval for *The Assayer* six years earlier, was now Master of the Sacred Palace and thus ultimately responsible for all publication permissions. In addition, Galileo was still in high favor with Urban VIII, whose nephew Cardinal Francesco Barberini remarked to Galileo that he had "no better friend than the pope and himself."[32] Indeed, the pope made Galileo a cathedral canon of Pisa, for which he was tonsured and received a modest church pension. Galileo, like Copernicus, had become a non-ordained member of the clergy. It should be pointed out that the Council of Trent laid down as a necessary qualification for cathedral canons that they be men of piety and examples to others.

After pressure from some of Galileo's high-placed friends in Rome, Riccardi agreed to grant the *imprimatur,* but only if Galileo rewrote the preface and the conclusion. As for the rest of the *Dialogue,* which Riccardi had not yet read, he insisted that he would read it and correct it page by page as it came off the press. Riccardi would later maintain that he had been ordered by Urban himself to grant final permission for publication of the *Dialogue,* though Urban denied this.[33]

Galileo left for Florence on June 26, 1630, confident that his book would soon appear, but then an outbreak of the plague, which claimed the life of Galileo's brother in Germany, made travel and communications between Florence and Rome difficult. Galileo asked if his book could be published in Florence instead, to which Riccardi agreed, as long as the inquisitor in Florence approved the book. Inquisition officials in Florence, however, issued an *imprimatur* after only a cursory perusal of Galileo's book, confident that the *imprimatur* granted by Riccardi already had involved a thorough reading of the text.

It was not until February 1632 that the first copies appeared, which were an immediate success among those sympathetic to Copernicanism. The *Dialogue* was structured as a conversation about the universe among three friends over the course of four days in a palace in Venice. Salviati, who is the mouthpiece for Galileo, was a tribute to his deceased friend Filippo Salviati (1582–1614). In the character of Salviati, Galileo felt free to make brilliant arguments in support of Copernicanism, since he was doing so under the guise of a fictional character.

The character Sagredo, an open-minded intellectual not yet convinced of the truth of Copernicanism but leaning strongly in that direction, undoubtedly honored Galileo's other deceased friend Gianfrancesco Sagredo (1571–1620). The character Simplicio was likely modeled on Ludovico delle Colombe, as well as the ancient philosopher Simplicius (490–560), who had written a commentary on Aristotle. It is not surprising that he represents the Aristotelian point of view and offers weak challenges to Salviati's arguments in favor of Copernicanism.

The *Dialogue* continued Galileo's sharp critique of Aristotelianism and affirmation of Copernicanism. Yet there was no new evidence to support it. Galileo's central argument was still his belief that the tides could be caused only by the revolution and orbit of the earth, in spite of the fact that Johannes Kepler had already argued that the tides were in fact caused by the moon. Salviati/Galileo does not even mention the universe system of Danish astronomer Tycho Brahe (1546–1601), according to which all the other planets revolved around the sun, all of which together revolved around a motionless earth. Although Brahe's system is now known to be incorrect, it accommodated all of Galileo's discoveries about Jupiter, Venus, and sunspots, while still retaining the earth at the center of the universe. Many leading astronomers adhered to it, including Christopher Clavius, who had died in 1612. Clavius realized that Galileo's observations rendered untenable the Ptolemaic universe as it had been previously understood, but, concerned that Copernicanism contradicted scripture, he embraced the model of Brahe as the more orthodox hypothesis.

The only caveat about Copernicanism was found in the words of Simplicio to Salviati: "I am not entirely convinced . . . keeping always before my mind's eye a most solid doctrine that I once heard from a most eminent and learned person." Assuming for the sake of argument that Salviati and Sagredo would agree that God can do many things in nature that are incomprehensible to us, Simplicio concludes that "it would be excessive boldness for anyone to limit and restrict the divine power and wisdom to some particular fancy of his own."[34] It was the very same point that Urban had raised in conversation with Galileo in the aftermath of reading *The Assayer*.

Galileo's detractors seized on this point and convinced Pope Urban that Galileo had in fact mocked him through the character of Simplicio. It almost certainly had not been Galileo's intention, since he enjoyed a close friendship with Urban and would have gained nothing by such a brazen insult. Nevertheless, feeling that their friendship had been abused and betrayed, Urban ordered publication of the book stopped, and all copies retrieved. A special papal commission in September 1632 alleged that Galileo had defended Copernicanism as fact, wrongly attributed the tides to the motion of the earth, and most surprisingly to Pope Urban VIII, had violated the terms of a purported Holy Office injunction (1616) not to treat Copernicanism in *any* way.[35]

Another Summons to Rome

Galileo was summoned to Rome in October 1632, unaware of the exact charges against him. After unsuccessfully convincing church authorities that he was too ill to travel, he finally arrived on February 13, 1633, just two days shy of his seventieth birthday. Instead of imprisonment, he was housed for two months at the Tuscan Embassy in the stately Villa Medici before being transferred to the headquarters of the Holy Office. There, he was given a suite of rooms, a personal servant, and meals sent daily from the Tuscan Embassy. While at the Tuscan Embassy, Galileo received a letter of support from his daughter and was no doubt moved to discover that she had signed her letter *S. M. Celeste Galilei,* using their family name in correspondence with him for the first time.[36]

The trial began in April 1633. The commissary general in charge of the proceedings was Dominican cardinal Vincenzo Maculano (1578–1667), who in fact was quite sympathetic to Copernicanism. When he asked Galileo to recount what had happened seventeen years earlier, in 1616, Galileo narrated the sequence of events as recorded in the letter written by Bellarmine. Then, to everyone's surprise, Galileo produced the letter itself for all to read.

After the panel had examined the letter, a document from the Holy Office was produced, dated February 26, 1616, which portrayed a very different version of events. It stated that Galileo had in fact been ordered in the name of His Holiness the Pope, and that of the Congregation of the Holy Office, to relinquish altogether the said opinion, namely, that the sun is at the center of the universe and immobile, and that the earth moves; nor henceforth to hold, teach, or defend it in any way, either verbally or in writing. Otherwise, proceedings would be taken against him by the Holy Office. The said Galileo acquiesced in this ruling and promised to obey it.[37]

Though the authenticity of the document has been established by modern scholars, it was unsigned, not notarized, and never published, which meant that it should not have been considered an official document or canonical decision of the Holy Office. What then, was it?

It has been suggested that it was minutes taken by an anonymous individual at the proceedings. This would mean that although it was not an official document, Galileo [and Bellarmine] had lied about the sequence of events. Another suggested scenario is that in the meeting, before Galileo had agreed to Bellarmine's admonition, the commissary general intervened with the more strongly worded statement, and Galileo agreed to it out of confusion. Bellarmine then told Galileo that the commissary general had overstepped his bounds and that he was not obliged to follow the more strongly worded admonition.[38]

A third, simpler possibility exists, however. The content of the document is strikingly similar to what Paul V had told Bellarmine would happen if Galileo did *not* acquiesce to an admonition to abandon Copernicanism. It seems plausible, then, that the document had been drawn up in the event that Galileo balked at the gentler admonition, which would explain why it was unsigned and not notarized. It would have been easy for such a document to find its way into the files of the Holy Office and, without any explanation as to its purpose, *appear* seventeen years later to be a formal admonition against Galileo.

The panel, however, assumed the worst, and began to question Galileo as to whether this in fact *had* been the decision during his interview with the Holy Office in 1616. Galileo countered that he remembered only being admonished not to treat Copernicanism as more than just a theory, as reflected in Bellarmine's letter. At age sixty-nine and in poor health, however, he could not say with certainty that nothing else had been said. But he insisted in spite of what might have been said, the most important document was Bellarmine's letter, which had formed the basis of his subsequent actions with regard to Copernicanism.[39]

Asked whether he had revealed the alleged formal injunction of 1616 when seeking permission to publish his *Dialogue,* Galileo again denied active knowledge of it and insisted that he had abided by the terms of Bellarmine's letter. In the end, the commission focused on the fact that in his *Dialogue*, Galileo had upheld Copernicanism, had ridiculed Ptolemy and Aristotelianism, and had attempted to establish further proofs of a heliocentric universe. It was an accurate assessment, if one discounts the fact that Galileo was speaking through fictional characters.

Commissary general Maculano and Urban VIII's nephew, Cardinal Barberini, however, were by no means enemies of Galileo. They worked out a plea bargain, in which Galileo would admit he had overstepped bounds in his book in return for a light sentence of a penance and temporary house arrest until corrections were made in the *Dialogue*. Galileo agreed, and in a statement of contrition (April 30th), he admitted that his evidence in support of Copernicanism was inconclusive and contrary to how he portrayed it in his *Dialogue,* and that his error was one of "vainglorious ambition and of ignorance and inadvertence." His initial interview over, Galileo was allowed to move back to the Tuscan Embassy at Villa Medici.[40]

Unfortunately, the plea bargain was unacceptable to Pope Urban, who insisted that Galileo's true intent in writing the *Dialogue* be found, "even with the threat of torture." He was then to abjure formally before the Holy Office, after which he was to be sentenced to prison, the length of which was to be determined by the Holy Office. Furthermore, Galileo's *Dialogue concerning the Two Chief World Systems* was to be prohibited, and he was not to discuss heliocentrism any further, either in print or verbally.

It must be pointed out that the threat of torture was formulaic language in Holy Office investigations and that even Galileo likely realized that it would never have been used on someone of his advanced age or state of poor health, particularly given his friendship, albeit strained, with Urban VIII. Furthermore, contrary to the play *Galileo*, by Bertolt Brecht (1898–1956), Galileo was *never* shown the instruments of torture.

Cardinal Maculano was striving to show leniency toward Galileo but, in accordance with the decision of Pope Urban, questioned him on June 21 about his true intent in writing his *Dialogue*.[41] It was at this point that Galileo committed perhaps one of his greatest blunders. Foolishly, he tried to argue that his *Dialogue* was *against* rather than *for* Copernicanism and that he had subscribed to the Aristotelian/Ptolemaic view of the universe since 1616. Understandably, many in the Holy Office felt that their intelligence had been insulted.

The final decision of the Holy Office was that Galileo was "vehemently suspected of heresy" for adhering to heliocentrism and for believing that "any opinion may be held and defended as probable after it has been declared and defined contrary to Holy Scripture." Consistent with the wishes of Pope Urban, Galileo would receive absolution after he had abjured himself before representatives of the Holy Office, and his *Dialogue Concerning the Two Chief World Systems* would be prohibited altogether. Furthermore, he was to be incarcerated in a formal prison of the Holy Office and, for three years, was to recite the seven penitential psalms each week.[42] Cardinals Barberini, Laudivio Zacchia, and Gasparo Borgia (1580–1645) refused to join the other seven cardinals of the Holy Office in signing the decree against Galileo.

On June 22, 1633, Galileo knelt before representatives of the Holy Office in the church of Santa Maria Sopra Minerva as the sentence against him was read.[43] He then formally abjured but only after convincing officials to remove from his oath the implication that he was not a good Catholic and the suggestion that he had gained an *imprimatur* for his *Dialogue* by trickery. He admitted upholding heliocentrism in his *Dialogue,* in spite of the prohibition against Copernicanism (1616), and promised never to discuss heliocentrism again, in any way, shape, or form. Contrary to the long-standing myth, after forsaking the notion of a stationary sun and an orbiting earth, Galileo did not in fact mutter under his breath, "Yet it does move!"

Galileo then received absolution, and almost immediately, the sentence against him was softened. His imprisonment took the form of house arrest in the spacious buildings and gardens of the Villa Medici, which led his daughter Sister Maria Celeste to remark that it was "a promise of leniency demonstrated toward you, Sire, by His Holiness, who has destined for your prison a place so delightful, whereby it appears we may anticipate another commutation of your sentence conforming even more closely with all your and our wishes."[44] Sure enough, Sister Maria Celeste was soon allowed to recite the seven penitential psalms for the next three years in place of her father, which she was delighted to do.

On July 6, 1633, after just two weeks at the Villa Medici, Galileo left Rome for the last time, when Urban VIII allowed him to travel to Siena to stay with his friend, scholar and mathematician Archbishop Ascanio Piccolomini (1590–1671), whose family had produced two popes. Instead of being treated as a penitent prisoner, Galileo became a guest of honor and enjoyed numerous evening meals at the archbishop's residence, which was also frequented by influential persons who sympathized with Galileo. Finally, in December 1633, Galileo was given permission to return to his villa at Arcetri, just outside Florence.

One of the bitterest blows to Galileo was the death of his daughter Sister Maria Celeste in 1634, shortly after he had returned to Florence. Though no longer allowed to write on Copernicanism and blind from 1637 on, the despondent Galileo could still write on other aspects of physics. Accordingly, he spent the remainder of his days working on his *Discourses on Two New*

Sciences (1638), which reprised the characters of Sagredo, Simplicio, and Salviati, though with language much more subdued than previously, and no longer addressing the issue of Copernicanism. The *Dialogue concerning the Two Chief Systems of the Word*, however, would gain new life and have an impact on the scientific world, when in 1635, a Latin translation was published in Protestant Strasbourg, beyond the jurisdiction of the inquisition.

Galileo was technically forbidden to receive any visitors at his villa in Florence other than family, lest he discuss Copernicanism, but this proved unenforceable. In addition to famed Dutch legal scholar and theologian Hugo Grotius (1583–1645), Galileo was visited in 1636 by Thomas Hobbes (1588–1679). The English philosopher was particularly fascinated by Galileo's theory of reverse dynamics, which held that the natural state of objects was, in fact, motion, until they were stopped—a concept that Hobbes subsequently attempted to apply to social philosophy. Hobbes was followed in 1638 by author John Milton (1608–1674), who had read Galileo's *Dialogue* and would later write in his *Areopagitica* of his visit to "the famous Galileo, grown old, a prisoner to the Inquisition, for thinking in astronomy otherwise than the Franciscan and Dominican licensers thought." Milton would also write in *Paradise Lost* of "the moon, whose orb, through optic glass, the Tuscan artist views, at evening from the top of Fiesole."

Galileo died quietly of apparent kidney failure in Florence, a month shy of seventy-nine, on January 8, 1642, the same year that Isaac Newton was born. Under pressure from Rome, his burial in Florence was not in the church proper of Santa Croce but rather in a hallway between the transept and the sacristy. When Pope Urban died two years later, however, he would also experience a degree of posthumous ignominy, when a statue of him in the courtyard of the Roman College was defaced, not over the Galileo affair but because of his support for various military campaigns in Italy.[45]

Contrary to the popular perception, it did not take long for the church to come to a deeper appreciation of Galileo. In 1737, his body was brought to the main part of the church of Santa Croce and placed in an ornate mausoleum, along with the remains of his daughter Sister Maria Celeste. In 1741, Pope Benedict XIV (1740–1758) instructed the Holy Office to grant an *imprimatur* to the first complete edition of Galileo's works, with the exception of the *Dialogue concerning the Two Chief World Systems*, and, in 1758, the general ban on Copernican works was lifted. In 1822, specific prohibitions of Copernican works were officially removed from the Index of Forbidden Books, and, in 1835, Galileo's *Dialogue* was finally removed.

In recent years, the Vatican has taken steps that eventually would lead to concrete validation of Galileo's theories, both scientific and religious. The Second Vatican Council, in its decree *Gaudium et Spes*, rejected the notion of the mutual opposition of faith and science, "for earthly matters and the concerns of faith derive from the same God." The humble and steady mind, as long as it is in conformity with moral norms, is "being led by the hand of God, who holds all things in existence, and gives them their identity." The decree goes on to deplore "certain attitudes which have existed among Christians themselves, insufficiently attentive to the legitimate autonomy of science." Many minds have concluded that faith and science are mutually opposed because they are sources of tensions and conflicts. Because of dissent among some participants in the council, the decree never mentions Galileo by name, but his complete works are clearly footnoted in this section of the decree.

Pope Paul VI praised Galileo during a visit to his tomb in 1965 and in a homily the same year to the National Eucharistic Congress of Italy meeting in Pisa. He spoke of "the celebrated immortal memory of the great men of Tuscany, Galileo, Michelangelo, and Dante."

Then, on November 10, 1979, in an address to the Pontifical Academy of Sciences commemorating the first centenary of the birth of Albert Einstein, Pope John Paul II spoke of the suffering that Galileo had endured "at the hands of men and organisms of the Church." The pope then quoted the above-cited passage from *Gaudium et Spes* which had decried the notion of mutual opposition between faith and science and stated his wish "that theologians, scholars and historians . . . might examine more deeply the Galileo case, and, in an honest recognition of wrongs on whatever side they occur, might make disappear the obstacles that this affair still sets up in many minds, to a fruitful concord between science and faith, between the church and world."

In praising Galileo, whom John Paul II stated is "rightly called the founder of modern physics," he quotes from his *Letter to Castelli* and his *Letter to the Grand Duchess Christina*, and insists that Galileo's beliefs on the proper interpretation of scripture with regard to matters of science is the correct one and fully conforms to the norms of the church today. He also praises Galileo's "confession of divine illumination in the mind of the scientist" in *The Starry Messenger*, which led him to believe that the discoveries he made with his telescope were only because of God's grace. In Rome, 346 years after Galileo had knelt and abjured in the church of Santa Maria Sopra Minerva, Pope John Paul II had essentially reopened the case.

A special papal study commission for a formal reexamination of the Galileo affair was created on July 3, 1981. It completed its work ten years later and submitted its findings on October 31, 1992—the year of the 350th anniversary of the death of Galileo. In his speech responding to the work of the commission, John Paul II saw in the Galileo affair the great lesson that experts in science and religion must be aware of the "limits of their competencies" in the event that they find themselves one day in a similar situation with regard to tension between science and faith.

John Paul II also gave unequivocal affirmation to Galileo's exegetical skills, stating that Galileo "showed himself to be more perceptive in this regard than the theologians who opposed him," and reiterated the importance of the *Letter to Castelli* and the *Letter to the Grand Duchess Christina*, which he had already noted in his speech in 1979. Overall, the pope deemed the Galileo affair a "tragic mutual incomprehension" that has "been interpreted as the reflection of a fundamental opposition between science and faith," and declared that because of the work of the commission, this "sad misunderstanding now belongs to the past." Galileo had officially been rehabilitated.

The Myth of Science Versus Religion

Yet false perceptions remain. The simplistic view of a brilliant Galileo struggling against an oppressive church that placed no value on intellectual discovery or innovation is still quite common. The genius of Galileo is beyond question. Yet he was a genius with flaws. Though geocentrism was never a doctrine of the church, it had been part of the Christian worldview for 1,600 years, and Galileo was now asking the world to believe something different, on the basis of "his authority alone," without having offered conclusive proof of its validity, and on the basis of some scientific conclusions that would later prove to be completely wrong. Though never excommunicated, he had attempted to skirt the church authorities and overplayed his hand. Galileo's apparent inability to engage in civil discourse, combined with his belief that he had somehow been designated by God to be the herald of the new science, made collaboration with others almost unthinkable. Thus, he ignored Kepler's correct theory about elliptical orbits and the moon as the true cause of the tides. Instead, Galileo chose the path of polemic and alienation, leading one scholar to remark that "the triumph of truth and the glorification of Galileo tended to merge into one."[46]

And it was not just his opponents who were alienated. When it came to weighing friendship against his quest for acceptance and affirmation of his theories, Galileo came up short. Clavius and the rest of the Jesuits had given him clear support, which Galileo repaid with an attack on Grassi, who in the end felt that Galileo had ruined himself by becoming "infatuated with his own genius and by wholly disdaining that of others." Christopher Grienberger, S.J. (1561–1580), successor to Clavius at the Roman College and privately sympathetic to Copernicanism, put it more diplomatically: "If Galileo had known how to retain the affection of the Fathers of this College, he would have lived gloriously before the world, and none of his misfortunes would have happened, and he would have been able to write as he chose about everything, including the motion of the earth."[47]

Most important, of course, was the damage Galileo did to his friendship with Pope Urban VIII. Nothing could illustrate this better than the very fact that although Galileo was almost certainly not trying to mock Urban VIII through the character of Simplicio, he still lacked the relational astuteness to realize that this is how the pontiff would interpret it. Without the *Dialogue,* there would have been no *Simplicio,* and without *Simplicio,* there almost certainly would not have been a trial in 1633.

Yet in spite of his character flaws and strategic blunders, Galileo was both brilliant scientist and loyal Catholic, whose two daughters had become nuns, and whose grandson, Cosimo Galilei, would become a Vincentian priest. In the end, it seems appropriate to let him have the last words, which are found in a letter dated February 21, 1635: "I have two sources of perpetual comfort: first, that in my writings there cannot be found the faintest shadow of irreverence towards the Holy Church; and second, the testimony of my own conscience, which only I and God in Heaven thoroughly know. And He knows that in this cause for which I suffer, though many might have spoken with more learning, none, not even the ancient Fathers, has spoken with more piety or with greater zeal for the Church than I."

Questions for Reflection and Discussion

1. Did the Galileo affair signal an inherent incompatibility between religion and science?

2. What do you think was Galileo's greatest error during the course of his career? What do you think was the greatest error on the part of church authorities?

3. Can you think of contemporary scientific discoveries that might cause similar tensions between the scientific community and the Catholic Church?

7

Pius XII and Nazi Germany

The alleged silence of Pope Pius XII during the Holocaust is a fairly recent perception that does not square with widespread praise that the pope received from prominent Jewish leaders after World War II. Yet in their efforts to defend him, Pius XII's supporters have tended to the opposite extreme, praising almost his every action during World War II during what was clearly the most complex period in his pontificate. An objective assessment must not only look at the pontificate of Pius XII but must also assess whether his actions during World War II were unique or were, in fact, consistent with papal policies that had been in place since World War I.

———◀○▶———

Nothing can be useful, if it is not at the same time morally good.
—Cicero, *Offices*, ii. 30

Neither of the denominations—Catholic or Protestant, they are both the same—has any future left. At least not for the Germans. Fascism may perhaps make its peace with the Church in God's name. I will do it too. Why not? But that won't stop me from stamping out Christianity in Germany, root and branch. One is either Christian or German. You can't be both.
—Adolf Hitler (1933)

The reign of Pius XII has become the most controversial pontificate of the modern period, over allegations of silence about the Holocaust in Nazi Germany. Fundamental to negative assessments of the pope is a presumptive moral failure on the part of the Catholic Church, exemplified by books such

151

as political scientist Daniel Goldhagen's *A Moral Reckoning: The Role of the Catholic Church in the Holocaust and Its Unfulfilled Duty of Repair* and journalist John Cornwell's *Hitler's Pope: The Secret History of Pius XII*.[1] This has led to a slew of books in defense of Pius XII, which like those that condemn Pius XII, are mostly written by non-historians from a highly polarized perspective.

Remarkably absent in most discussions is an adequate inclusion and understanding of the evolution of Pius XII's posture toward the Nazi regime during his many years as Eugenio Pacelli, papal nuncio to Germany. Furthermore, often neglected is consideration of the fact that as pope, Pius XII fought to preserve the existence of Christianity itself in Germany, which Hitler aspired to eradicate through persecution and executions. Historical perspective seems only to have sharpened and further polarized the debate, which has become more heated with initiation of the canonization process for the pontiff. How, then, is one to understand the matter objectively and get a sense of the intense struggles faced by the Jews of Europe, the Catholic Church, and Pius XII in the face of a totalitarian regime and genocide program unlike anything the world had ever seen? One must begin with a review of wartime and postwar perceptions of Pius XII, followed by an examination of his role as papal nuncio and as pope.

In 1940, Albert Einstein, who had fled Nazi Germany, wrote that "only the Church stood squarely across the path of Hitler's campaign for suppressing the truth . . . I am forced thus to confess that what I once despised I now praise unreservedly." First president of Israel, Chaim Weizmann (1874–1952), attested during the war to the significant assistance to Jews given by Pius XII, and, during a wartime meeting with the pope, Israel's second prime minister, Moshe Sharett (1894–1965), expressed his gratitude. Isaac Herzog (1888–1959), the chief rabbi of Jerusalem, conveyed through an intermediary his gratitude to Pius XII for the "invaluable help given by the Catholic Church to the Jewish people" and his "assurance that the people of Israel know how to value his assistance and his attitude."[2]

The immediate aftermath of World War II saw a continuation of praise for Pope Pius XII. Herzog sent a special blessing to the pontiff and again thanked him for his help, and similar expressions of gratitude came from the chief rabbis of Egypt, London, and France. Israel Zolli (1881–1956), the chief rabbi of Rome, even became a Roman Catholic and took the name Eugenio—Pius XII's given name. Dr. Nahum Goldmann (1894–1982), president of the World Jewish Congress, donated $20,000 to Vatican charities, remarking that "with special gratitude we remember all he [Pius XII] has done for the persecuted Jews during one of the darkest periods in their entire history."

This praise was not simply temporary postwar euphoria. On the death of Pius XII in 1958, Pinchas E. Lapide (1922–1997), who had fought in Italy in General Montgomery's Jewish-English brigade and after the war served as Israeli consul in Italy, stated that "the Catholic Church saved more Jewish lives during the war than all the other churches, religious institutions and rescue organizations put together," and credited the Holy See with saving the lives of hundreds of thousands of Jews. First female prime minister of Israel, Golda Meir (1898–1978), at the time foreign minister, remarked in a speech to the United Nations that Pius XII "affirmed the high ideals of peace and compassion" and that "during the ten years of Nazi terror . . . the Pope raised his voice to condemn the persecutors and to commiserate with their victims."

Remarkably, and without any supporting evidence whatsoever, Goldhagen dismisses the above-mentioned praise as coming from "Jews who were more concerned with contemporary politics, with inhibiting the expression of more anti-Semitism, and with trying, in vain, to get the powerful Church to take a more favorable position on Israel."[3] Yet one must understand that Goldhagen is operating on the basis of a forty-year canon of perception about Pius XII, which had its beginnings not in historical revelations based on newly discovered documents but rather in a German play.

In June 1963, *The Deputy* (*Der Stellvertreter*) was published by German author Rolf Hochhuth (b. 1931).[4] The play is a stinging indictment of Pius XII and his handling of the extermination policies of Nazi Germany. The two central characters are German SS Lieutenant Kurt Gerstein and Italian-German Jesuit Riccardo Fontana. Kurt Gerstein (1905–1945) was a historical, though highly enigmatic, figure, who claimed at the end of the war that he had only joined the SS in order to work secretly on behalf of Jews and tell the world what was happening in the concentration camps. Though Fontana is fictional, his character is based on Fr. Bernhard Lichtenberg (1875–1943), provost of the Berlin cathedral, who died on the way to Dachau after offering public prayers on behalf of the Jews.

Gerstein is unable to convince the papal nuncio in Berlin of the genocide but does convince the nuncio's secretary, Fontana, who in turn, in a meeting that never actually took place, attempted to convince Pope Pius XII to speak out forcefully against Hitler's policies of extermination. Pius XII's response is that of a cold, fist-pounding, angry bureaucrat, who is more interested in Vatican finances than listening attentively to Fontana. The pope is likened to the notorious Renaissance pope Alexander VI and the soul in Dante's *Inferno* who, through cowardice, had made "the great refusal." He is Pilate, who has washed his hands of the Jews, and a "criminal," whose "silence . . . in favor of the murderers" makes the entire church guilty.[5]

On June 21, 1963, a letter to the editor was received at the office of the widely read Catholic periodical *London Tablet*, which questioned the veracity of the Hochhuth play, and which it described not as historical reality but rather a "distorted representational pseudoreality." Though the letter had been written by Cardinal Giovanni Montini, who just hours earlier had been elected Pope Paul VI, it had little positive impact. After all, the preface to *The Deputy* had been written by Nobel Prize-winning humanitarian Albert Schweitzer (1875–1965), who declared it "an indictment of an historical personality who placed upon himself the great responsibility of silence" and insisted that the Catholic Church bore "the greater guilt" for what happened in Nazi Germany, since the Protestant church "was an unorganized, impotent, national power."

This perception that Pius XII was the only one who could have stopped the Holocaust, and failed to do so, grew steadily. The difficulty, however, is that the play of the non-historian Hochhuth is fatally flawed in its facts. Even John Cornwell, whose book *Hitler's Pope* is otherwise harshly critical of Pius XII, calls the Hochhuth play "historical fiction based on scant documentation" and terms the portrayal of Pius XII "ludicrous." *The Deputy,* in Cornwell's words, "offends the most basic criteria of documentary: that such stories and portrayals are valid only if they are demonstrably true." [6] What then, *are* some of the demonstrably true facts concerning Pius XII and the Nazi regime?

Responses to the Rise of the Nazi Party

On March 2, 1939, on the third round of voting in the shortest conclave since 1623, Vatican secretary of state Eugenio Pacelli became Pope Pius XII, receiving forty-eight out of fifty-three votes. No Vatican secretary of state had been elected pope since 1667, and no Roman since 1721. Though a titular archbishop, Pacelli had never actually administered a diocese. Yet he had seemed the only logical choice. An experienced papal diplomat fluent in German, he represented the Vatican in Germany from 1917 to 1930 and would be the most able to deal with the inevitable initiation of hostilities from Hitler's Germany. Few at his papal installation, however, would have guessed that the outbreak of hostilities was only three days away.

Born in Rome in 1876 to an aristocratic family that had already produced a number of civil lawyers as well as canon lawyers, there was never a doubt that Eugenio Pacelli would also have a church career. He received the extraordinarily rare permission, however, to do his seminary studies as a day student and live at home, ostensibly because seminary food did not agree with him. Intensely shy, Pacelli did additional studies at the Gregorian University as well as at other

Roman universities, and was ordained to the priesthood in 1899. By 1904, his career as a papal diplomat was set when he became secretary to Vatican secretary of state Cardinal Pietro Gasparri (1852–1934). After a brief teaching stint, Pacelli was made a titular archbishop in 1917 and dispatched as papal nuncio to Munich to find out Germany's preconditions for peace talks. And it would be in Munich that Pacelli was first exposed to what would become his own wartime policy as Pius XII.

Benedict XV (1914–1922), who felt that World War I had turned Europe into a charnel house, would not even allow military chaplains to wear their uniforms within the Vatican. He was determined to bring the conflict to an end with a threefold strategy. First, he insisted on absolute impartiality for the Vatican. Only in this way, he believed, could he play an effective and credible role as peacemaker. Second, he insisted on doing what he could to alleviate the suffering of those affected by the war. He utilized both his family inheritance as well as Vatican funds in this pursuit, to the extent that on his death there was only $20,000 left in the Vatican treasury and a loan was necessary for the conclave that elected his successor. Finally, Benedict declared the futility of war in his encyclical *Ad Beatissimi* (September 1914) and in 1915 instituted the worldwide Prayer for Peace.

In Germany, Pacelli became an important part of implementing the peace-brokering element of the pope's war strategy and, after the war, stayed on as nuncio to the newly created Weimar Republic. Few historians would deny that the Versailles Treaty (1919), which ended World War I, was designed to punish Germany economically. The collapse of the German economy led to severe food shortages and hyperinflation so great that people literally used wheelbarrows to transport money for shopping trips. Pacelli observed this suffering first-hand and developed a great degree of sympathy for the German people. Benedict XV's successor, Pius XI (1922–1939), had similar sentiments, which led some to sarcastically refer to the official Vatican newspaper *Osservatore Romano* as *Osservatore Tedesco* ("The German Observer").

Pacelli was also deeply concerned about preserving the rights of Catholics in Germany, long-regarded as second-class and disloyal citizens, after nineteenth-century German chancellor Otto von Bismarck (1815–1898) had insisted that the pope and Catholic clergy were foreign interlopers.[7] The marginalization of Catholics in the political and social life of Germany led Pacelli to negotiate concordats with Bavaria (1924), Prussia (1929), and Baden (1932) in an effort to guarantee them a fair juridical status. Then, in 1929, after twelve years in Germany, Pacelli was recalled to Rome, where Pius XI made him a cardinal and appointed him the new Vatican secretary of state.

Meanwhile, in Germany, the Nationalsozialistische Deutsche Arbeiterpartei (National Socialist Worker's Party), abbreviated to Nazi, was gaining ground under the leadership of Adolf Hitler (1889–1945). In his charismatic speeches, the Austrian-born veteran of World War I hit the raw nerve that affected almost every German—the lack of national self-esteem and the shattered economy in the aftermath of the Versailles Treaty. Convinced that Hitler would restore national pride and rebuild the economy, membership in the party soared. The economic devastation of Weimar Germany, however, was also a fertile ground for anti-Semitic scapegoating. Hitler explicitly blamed the Jews for many of the afflictions that had beset Germany and made the restoration of a pure Aryan race an integral part of his program, though what this fully entailed would be kept hidden until the Wannsee Conference on January 20, 1942, when the "final solution" of the "Jewish question" was developed.

There were objections to Nazi ideology as early as 1929, when the archbishop of Mainz, Ludwig Maria Hugo (1871–1935), declared that a Catholic could not belong to the Nazi party and barred members from receiving the sacraments. In 1931, cardinals Adolf Bertram (1859–1945) of Breslau and Michael von Faulhaber (1869–1952) of Munich condemned National Socialism, as did the bishops of Bavaria, who declared it to be a type of heresy. By 1932, the German episcopacy as a body had endorsed a ban on membership in the Nazi party, though there were individual bishops who dissented.[8]

The objections of the bishops, however, were explicitly about Hitler's emphasis on the superiority of the state and threatened curtailment of religious liberties rather than about anti-Semitism, which had been a reality since A.D. 69, when Christians denied their Jewish roots after the Roman destruction of the Temple in Jerusalem. Throughout the Middle Ages, Jews were the scapegoats for all that went wrong in society, which sometimes led to violent pogroms. Canon 68 of the ecumenical Fourth Lateran Council (1215) even required that Jews wear distinguishing dress. In France, between 1870 and 1894, approximately one third of all anti-Semitic literature was written by Catholic priests, and anti-Semitism had also been assimilated by many nineteenth century Germans.[9]

That having been said, a subtle but important distinction must be made between *religious* anti-Semitism and *racial* anti-Semitism. Religious anti-Semitism perceived the Jews negatively for their rejection of Christian salvation, though if a Jew were to be baptized, he would be considered an equal to other Christians (this belief, however, was not shared in fifteenth- and sixteenth-century Spain). Racial anti-Semitism, however, held that no matter what a Jew believed, even if baptized, he was still a Jew and would always be inferior. This latter view would eventually lead to a large number of Jewish Catholics being sent to concentration camps.

Furthermore, the connection between social/religious anti-Semitism and the early racial anti-Semitism of Hitler was not clearly seen on either side of the Atlantic in the 1930s. The German Bund in the United States embraced Nazi ideology and boasted an official membership of 25,000. Influential icons such as Henry Ford (1863–1947), Joseph P. Kennedy (1888–1969), and Charles Lindbergh (1902–1974) were outspoken and unapologetic about their belief in the harm Jews were doing to America. Nor were Catholics immune to such thinking. The virulently anti-Semitic and racist weekly radio broadcasts from Detroit of Canadian-born priest Fr. Charles Coughlin (1891–1979) were avidly followed by 40 million listeners, and older Catholics today will remember that until the Second Vatican Council (1962–1965), one always paused briefly during Good Friday services to "pray for the perfidious Jews."

President Roosevelt made it clear that he did not want to get into the war in Europe over persecution of Jews and made Jewish emigration almost impossible. One need only recall the tragic story of the *S.S. St. Louis*, which in May 1939 carried 930 German Jewish asylum-seekers to Florida, only to be forced back to Germany when Roosevelt refused them entry. The first concrete step Roosevelt would take on behalf of European Jews would not be until the establishment of the War Refugee Board in January 1944, a full seventeen months after he had learned of the extermination policies being carried out by the Nazi regime.

In spite of the objections of the German bishops to elements of Nazi ideology, they faced a dilemma in January of 1933, when Hitler became the legitimately elected chancellor of Germany. How could they continue to critique Nazi ideology and forbid membership in the party without exposing Catholics to charges of national disloyalty? Hitler, who was a baptized Catholic and had been educated by the Benedictines, mollified their concerns by assurances that he was a friend of the church, which was an important part of Germany's future. He also insisted that his government was the only power that could stand up to the westward spread of communism, which would surely lead to the destruction of the church.

The bishops began to soften their objections and removed the ban on membership in the party, and, in the words of one scholar, opposition "evaporated into meaningless generalities." One must not jump to the conclusion, however, that Catholic support for Hitler meant acceptance of his ultimate plan for the Jews, which in fact was an aspect of his ideology, along with his intent on eradicating Christianity, which was still well hidden.[10]

Two months later, after Hitler promised peace gestures toward France, England, and the Soviet Union, the Catholic Center Party provided Hitler the necessary votes to pass the Enabling Act, which now made the newly elected chancellor independent of the president of Germany. Four months later, in July

1933, Pius XI commissioned his secretary of state, Eugenio Pacelli, to negotiate a concordat with the new German government. The concordat, as all papal concordats, was in no way meant as an approval of a government or its teachings but was rather a pragmatic tool designed to provide Catholics a juridical base and preserve basic religious freedoms. It had no political significance. This point was made clear in *Osservatore Romano*.[11] Many Catholics in Germany, however, saw it as approval of Nazi policies, and regrettably, the bishops did little to educate people to the contrary.

In *The Deputy*, the concordat is portrayed as a vain grasp for self-aggrandizement by Pacelli, and it ultimately enabled fascism by giving the Nazi regime a sense of legitimacy. There is no doubt that Hitler exploited the concordat, which he called an "indescribable success." Furthermore, he secretly intended to do away with the parts of it that he did not care for. But for the time being, Hitler needed the church in order to maintain good relations with the Catholic Center Party, which still had enough deputies to block some of his votes, and he was thus willing to make concessions. From the Vatican perspective, a concordat was the best deal they could get, if the sacramental life of the church was to continue in Germany.[12]

Escalating Conflict

There was a growing lack of episcopal unity and leadership after the concordat, and Pacelli felt the bishops were, in fact, too conciliatory toward the Nazi regime. The insistence of the bishop of Berlin, Konrad von Preysing (1880–1950), at the National Conference of Bishops in 1933 that the Nazi regime be rejected and that a clear statement from the bishops be made about the errors of its ideology was unfortunately the exception rather than the rule.[13] Even after the Nuremberg Laws of September 1935, which prohibited marriage between Jews and non-Jews and stripped German Jews of their citizenship, exiled German Catholic writer Waldemar Gurian (1903–1954) and Fr. Bernhard Lichtenberg were among the handful who saw the fuller implications for Jews.

In a pastoral letter of 1937, the German bishops urged support of the Nazi regime as a bulwark against communism. With each political and military victory of the Nazi regime, however, Hitler found it less and less necessary to abide by the concordat. Pacelli, along with Faulhaber, von Preysing, Bertram, and Cardinal Clemens von Galen (1878–1946), became concerned that the church needed to take a stand against the regime. Thus, with the approval of Pius XI, Pacelli and Faulhaber drafted a papal encyclical, which the pope issued on Passion Sunday, 1937, under the title *Mit Brennender Sorge* ("With Burning Concern").

The Catholic press in Germany had been shut down by the government, so the following Sunday, couriers secretly distributed the encyclical, which was read from all Catholic pulpits before a single copy had been seen by Nazi officials. Written in response to "things hard and unpleasant" that had been conveyed to the pope by representatives of the German episcopate, the document declares that the "emasculation and distortion" of the concordat of 1933 has "fixed responsibilities and laid bare intrigues, which from the outset only aimed at a war of extermination" [of Christianity]. The pope rejects the "pantheistic confusion" of the "so-called pre-Christian Germanic conception of substituting a dark and impersonal destiny for the personal God." Any exaltation to an idolatrous level of race, people, the state, a particular form of the state, or a depository of power distorts and perverts God's order of creation. It is an "aggressive paganism" that promotes the "so-called myth of race and blood" above religion, and the faithful are exhorted to resist the "seduction of a national German Church," which is a "Christianity not of Christ."

Furious, Hitler threatened to cancel the concordat entirely but backed off when he realized that he would still need to be perceived as having harmonious relations with the Catholic Church, in view of his intended annexation of Catholic Austria. As for Pacelli, his role in the encyclical was well known, and he was quickly portrayed in an SS cartoon as a "Jew-lover."[14]

But Pius XI had additional plans afoot to stand up to the regime. In the summer of 1938, he recruited American Jesuit John LaFarge (1880–1963), French Jesuit Gustave Desbuquois (1869–1959), and German Jesuit Gustav Gundlach (1892–1963) to work in secret on a papal encyclical specifically denouncing Hitler's racial policies. Though *Humani Generis Unitas* ("The Unity of the Human Race") allowed that a certain level of *religious* anti-Semitism was justified, it unequivocally condemned racial anti-Semitism as misguided and cruel. Before it could be promulgated, however, Pius XI died, on February 10, 1939. The document would not see the light of day again until 1997, when several different working manuscripts were painstakingly reconstructed by two scholars.[15]

That Pius XI took seriously the danger of anti-Semitism, however, is clear. In one of his last public speeches, he compared Hitler to the emperors Nero and Julian the Apostate and insisted that it was impossible for a Christian to take part in anti-Semitism, since we were *all* Semites spiritually. In response, a Nazi periodical labeled Pius XI the "chief rabbi of the Christian world." But what would the Nazi regime now think of the just-elected Pius XII, who knew Germany so well but was also so clearly in league with the increasingly confrontational stance of his predecessor?

When German troops invaded Czechoslovakia and took Prague just three days after the election of Pius XII, it was clearly the prelude to something larger. Almost immediately, Hitler insisted that Poland return the Danzig Corridor, which Germany had been forced to cede at the end of World War I, and also allow for free communications with East Prussia. It was very clear to the newly elected pope that there would be only one central item on the agenda for his new pontificate—preservation of the peace of Europe.

Events then moved very quickly. On March 31, British prime minister Neville Chamberlain (1869–1940), anxious to contain the Soviet Union, informed the House of Commons that any overt action against Poland would lead England to assist her. The following month, France pledged the same, though the British and French now added Romania and Greece as countries that were not to be touched. Then, in a move that was utterly consistent with the wartime policies and attitudes of Benedict XV, Pius XII on May 3 requested that Vatican secretary of state Cardinal Maglione (1877–1944) invite representatives of France, Germany, England, and Poland to an international peace conference in hopes of settling their differences.

The French, the British, and the Poles paid little attention to the papal proposal. Hitler, however, brought the papal nuncio to Germany, Archbishop Cesare Orsenigo (1873–1946), to his mountaintop retreat at Berchtesgaden. There, during a cordial meeting with foreign minister Joachim von Ribbentrop (1893–1946) and Hitler, Orsenigo was assured that the war would not spread and that Germany was not interested in an alliance with Italy. Just days later, the German ambassador to the Holy See informed secretary of state Cardinal Maglione that the pope should drop his attempt at organizing a peace conference. Then, on May 22, 1939, Germany and Italy entered into a formal alliance, setting the stage for further conflict. Pius XII now unsuccessfully appealed to Mussolini to dissuade Hitler from further hostilities.

For their part, the Polish government knew that the return of Danzig would only be the pretext for attacking the rest of Poland and gaining access to the oil-fields of the Ukraine and Romania, but it was confident that Western assistance would be forthcoming and that the Soviet Union would not stand for a German takeover of Poland. They would have been far more concerned, had they known that Hitler and Stalin had a secret understanding for dividing up Poland.

On August 24, the day after a non-aggression pact between the Soviet Union and Germany was announced, a steady stream of ambassadors visited the Vatican secretariat of state—the French, the English, the Italians, and the Yugoslavians. All wanted to avoid war, and the French and English wanted the pope to condemn any aggression against a Catholic country. That evening on Vatican Radio, using a text prepared by Fr. Giovanni Montini, the future Pope Paul VI, Pius XII addressed the world. He warned of the "grave hour that sounds for the whole human family" and invoked his God-given power "to guide souls along the paths of justice and of peace . . . through reason and not through arms." Empires that are not based "on peace are not blessed by God. . . . Nothing is lost with peace. Everything can be lost by war."

Though some would regard the comments of the pope as vague and general, it must be understood that his speech, like most formal papal documents that deal with controversy, place great value on upholding the larger moral and ethical principles without necessarily citing specific infractions or individuals. The sweeping condemnation of Protestant doctrine found in the extensive decrees of the Council of Trent never once mentions a Protestant reformer by name, though none doubted the target of the decrees.

Though it likely had little to do with the pope's speech, Hitler suspended his order to attack Poland and tried one last time to convince England and France not to support Poland, expressing his desire for friendship with England. In the interval, the British pressured Pius XII to make a public statement on behalf of Poland, especially given its strong Catholic population, but Pius XII refused, concerned about being seen as an ally of England and France and about German repercussions against the 40 million Catholics in Germany and Austria.

Diplomatic Mistakes

Pius XII again tried to influence Hitler through Mussolini, who insisted to the pope that the loss of Danzig would have to be the starting point for any negotiations between Germany and Poland but would be a small price for peace. Secretary of the curia, Msgr. Domenico Tardini (1888–1961), advised Pius XII that it would be playing right into Hitler's hands, but the pope accepted the proposal, which he communicated to Warsaw. On September 1, 1939, the day after the pope renewed his call for an international peace conference, the German *Wehrmacht* seized the Danzig Corridor. The next day, as France mobilized its military, Mussolini suggested to Hitler a peace conference on September 5, but England and France would only participate if German troops withdrew from Poland. Hitler, of course, refused, and on September 3, 1939, England and France declared war on Germany.

However well intentioned he may have been, Pius XII had committed perhaps the biggest diplomatic blunder of his career. Now, with official declarations of war, he sought ways to keep Italy out of the war, in spite of its alliance with Germany. Matters quickly spiraled out of control. As Russia and Germany divided up Poland and Russia took over the Baltic States, the British became incensed with the Vatican policy of impartiality, and no one seemed interested any longer in peace conferences.

Pius XII addressed the worsening situation in his encyclical *Summi Pontificatus* (October 1939), which condemned the political and religious policies of both the Soviet Union and Germany, though not by name. The pope contrasted the "soldiers of Christ" with the "ever-increasing host of Christ's enemies" who break God's commandments. The growing conflict was an "Hour of Darkness" for those nations who were being "swept into the tragic whirlpool of war." For Pius XII, the heart of the conflict was the arrogation of absolute power to the state without any mandate from the people. Though written in the carefully crafted and subtle language of a career diplomat, the encyclical was, nevertheless, sufficiently confrontational for Nazi authorities to forbid its publication in Germany.

That Pius XII understood his mistake in expecting Hitler to sit down to the negotiating table was perhaps best demonstrated as early as January 1940, when he became indirectly involved in a plot to assassinate Hitler. Three high-ranking German officers, all Protestant and one of them married to the sister of Lutheran pastor and later Dachau martyr Dietrich Bonhoeffer (1906–1945), planned to remove Hitler and negotiate peace with the allies. It was essential, however, that they know the British terms for peace, and that there would be at least a one-week cessation of hostilities in the aftermath of Hitler's death. They approached Catholic lawyer Dr. Josef Müller (1898–1979), who had known Pius XII while still nuncio to Germany and who had also been arrested by the SS numerous times on suspicion of disloyalty. Müller, in turn, contacted his friend, German Jesuit Robert Leiber (1887–1967), who was personal secretary to Pius XII.

Pius XII agreed immediately to be the intermediary between the German generals and the British ambassador to the Vatican, Sir Francis D'Arcy Osborne. The matter, however, had to be handled with utmost caution. Müller gave the pope written questions from the generals, and Pius XII in turn gave them to Osborne, who then consulted with the British government in London. Osborne's replies to the pope were then communicated to Leiber, who passed them on to Müller, who by February 1, 1940, was on his way to Germany with a written proposal. But for unknown reasons, this particular assassination attempt against Hitler never materialized, and the plan came to nothing.

The failed plot, however, had provided Pius XII with an important contact in the person of Dr. Müller. The head of German military intelligence, Admiral Wilhelm Canaris (1887–1945), who would later be executed for his efforts to overthrow Hitler, supplied Müller with regular, high-quality intelligence on the atrocities committed against the Poles, both Catholic and Jewish, and Müller relayed these reports to Pius XII. On December 23, 1940, the very day on which the above-mentioned comments of Albert Einstein appeared in *Time Magazine*, Pius XII took action in a secret letter to the European bishops entitled *Opere et caritate* ("By Work and by Charity"), which instructed them to do all they could on behalf of those persecuted by the Nazi regime because of religion or ethnicity.

In *The Deputy,* the characters suggest a temporary takeover of Vatican Radio in light of the pope's refusal to let the world know of atrocities against Jews. The reality was that the British hampered the ability of the pope to use Vatican Radio with full effectiveness. In January 1940, Vatican Radio unequivocally declared that Germany had plunged Poland into a state of terror and barbarism, after Cardinal August Hlond (1881–1948) of Poland had escaped to the West and detailed for Pius XII the German persecution of Poles. British intelligence rebroadcast the transmission throughout Europe in order to give the impression that the Vatican had finally sided with England. That this was their intent is supported by a high official in the British Foreign Office, who remarked that "the Vatican Wireless has been of the greatest service to our propaganda and we have exploited it to the full."[16]

The perception that the Vatican was allied with England, or with *anyone* for that matter, was precisely what Pius XII tenaciously wanted to avoid, so further broadcasts omitted specific mention of Germany. London disingenuously professed astonishment and outrage and, in a blatantly manipulative formal protest, attributed the change in policy to successful German pressure and asked how Catholics would view their church after the inevitable Allied victory, "if it may be said of their church that, after at first standing courageously against Nazi paganism, it subsequently consented, by surrender and silence, to discredit the principles on which it is based and by which it lives?"[17]

In Germany, a few bishops *embraced* Nazi ideology. Konrad Gröber (1872–1948), the archbishop of Freiburg im Breisgau, had been a convinced Nazi since 1933, and Franz Rarkowski (1873–1950), official Catholic bishop of the German military, called Hitler "the shining example of a true warrior, the first and most valiant soldier of the Greater German Reich." As a body, however, the bishops began to take a stand. A joint pastoral letter read on June 26, 1941, in all parishes spoke of "sacred obligations of conscience from which no one has the power to release us and which we must fulfill even if it costs us our lives. Never under any circumstances may a human being kill an innocent person apart from war and legitimate self-defense." Five weeks later, on August 3, Cardinal von Galen, known as the Lion of Münster, railed in his cathedral against Hitler's euthanasia program for the mentally retarded and disabled. Remarkably, Hitler halted the program, though only temporarily.

The United States and British declaration of war against Japan on December 8, 1941, and the German declaration of war against the United States which followed three days later were of grave concern to Pius XII. Yet, even as the crisis escalated, his ability to call for peace negotiations was effectively stripped from him by a personal visit on September 19, 1942, of the U.S. special envoy to the Vatican, Myron Taylor (1874–1959). It was no time for diplomacy, Taylor insisted, and the Allies were interested only in total victory. Any peace proposals would thus be considered Axis-inspired and would be considered a strike against the Allies. In other words, *any* future peace efforts by Pius XII would be regarded by the United States as Vatican cooperation with, and partiality toward, Germany.

No longer able to speak publicly of a negotiated peace, in 1942 Pius XII used his Christmas message, *The Internal Order of States and People,* to speak out against the antireligious and racist policies of Hitler. In a world "plunged in darkness by fatal errors," the church would "be untrue to herself" if she ignored the suffering of "*every* [emphasis mine] class of the human family." Pius XII acknowledged the courage and sacrifice of "those peoples," and his tie "to each and every one of them without exception, by a deep, all-embracing, unmovable affection, and by an immense desire to bring them every solace and help which is in any way at Our command." The root cause of the war is a social order "which hid its mortal weakness and its unbridled lust for gain and power," which has led to "numberless exiles . . . torn from their native land" and "hundreds of thousands of persons who, without any fault on their part, sometimes only because of their nationality or race, have been consigned to death or to a slow decline."

The Allies maintained that the speech was not strong enough, and *The Deputy* writes of the Christmas message that "the murderers ignored it." Hochhuth believed that the only thing that could have stopped the genocide was "a papal anathema to chill the blood of every last man on earth," which would have led "500 million Catholics to make Christian protest."[18] Popes might have wielded such spiritual authority in the Middle Ages, but the disregard that secular powers in the nineteenth century exhibited for Pope Pius IX, who eventually became, in his words, "a prisoner of the Vatican," had clearly demonstrated that papal pronouncements and excommunications were no longer an effective tool of influencing state policies.

Even today, critics of Pius XII attach little positive significance to his Christmas message. Goldhagen dismisses it as "wan, elliptical, evasive statements" that are "not even superficially credible" in terms of demonstrating any kind of support for the Jews.[19] Yet a *New York Times* editorial at the time called

Pius XII's speech a "lonely voice crying out of the silence of a continent." Furthermore, the Nazi regime clearly understood the intentions of the pope's speech. An official German government report stated that Pius XII had "repudiated the National Socialist New European Order" and that though he mentioned no names, his speech was "one long attack on behalf of the Jews" and that the pope himself was in fact the "mouthpiece of the Jewish war criminals."[20] The German ambassador to the Holy See was ordered to warn the pope that Germany would retaliate if the Vatican abandoned its neutrality.

Pius XII was fully aware of the ability of the Nazi regime to retaliate on a national level. By June 1942, most of the 2,700 clergy in Dachau were Catholic priests from Poland, and there had been numerous arrests and even executions of priests in Germany. Franz Reinisch (1903–1942), a Pallotine father and military chaplain, was beheaded for his refusal to take the new oath of allegiance to the German military, which he stated in his final words represented "a nihilistic government that has attained power only through force, lies, and deceit."[21] The arrest and transfer to Dachau of Berlin cathedral provost Bernhard Lichtenberg has already been mentioned and in the months to come there would be more.

Pius XII was also aware that Hitler saw kidnapping the pope as a legitimate option if the Vatican abandoned its impartiality. Baron Ernst von Weizsäcker (1882–1951), German ambassador to the Holy See, had advised him of this early on. Though von Weizsäcker is portrayed in *The Deputy* as "Hitler's pure and stainless front,"[22] he was in fact a "cautious enemy of the Nazi regime," who regularly advised the pope as to just how far he could antagonize Hitler without severe retaliation, and at times he even fabricated reports to Berlin in order to give the appearance that Pius XII was cooperative with German objectives.

Though some might see kidnapping the pope as unlikely, there was clear and recent historical precedent. In 1809, troops of Napoleon arrested Pope Pius VII, who spent five long years in Paris, able to exercise very few of his papal responsibilities. It is doubtful that Pius XII was concerned for his personal safety. Contrary to many current perceptions, he was known for personal resolve and courage, albeit of a quiet, diplomatic variety. After the war, the British ambassador to the Holy See, Sir Francis D'Arcy Osborne, who had come to know Pius XII quite well, remarked that with regard to the war, the pope "without the slightest doubt . . . would have been ready and glad to give his life to redeem humanity from its consequences. And this quite irrespective of nationality or faith."[23]

Just as he had directed other European bishops to do in their own dioceses, Pius XII undertook efforts on behalf of the Jews of Rome. Vatican buildings throughout Rome, which were sovereign territory though not contiguous with Vatican City itself, were used at the behest of Pius XII to shelter approximately

5,000 Jewish refugees, some of them in the Vatican itself. False baptismal certificates were often issued to Jews in order to protect them from the authorities, and the pope also exhorted priests and members of religious orders to assist. That his exhortation was heeded is exemplified by Capuchin monk Pierre-Marie Benoît (1895–1990), who saved the lives of some 4,000 Polish Jews in Italy, and the famous "Assisi underground" of Fr. Rufino Niccacci.

Hochhuth asserts that Pius XII allowed the deportation of Roman Jews "in the shadow of the Vatican," when in fact the pope intervened immediately with von Weizsäcker to halt the deportations, though not before approximately 1,000 of the 8,000 intended deportations had taken place. Pius XII himself provided a large amount of gold as a bribe for the German chief of police in Rome in order to prevent him from sending two hundred Roman Jews to the Russian front.

On April 15, 1945, three days after the death of Franklin Roosevelt and the Allied liberation of the Buchenwald and Belsen concentration camps, and the day before Soviet troops began their final assault on Berlin, Pius XII addressed the world in his encyclical *Communium Interpretes Dolorum*. He prayed for a quick end to the destruction, for "too many tears have been shed, and too much blood has been spilled . . . divine and human rights demand unequivocally that such hideous slaughter cease as soon as possible." It must, however, be a sincere peace founded on justice and equity, for "if these matters are not resolved, it would be detrimental both for the victors and the vanquished, since then their solutions could themselves bear the seeds of future wars." Two weeks later, Hitler was dead, and three weeks later, on May 7, 1945, the Allies achieved their objective of an unconditional surrender of all German forces.

Re-assessments

The Second Vatican Council went to unprecedented lengths to rid the church of religious anti-Semitism, and Pope John Paul II made the mending of fences with the Jewish community a major goal of his pontificate, as seen in the Vatican document *We Remember: A Reflection on the Shoah* (1998). Yet the alleged "silence of Pius XII" in *The Deputy* continues to be the starting point of any discussion of the Catholic Church during the Holocaust, and this view has gained new life with the release of the movie *Amen* in 2002, based on the Hochhuth play. The recent start of the canonization process for Pope Pius XII has only sharpened the rhetoric on both sides.

All told, it has been estimated that approximately 30,000 Jews in Italy alone, and hundreds of thousands of Jewish lives in greater Europe were saved directly as a result of clandestine Vatican intervention. "Whosoever saves a single life, saves the entire universe" says a well-known passage in the Talmud. German industrialist Oskar Schindler (1908–1974), for all of his personal shortcomings, spent his personal fortune to save the lives of 1,300 Polish Jews and has been deservedly memorialized in print and on film. Yet any such similar consideration of Pius XII is often overshadowed or even dismissed in favor of unanswerable speculative questions as to what *might* have occurred had the language of his public statements on behalf of the Jews been less general and more explicit.

What *can* be said without dispute is that an agonizingly complex maze of responsibilities and challenges required that Pius XII simultaneously preserve the seriously threatened Catholic Church in Germany and German-occupied Europe, stand up to the Nazi regime, and steer the long-charted papal course of impartiality in the face of Allied and Axis attempts to claim him as an ally, all the while struggling to uphold the rights of *every class of the human community* as the true nature of Hitler's racial policies began to become fully apparent.

How well he accomplished these things will always be a matter of debate, and the negative image of Pius XII will likely always persist to at least a certain degree, which is perhaps the normal price paid by major historical figures who lived in the midst of controversy. Rabbi David Dalin recently earned considerable enmity among fellow Jews when he argued that Pius XII should be considered a "Righteous Gentile" for what he did on behalf of the Jews of Europe. Yet, this is a question that must be examined carefully, honestly, and objectively by the Jewish community, just as the Vatican must honestly and objectively examine the actions of Pius XII during canonization enquiries. In the end, whatever the outcome, characterizations, misrepresentations, and presumed realities, either positive or negative, must be replaced by fair and professional historical scrutiny.

Questions for Reflection and Discussion

1. Do you think that the papal policy of impartiality pursued by Pius XII during World War II was appropriate, or should he have taken a clear side in the conflict?

2. Was Pius XII truly silent with regard to the plight of German Jews?

3. If you had been Pius XII, how would you have balanced the need to protect the Catholic Church in Germany with the need to address the anti-Semitism of the Nazi regime?

4. Can you think of recent instances in which papal intervention has prevented or reduced instances of genocide?

Notes

1. People of the Book

1. Reuven Firestone, *Jihad: The Origin of Holy War in Islam* (New York: Oxford University Press, 1999), 25–27.

2. Karen Armstrong, *Muhammad: A Biography of the Prophet* (New York: HarperCollins, 1992), 79.

3. Reuven Firestone, *Journeys in Holy Lands: The Evolution of the Abraham-Ishmael Legends in Islamic Exegesis* (Albany: State University of New York Press, 1990), 158.

4. Firestone, *Journeys in Holy Lands,* 4–5; Richard Bell, *The Origin of Islam in Its Christian Environment* (London: Macmillan, 1926), 14–16.

5. Firestone, *Jihad,* 22, 30.

6. Bell, *Origin of Islam,* 20; Firestone, *Jihad,* 13.

7. Bell, *Origin of Islam,* 43.

8. Bell, *Origins of Islam,* 19, 69; Armstrong, *Muhammad,* 76.

9. Bell, *Origins of Islam,* 29; Armstrong, *Muhammad,* 67.

10. Bell, *Origins of Islam,* 117.

11. Armstrong, *Muhammad,* 97; Bell, *Origins of Islam,* 104, 201.

12. Bell, *Origins of Islam,* 82.

13. Armstrong, *Muhammad,* 107, 110; Bell, *Origins of Islam,* 56.

14. Bell, *Origins of Islam,* 125.

15. Firestone, *Jihad,* 38.

16. Ibid., 45.

17. Firestone, *Journeys in Holy Lands,* 15, 156; Bell, *Origins of Islam,* 112.

18. Bell, *Origins of Islam,* 127, 145.

19. Firestone, *Journeys in Holy Lands,* 3.

20. Bell, *Origins of Islam,* 130–31; Firestone, *Journeys in Holy Lands,* 19, 61.

21. Bell, *Origins of Islam,* 123.

22. Firestone, *Jihad,* 38, 57.

23. Bell, *Origins of Islam,* 145.

24. Armstrong, *Muhammad,* 206–7.

25. Bell, *Origins of Islam,* 150.

26. Ibid., 178–79.

27. Bell, *Origins of Islam,* 50, 90, 116, 142–43; Armstrong, *Muhammad,* 101.

28. Bell, *Origins of Islam,* 140, 150; Sura 3:45–49; 4:154–59.

29. Bell, *Origins of Islam,* 58; Armstrong, *Muhammad,* 70, 236.

30. Armstrong, *Muhammad*, 243; Firestone, *Journeys in Holy Lands*, 96–100; Firestone, *Jihad*, 21–23.

31. Bell, *Origins of Islam*, 7, 136, 158–62; Firestone, *Journeys in Holy Lands*, 6.

32. Bell, *Origins of Islam*, 2, 174, 180–86.

33. R. W. Southern, *Western Views of Islam in the Middle Ages* (Cambridge, Mass.: Harvard University Press, 1962), 29.

34. Tor Andrae, *Mohammed: The Man and His Faith* (London, 1936), viii.

35. Firestone, *Jihad*, 10, 16–17.

36. Sura 22:39–40; Firestone, *Jihad*, 47, 73.

37. Firestone, *Jihad*, 14, 68, 83–84.

38. John Paul II, *Address to the Young Muslims of Morocco*, August 19, 1985; *Nostra Aetate* 3, October 28, 1965.

39. Philip Jenkins, *The Next Christendom: The Coming of Global Christianity* (New York: Oxford University Press, 2002), 181.

2. Neither for Money Nor Honor

1. Jonathan Riley-Smith, *The First Crusaders: 1095–1131* (henceforth *Crusaders*) (Cambridge: Cambridge University Press, 1997), 12

2. Frederic Duncalf, "The Councils of Piacenza and Clermont" (henceforth "Councils"), in *A History of the Crusades,* ed. Kenneth Setton (Madison: University of Wisconsin Press, 1969), 1.229.

3. Riley-Smith, *Crusaders,* 68; Duncalf, "Councils," in *A History of the Crusades,* ed. Setton, 1.237, 242.

4. Steven Runciman, *The First Crusade* (henceforth *Crusade*) (Cambridge: Cambridge University Press, 1980), 1, 8, 10–11, 35.

5. Steven Runciman, "Pilgrimages to Palestine before 1095," in *A History of the Crusades,* ed. Setton, 1.78.

6. Duncalf, "Councils," in *A History of the Crusades,* ed. Setton, 1.222–33.

7. Riley-Smith, *Crusaders,* 42, 48; Jonathan Riley-Smith, *What Were the Crusades?* (henceforth *Crusades*) (San Francisco: Ignatius, 2002), 4.

8. Duncalf, "The First Crusade: Clermont to Constantinople" (henceforth "Crusade"), in *A History of the Crusades,* ed. Setton, 1.272.

9. Riley-Smith, *Crusades,* 57, 64.

10. Duncalf, "Councils," in *A History of the Crusades,* ed. Setton, 1.243; Runciman, "Pilgrimages to Palestine before 1095," in *A History of the Crusades,* ed. Setton, 1.68–72, 76; Riley-Smith, *Crusaders,* 25–26; Runciman, *Crusade,* 11–12.

11. Runciman, *Crusade,* 12.

12. Riley-Smith, *Crusaders,* 11; Duncalf, "Councils," in *A History of the Crusades,* ed. Setton, 1.247, 239; Riley-Smith, *Crusades,* 46.

13. Duncalf, "Councils," in *A History of the Crusades,* ed. Setton, 1.244; Riley-Smith, *Crusaders,* 15–20, 38–39, 68, 106, 112–13; Runciman, *Crusade,* 72; Riley-Smith, *Crusades,* 67.

14. Riley-Smith, *Crusaders,* 120; Riley-Smith, *Crusades,* 73.

15. Duncalf, " Crusade," in *A History of the Crusades,* ed. Setton, 1.253–54; Riley-Smith, *Crusaders,* 106; Riley-Smith, *Crusades,* 37, 69.

16. Riley-Smith, *Crusaders*, 56; Runciman, *Crusade*, 49; Duncalf, " Crusade," in *A History of the Crusades,* ed. Setton, 1.266.

17. Riley-Smith, *Crusaders*, 12; Duncalf, "Crusade," in *A History of the Crusades,* ed. Setton, 1.260, 264–65; Runciman, *Crusade*, 65–67.

18. Runciman, *Crusade*, 83–85.

19. Ibid., 79, 87.

20. Duncalf, " Crusade," in *A History of the Crusades,* ed. Setton, 1.258–59.

21. Runciman, "The First Crusade: Constantinople to Antioch," in *A History of the Crusades,* ed. Setton, 1.283–84; Runciman, *Crusade*, 58–61.

22. Duncalf, "Councils," in *A History of the Crusades,* ed. Setton, 1.252.

23. Runciman, *Crusade*, 74, 92, 97; Runciman, "The First Crusade: Constantinople to Antioch," in *A History of the Crusades,* ed. Setton, 1.279–80, 286; Duncalf, "Crusade," in *A History of the Crusades,* ed. Setton, 1.279, 271.

24. Runciman, "The First Crusade: Constantinople to Antioch," in *A History of the Crusades,* ed. Setton, 1.288, 291; Runciman, *Crusade,* 99.

25. Runciman, "The First Crusade: Antioch to Ascalon," in *A History of the Crusades,* ed. Setton, 1.309; Runciman, *Crusade*, 133.

26. Runciman, "The First Crusade: Constantinople to Antioch," in *A History of the Crusades,* ed. Setton, 1.304; Runciman, *Crusade*, 125.

27. Runciman, "The First Crusade: Antioch to Ascalon," in *A History of the Crusades,* ed. Setton, 1.315–16.

28. Runciman, "The First Crusade: Antioch to Ascalon," in *A History of the Crusades,* ed. Setton, 1.324; Runciman, *Crusade*, 160, 176.

29. Runciman, *Crusade*, 185.

30. Riley-Smith, *Crusaders*, 41.

31. Ibid., 8, 144, 149, 153–54.

32. Hamilton A. R. Gibb, "Zengi and the Fall of Edessa," in *A History of the Crusades,* ed. Setton, 1.449.

33. Riley-Smith, *Crusaders*, 186, 188; Harold S. Fink, "The Foundation of the Latin States, 1099–1118," in *A History of the Crusades,* ed. Setton, 1.370, 385.

34. Runciman, *Crusade*, 188.

35. Norman P. Tanner, ed., *Decrees of the Ecumenical Councils* (London: 1990) 191–92; Gibb, "Zengi and the Fall of Edessa," in *A History of the Crusades,* ed. Setton, 1.461; Virginia G. Berry, "The Second Crusade," in *A History of the Crusades,* ed. Setton, 1.463–64, 467.

36. Berry, "The Second Crusade," in *A History of the Crusades,* ed. Setton, 1.468, 471, 480.

37. Ibid., 479, 494.

38. Ibid., 476, 484, 488–92.

39. Riley-Smith, *Crusaders*, 160.

40. Berry, "The Second Crusade," in *A History of the Crusades,* ed. Setton, 1.511.

41. A. R. Gibb, "The Rise of Saladin: 1169–1189," in *A History of the Crusades,* ed. Setton, 1.564.

42. Gibb, "The Rise of Saladin: 1169–1189," in *A History of the Crusades,* ed. Setton, 1.584.

43. Marshall W. Baldwin, "The Decline and Fall of Jerusalem, 1174–1189," in *A History of the Crusades,* ed. Setton, 1.598; 605; Gibb, "The Rise of Saladin: 1169–1189," in *A History of the Crusades,* ed. Setton, 1.568, 579–80.

44. Baldwin, "The Decline and Fall of Jerusalem, 1174–1189," in *A History of the Crusades,* ed. Setton, 1.617, 620.

45. Gibb, "The Rise of Saladin: 1169–1189," in *A History of the Crusades,* ed. Setton, 1.564, 569; Sidney Painter, "The Third Crusade: Richard the Lionhearted and Philip Augustus," in *A History of the Crusades,* ed. Setton, 2.50, 56.

46. Painter, "The Third Crusade: Richard the Lionhearted and Philip Augustus," in *A History of the Crusades,* ed. Setton, 2.49, 73, 85.

47. Gibb, "The Rise of Saladin: 1169–1189," in *A History of the Crusades,* ed. Setton, 1.563.

48. Edgar H. McNeal and Robert Lee Wolff, "The Fourth Crusade," in *A History of the Crusades,* ed. Setton, 2.154.

49. Ibid., 156–57.

50. Ibid., 162–63.

51. Ibid., 169.

52. Ibid., 167.

53. Ibid., 175.

54. Nicetas Choniates, in *Translations and Reprints from the Original Sources of European History,* ed. D. C. Munro, series 1, vol 3:1 (Philadelphia: University of Pennsylvania Press, 1912), 15–16; Robert de Clari, chapter 73, in *Chroniques Gréco-Romanes,* ed. Karl Hopf (Berlin, 1873), 57–58.

55. *Patrologia Latina,* 215:699.

56. Robert Lee Wolff, "The Latin Empire of Constantinople, 1204–1261," in *A History of the Crusades,* ed. Setton, 2.191–93, 222–25; McNeal and Wolff, "The Fourth Crusade," in *A History of the Crusades,* ed. Setton, 2.185.

57. Norman P. Zacour, "The Children's Crusade," in *A History of the Crusades,* ed. Setton, 2.330, 340.

58. Riley-Smith, *Crusades,* 49.

59. T. S. Eliot, *Choruses from the Rock,* in T. S. Eliot, *Collected Poems 1909–1962* (New York: 1984), 165.

3. The Spanish Inquisition

1. Edward Peters, *Inquisition* (Berkeley: University of California Press, 1988), 7.

2. Ibid., 81.

3. Norman Tanner, S.J., *Decrees of the Ecumenical Councils* (London: Sheed & Ward, 1990), 1.266; Peters, *Inquisition, 78.*

4. Peters, *Inquisition,* 77, 81; Alastair Hamilton, *Heresy and Mysticism in Sixteenth-Century Spain* (henceforth, *Heresy*) (Toronto: University of Toronto Press, 1992), 7; Henry Kamen, *The Spanish Inquisition: An Historical Revision* (henceforth *Inquisition*) (New Haven: Yale University Press, 1998), 14.

5. Peters, *Inquisition,* 82–84.

6. Kamen, *Inquisition,* 16.

7. Ibid., 61, 6.

8. Peters, *Inquisition,* 28.

9. Peters, *Inquisition,* 24–26, 29, 41, 46, 57; Kamen, *Inquisition,* 158.

10. Tanner, *Decrees of the Ecumenical Councils,* 1.205ff.; Peters, *Inquisition,* 47–48, 50, 56.

11. James Given, *Inquisition and Medieval Society: Power, Discipline, and Resistance in Languedoc* (Ithaca, N.Y.: Cornell University Press, 1997), 11–12, 20, 22; Peters, *Inquisition,* 12, 52.

12. Given, *Inquisition and Medieval Society,* 13; Peters, *Inquisition,* 44, 51; Kamen, *Inquisition,* 202.

13. Peters, *Inquisition,* 54, 65–68; Given, *Inquisition and Medieval Society,* 15.

14. Peters, *Inquisition,* 60, 91; Given, *Inquisition and Medieval Society,* 4; Kamen, *Inquisition,* 144.

15. Peters, *Inquisition,* 58, 91; Kamen, *Inquisition,* 57–58, 174.

16. Kamen, *Inquisition,* 193–96; Peters, *Inquisition,* 66.

17. Peters, *Inquisition,* 67, 91; Kamen, *Inquisition,* 148–151.

18. Peters, *Inquisition,* 16, 65, 92; Kamen, *Inquisition,* 188.

19. Peters, *Inquisition,* 93–94; Kamen, *Inquisition,* 71, 198, 243.

20. Kamen, *Inquisition,* 45–47; Peters, *Inquisition,* 86–87.

21. Quoted in Kamen, *Inquisition,* 48–49.

22. Peters, *Inquisition,* 86.

23. Kamen, *Inquisition,* 15.

24. Ibid, 54–55.

25. Hamilton, *Heresy,* 66.

26. Kamen, *Inquisition,* 20.

27. Kamen, *Inquisition,* 26, 56; Peters, *Inquisition,* 97.

28. Kamen, *Inquisition,* 64, 255; Hamilton, *Heresy,* 8; Moshe Lazar, "Scorched Parchments and Tortured Memories: The 'Jewishness' of the Anussim (Crypto-Jews)," in *Cultural Encounters: The Impact of the Inquisition in Spain and the New World,* ed. Mary Elizabeth Perry and Anne J. Cruz (Berkeley: University of California Press, 1991), 176–206.

29. Peters, *Inquisition,* 132.

30. Kamen, *Inquisition,* 53, 57, 61, 215, 220.

31. Ibid, 78.

32. Kamen, *Inquisition,* 61, 217.

33. Hamilton, *Heresy,* 21, 43.

34. Ibid, 25, 51, 60–61.

35. Ibid, 113.

36. Ibid, 40.

37. Kamen, *Inquisition,* 245–47; Hamilton, *Heresy,* 96.

38. Hamilton, *Heresy,* 34.

39. Kamen, *Inquisition,* 85.

40. Kamen, *Inquisition,* 87–89; Hamilton, *Heresy,* 86.

41. Peters, *Inquisition,* 114; Hamilton, *Heresy,* 23.

42. Peters, *Inquisition,* 95; Hamilton, *Heresy,* 63.

43. Kamen, *Inquisition,* 95.

44. Hamilton, *Heresy,* 104; Peters, *Inquisition,* 89; Kamen, *Inquisition,* 160–62.

45. Hamilton, *Heresy,* 111, 121–22; Kamen, *Inquisition,* 129, 131.

46. Kamen, *Inquisition,* 224, 227.

47. Kamen, *Inquisition,* 267; Peters, *Inquisition,* 101.

48. Kamen, *Inquisition,* 262, 315.

49. Peters, *Inquisition,* 123, 133; Kamen, *Inquisition,* 307–8.

50. Peters, *Inquisition,* 153.

51. Ibid, 125, 157.

52. Ibid, 243, 154.

53. Ibid, 188, 229.

54. Henry Charles Lea, *A History of the Inquisition of Spain,* 4 vols. (New York: Macmillan, 1906–8); Given, *Inquisition and Medieval Society,* 2; Peters, *Inquisition,* 254, 280, 290–95, 315; Kamen, *Inquisition,* 312.

55. Kamen, *Inquisition,* 7.

4. A Squabble among Friars

1. *The Theologia Germanica of Martin Luther,* trans. Bengt Hoffman (New York: Paulist, 1980), xvi; for an argument in favor of Luther's mysticism, see E. See Iserloh, in *Catholic Scholars Dialogue with Luther,* ed. J. Wicks (Chicago: Loyola University Press, 1970), 37.

2. Erik H. Erikson, *Young Man Luther: A Study in Psychoanalysis and History* (New York: Norton, 1958).

3. *Luther's Works,* ed. Gottfried Krodel (Philadelphia: Fortress, 1972), 48.37, 42

4. Joseph Lortz, The *Reformation in Germany,* trans. Ronald Walls (New York: Herder & Herder, 1968), 1.119.

5. Ibid.

6. *Works of Martin Luther,* trans. and ed. Adolph Spaeth, L. D. Reed, Henry Eyster Jacobs, et al. (Philadelphia: A. J. Holman, 1915), 1.29–38.

7. Erwin Iserloh, *The Theses Were Not Posted: Luther between Reform and Reformation,* trans. Jared Wicks (Boston: Beacon, 1968).

8. *Luther's Works* 48.47–48.

9. Ibid., 31.234; 48.69.

10. Ibid., 48.88.

11. Ibid., 48.91.

12. Ibid., 31.259–260; 48.94.

13. Ibid., 48.96–100.

14. Ibid., 48.100–102.

15. Ibid., 48.125.

16. Ibid., 48.107.

17. Ibid., 31.323.

18. *Preface to the Complete Edition of Luther's Latin Works* (1545) by Dr. Martin Luther, 1483–1546, trans. Bro. Andrew Thornton, OSB, from the "Vorrede zu Band I der Opera Latina der Wittenberger Ausgabe. 1545" in vol. 4 of *Luthers Werke in Auswahl,* ed. Otto Clemen (Berlin: de Gruyter, 1967), 421–28.

19. Aristotle, *Nicomachean Ethics* 2.1–7; *Luther's Works* 48.25

20. *Luther's Works* 44.135; 48.172.

21. Ibid., 48.179.

22. Ibid., 31.343.

23. Ibid., 48.183.

24. Ibid., 48.188.

25. Ibid., 48.225.

26. Ibid., 48.329.

27. Ibid., 48.363.

28. Ibid., 48.364.

29. Ibid., 48.388, 402.

30. Ibid., 49.117.

31. David V. N. Bagchi, *Luther's Earliest Opponents: Catholic Controversialists 1518–1525* (Minneapolis: Fortress, 1991).

32. Heinrich Boehmer, quoted in *Catholic Scholars Dialogue with Luther*, ed. Wicks, 3.

33. Heinrich Denifle, O.P., *Luther und Luthertum in der ersten Entwicklung* (Mainz: Kirchheim, 1904–9).

34. Jared Wicks, S.J., *Luther and His Spiritual Legacy* (Wilmington, Del.: Michael Glazier, 1983), 21.

35. Lortz, "The Basic Elements of Luther's Intellectual Style," in *Catholic Scholars in Dialogue with Luther,* ed. Wicks, 3.

36. *The Lutheran–Catholic Quest for Visible Unity: Harvesting Thirty Years of Dialogue,* An Educational Paper Prepared by the Lutheran–Roman Catholic Coordinating Committee (Washington D.C.: United States Catholic Conference, 1998).

5. First Contact

1. Matthew Restall, *Seven Myths of the Spanish Conquest* (henceforth *Myths*) (Oxford: Oxford University Press, 2003) 7.

2. Restall, *Seven Myths of the Spanish Conquest,* 131.

3. Robert Ricard, *The Spiritual Conquest of Mexico: An Essay on the Apostolate and the Evangelizing Methods of the Mendicant Orders in New Spain: 1523–1572* (Berkeley: University of California Press, 1966) 15.

4. Restall, *Myths,* 35.

5. Ibid., 52.

6. Ibid., *Myths,* 87.

7. Ibid., 95.

8. Ibid., 96.

9. Ibid., 25, 124.

10. Robert Ricard, *The Spiritual Conquest of Mexico*, 260.

11. Ibid., 22.

12. John Phelan, *The Millennial Kingdom of the Franciscans in the New World* (Berkeley: University of California Press, 1970); Restall, *Myths,* 15, 113.

13. Ricard, *The Spiritual Conquest of Mexico*, 152.

14. Ibid., 97.

15. Fintan Warren, *Vasco de Quiroga and His Pueblo-Hospitals of Santa Fe* (Washington, D.C.: Academy of American Franciscan History, 1963).

16. Ricard, *The Spiritual Conquest of Mexico*, 105.

17. Ibid., 252.

18. Ibid., 90.

19. Ibid., 83.

20. Ibid., 32.

21. Ibid., 37.

22. Ibid., 40.

23. Ibid., 250.

24. Ibid., 191.

25. Antonine Tibesar, OFM, *Franciscan Beginnings in Colonial Peru* (Washington, D.C.: Academy of American Franciscan History, 1953) 39.

26. Tibesar, *Franciscan Beginnings,* 30, 41, 45.

27. Restall, *Myths,* 49.

28. Tibesar, *Franciscan Beginnings,* 21.

29. Restall, *Myths,* 122.

30. Restall, *Myths,* 71, 127; Ricard, *The Spiritual Conquest of Mexico,* 264, 273.

31. Restall, *Myths,* 12, 116.

32. Restall, *Myths,* 74; Ricard, *The Spiritual Conquest of Mexico,* 270.

33. John Thornton, "The Development of an African Catholic Church in the Kingdom of Kongo, 1491–1750," *Christianity and Missions: 1450–1800* (Brookfield, Vt.: Ashgate/Variorum, 1997), 148.

34. Ibid. , 237–58; 238.

35. Francis Rogers, *The Quest for Eastern Christians: Travels and Rumor in the Age of Discovery* (Minneapolis: University of Minnesota Press, 1962), 114–36.

36. Vincent Cronin, *A Pearl to India: The Life of Roberto de Nobili* (New York: Dutton, 1959).

37. C. R. Boxer, *The Christian Century in Japan: 1549–1650* (henceforth *Century*) (Berkeley: University of California Press, 1951) 36.

38. Neil S. Fujita, *Japan's Encounter with Christianity: The Catholic Mission in Pre-Modern Japan* (New York: Paulist Press, 1991) 13–38.

39. Michael Cooper, *Rodrigues the Interpreter: An Early Jesuit in Japan and China* (New York: Weatherhill, 1974) 19.

40. Josef Schütte, SJ, *Valignano's Mission Principles for Japan,* vol. 1 (St. Louis: Institute of Jesuit Sources, 1980).

41. Fujita, *Japan's Encounter with Christianity,* 132.

42. Boxer, *Christian Century,* 163–67.

43. Ibid., 362–68, 448.

44. Joseph Sebes, SJ, "The Precursors of Ricci," in *East Meets West: The Jesuits in China, 1582–1773,* ed. Charles Ronan, SJ, and Bonnie Oh (Chicago: Loyola University Press, 1988) 19–61, 30.

45. Sebes, "Precursors of Ricci," 33; George Dunne, SJ, *Generation of Giants: The Story of the Jesuits in China in the Last Decades of the Ming Dynasty* (Notre Dame: University of Notre Dame Press, 1962) 19.

46. Jonathan Spence, "Matteo Ricci and the Ascent to Peking," in *East Meets West,* ed. Ronan and Oh, 3–18, 7.

47. Ibid., 15.

48. Jonathan Spence, *The Memory Palace of Matteo Ricci* (New York: Penguin, 1983).

49. Sebes, "Precursors of Ricci," in *East Meets West,* 41.

50. Spence, "Matteo Ricci and the Ascent to Peking," 12.

51. Dunne, *Generation of Giants,* 79, 83.

52. George Minamiki, SJ, *The Chinese Rites Controversy from Its Beginning to Modern Times* (Chicago: Loyola University Press, 1985) 18.

53. Minamiki, *The Chinese Rites Controversy,* 183–203; John Paul II, *Message of Pope John Paul II to the Participants in the International Conference Commemorating the Fourth Centenary of the arrival in Beijing of Father Matteo Ricci* (October 24, 2001).

6. A Tragic Mutual Incomprehension

1. Richard S. Westfall, *Essays on the Trial of Galileo* (henceforth *Essays*) (Vatican City: Vatican Observatory, 1989); William A. Wallace, *Galileo and His Sources: The Heritage of the Collegio Romano in Galileo's Science* (Princeton, N.J.: Princeton University Press, 1984).

2. Jerome J. Langford, *Galileo, Science and the Church* (Ann Arbor: University of Michigan Press, 1966) 19.

3. William R. Shea and Mariano Artigas, *Galileo in Rome: The Rise and Fall of a Troublesome Genius* (henceforth *Galileo*) (Oxford: Oxford University Press, 2003) 19.

4. Shea and Artigas, *Galileo*, 37.

5. Dava Sobel, *Galileo's Daughter: A Historical Memoir of Science, Faith, and Love* (New York: Walker & Co., 2000) 44–45.

6. Westfall, *Essays*, 44.

7. Shea and Artigas, *Galileo*, 8; Westfall, *Essays*, 5, 10.

8. Westfall, *Essays*, 11; Shea and Artigas, *Galileo*, 35.

9. Shea and Artigas, *Galileo*, 43.

10. Ibid., 46.

11. Galileo Galilei, *The Starry Messenger*, in *Discoveries and Opinions of Galileo*, trans. Stillman Drake (Garden City, N.Y.: Doubleday, 1957) 11.

12. Westfall, *Essays*, 2.

13. Shea and Artigas, *Galileo*, 59, 61; Langford, *Galileo, Science and the Church*, 56.

14. Westfall, *Essays*, 37; Shea and Artigas, *Galileo*, 51.

15. Langford, *Galileo, Science and the Church*, 59.

16. Ibid., 62.

17. Shea and Artigas, *Galileo*, 26; Westfall, *Essays*, 27.

18. Westfall, *Essays*, 3.

19. Shea and Artigas, *Galileo*, 81; Westfall, *Essays*, 48.

20. Langford, *Galileo, Science and the Church*, 68.

21. Westfall, *Essays*, 21, 66.

22. Shea and Artigas, *Galileo*, 54, 85; Langford, *Galileo, Science and the Church*, 105.

23. Shea and Artigas, *Galileo*, 64, 90.

24. Ibid., 91.

25. Langford, *Galileo, Science and the Church*, 106.

26. Westfall, *Essays*, 51.

27. Ibid., 59.

28. Langford, *Galileo, Science and the Church*, 115.

29. Shea and Artigas, *Galileo*, 113.

30. Shea and Artigas, *Galileo*, 118; Langford, *Galileo, Science and the Church*, 116.

31. Sobel, *Galileo's Daughter*, 164–65, 223.

32. Westfall, *Essays*, 60; Shea and Artigas, *Galileo*, 140.

33. Shea and Artigas, *Galileo*, 152; Westfall, *Essays*, 73.

34. Galileo Galilei, *Dialogue on the Great Systems of the World*, trans. Stillman Drake (Berkeley: University of California Press, 1962) 464.

35. Shea and Artigas, *Galileo*, 140; Langford, *Galileo, Science and the Church*, 135.

36. Sobel, *Galileo's Daughter*, 239.

37. Langford, *Galileo, Science and the Church,* 92.

38. Shea and Artigas, *Galileo,* 82; Langford, *Galileo, Science and the Church,* 97.

39. Shea and Artigas, *Galileo,* 83, 186.

40. Langford, *Galileo, Science and the Church,* 144.

41. Shea and Artigas, *Galileo,* 189.

42. Langford, *Galileo, Science and the Church,* 153.

43. Shea and Artigas, *Galileo,* 193.

44. Sobel, *Galileo's Daughter,* 279.

45. Ibid., 362.

46. Westfall, *Essays,* 69.

47. Ibid., 52.

7. Pius XII and Nazi Germany

1. Daniel Goldhagen, *A Moral Reckoning: The Role of the Catholic Church in the Holocaust and Its Unfulfilled Duty of Repair* (New York: Vintage Books, 2002); John Cornwell, *Hitler's Pope: The Secret History of Pius XII* (New York: Viking, 1999).

2. J. Derek Holmes, *The Papacy in the Modern World 1914–1978* (henceforth *Papacy*) (New York: Crossroad, 1981) 159.

3. Goldhagen, *Moral Reckoning,* 12.

4. Rolf Hochhuth, *The Deputy,* trans. Richard Winston and Clara Winston (Baltimore: Johns Hopkins University Press, 1964).

5. Hochhuth, *Deputy,* 102, 156–57, 193, 214, 219.

6. Cornwell, *Hitler's Pope,* 375.

7. Donald Dietrich, *Catholic Citizens in the Third Reich: Psycho-Social Principles and Moral Reasoning* (henceforth *Citizens*) (New Brunswick: Transaction, 1988), 5, 9.

8. Dietrich, *Citizens,* 97.

9. Ibid., 12–13.

10. Ibid., *Citizens,* 83, 98.

11. Ibid., 102.

12. Hochhuth, *Deputy,* 55, 120; Dietrich, *Citizens,* 104.

13. Dietrich, *Citizens,* 139, 142.

14. Holmes, *Papacy,* 90.

15. Georges Passelecq and Bernard Suchecky, *The Hidden Encyclical of Pius XI* (New York: Harvest, 1998).

16. Hochhuth, *Deputy,* 158; Holmes, *Papacy,* 131.

17. Holmes, *Papacy,* 131.

18. Hochhuth, *Deputy,* 102, 201, 204.

19. Goldhagen, *Moral Reckoning,* 114–15.

20. Holmes, *Papacy,* 140.

21. Ibid., 143.

22. Hochhuth, *Deputy,* 122–24.

23. Cited in Cornwell, *Hitler's Pope,* 381.

Index

Of Related Interest

MARK J. MASSA

ANTI-CATHOLICISM IN AMERICA
The Last Acceptable Prejudice

One of the most important books in contemporary religious publishing is a work of scholarly rigor, story-telling, and humor. In this authoritative study, Mark Massa, Program Director of Fordham University's Center for American Catholic Studies, reveals how American Catholics' distinctive way of viewing the world is constantly misunderstood—and attacked—by outsiders.

"An explosion of creative insight."
—Andrew Greeley

0-8245-23628
$19.95 paperback

Check your local bookstore for availability. To order directly from the publisher, please call 1-800-707-0670 for Customer Service or visit our website at www.cpcbooks.com. For catalog orders, please send request to the address below.

THE CROSSROAD PUBLISHING COMPANY
16 PENN PLAZA, SUITE 1550
NEW YORK, NY 10001

crossroad